A Seriously Useful Author's Guide

How To Get a Break As A Writer

A Seriously Useful Author's Guide

How to Get a Break As a Writer

Neil Nixon

t

Troubador Publishing Ltd
5 Weir Road
Kibworth Beauchamp
Leics LE8 0LQ, UK
Tel: (+44) 116 279 2299
Email: books@troubador.co.uk
Web: www.troubador.co.uk

ISBN 978-184876-564-1

A Cataloguing-in-Publication (CIP) catalogue record for this book is available from the British Library.

Typeset in 11pt Baskerville by Troubador Publishing Ltd, Leics, UK

Printed in Great Britain by the MPG Books Group, Bodmin and King's Lynn

Contents

Introduction

Not Another Book About Writing?

Yes, but for all the right reasons. This book deals with an area of writing for a living that remains virtually untouched by most other titles. This is a book about getting breaks, making your own luck and the kind of 'ducking and diving' that gets hopeful writers to the stage of being taken seriously. When other books do cover some of this ground they usually discuss how you'll sell one book or one script. This book does not assume you want to write that one novel that will change the world. It assumes only the following things:

1. You have ideas, and they come to often enough to suggest you might be happy in a creative career.
2. You have some general notions of how this creative career might work, but you also have a lot of uncertainty about the kind of opportunities that exist in the working world.
3. You are prepared to put in the work to make yourself more successful.
4. This work will involve you producing writing, and trying to sell your ideas.
5. You are prepared to be open-mined and consider a range

of options, including some that don't really appeal too much at first glance.

This is a book that addresses the age-old problem of not being able to get a break without experience and not being able to get experience without getting a break. This is also a book based on solid research and evidence. I started this book ten years after I founded the UK's first full-time university course in Professional Writing.

A lot of what follows are examples of how people with no experience and limited options went on to make things happen and kick-start their writing careers. In some cases I met students who told me they wanted to be writers and during the years we worked together both of us realized that 'writing' in the sense of writing words and trying to sell them, wasn't the right way forward for these people. The solutions we identified often involved creative jobs, including some writing, but also a great deal else; like working in teams, thinking up ideas and working with people.

This book assumes you are like the people I have met over the years. You know you are creative, you have ideas you want to share. You believe these ideas can earn you money and you believe you will be happier and feel more alive if you can find a way of earning good, regular money as a creative person.

What follows has worked for people I have taught, and many of the professionals with whom I work. I can't promise you a miracle in your own life. However, I can promise that this book will offer ideas, exercises and opportunities to make you more likely to get a break as a writer. I can also promise that this book was designed to be as useful as possible. If you are just starting on a writing career it can be read from beginning to end. If you are already underway each chapter can serve as a self-help manual for the skills you still need to develop, allowing you to dip into the book and come away with some positive possibilities in return for a few minutes reading and thinking.

If you are reading this with a view to buying the book, you might want to know what is coming. Here is a brief round up of the remaining chapters:

1 - The Talent

Considering strengths and abilities you may have. Drawing connections between your talents and a range of opportunities in the working world. Showing you that lack of ideas, lack of contacts or lack of time need not be impossible barriers when it comes to getting your work out there and making money. Giving you some exercises to help you identify the best routes to getting a break.

2 – The Job

A detailed look at professional writing, taking into account the range of the work on offer. Discussion of pros and cons of different areas of work. Concluding statements about the nature of professional writing work at present and in the future. Consideration of likely earnings in the different areas of work.

3 – Get Yourself Connected

Practical strategies to build the gap between chapters one and two. Starting with a list of strategies for generating a 'writer's CV' and exploring several case studies down to the specifics of likely income, level of difficulty and the pros and cons of each strategy. Examples considered include bypassing normal routes and going directly to a company, aiming for the softest targets available: such as charities.

4 – Are You Engaged?

Case studies of how to build relationships with those offering opportunities for writers. Consideration of professional development, and building self-confidence as work develops.

5 – Put Up or Shut Up

Chapter devoted to the development and sale of big ideas – like book and film submissions – detailing what agents and producers look for, formats for submission and examples of successful, and unsuccessful, submissions.

6 – Agents of Change

Chapter on getting and finding agents, also looking at other areas of help and mentorship available including websites, courses, professional mentors etc. Comments from agents and others involved in finding and managing talent.

7 – Out of the Box

Alternative strategies for making things happen. Case studies of writing success through unorthodox routes.

8 – In POD we Trust

Print-on-demand publishing, and other developing areas of low-cost independent publication for writers. Interviews and comments from those closely involved in these areas of work.

9 – The Write Stuff – AKA 'Sources'

Round up of major contacts and sources with ideas of how to use these contacts. Discussion of how to build on work covered in book through use of reference works and web sites.

Glossary

A round up of the terminology used in the book that may confuse you. Explaining what terms like 'development production' really mean and why they might matter to you.

So, it's time to get started. And, if you are leafing through this book in a bookshop, it's probably time to decide if you are going to take it to the till and give the next nine chapters a chance to change your life. Obviously I'd like you to do that, so I will include a section listing ten good reasons to consider turning your writing into part of your working life.

10 Reasons to Think About Professional Writing

1. The costs of making work are dropping against inflation, and they show no sign of stopping this trend. Break even cost of piece of written work can now be very low.
2. Low costs of work mean many new 'niche' markets are opening up, allowing opportunities for more writers to get work accepted.
3. The skills you will develop in writing and engaging with markets can be transferred into many other situations, giving you the basis for a varied and exciting career.
4. You have ideas and interests. In short; you have passions, they matter to you and they matter to others. You can reach people who think and feel the way you do.
5. This is one area of work that is incredibly flexible. The skills you develop will allow you to work around children, other work commitments and a range of other obstacles that would halt a more rigid career in its tracks.
6. Despite what some people will tell you, writing can be fun, exciting, and completely fulfilling.
7. Writing and creative careers can accommodate a range of different talents. Your creative talent can help you find a niche but, surprisingly, this is an area in which people without a huge amount of creative flair can make a good living.

8. The fringe benefits, like access to people, places and things you want (like free clothes, hotel rooms etc) can be a real bonus.
9. Writing and creative careers will give you surprises, and when you have been working for a long time, these surprises will serve to keep you interested in life. This is not something everyone with years of experience in other jobs will come to expect.
10. You want it, or you wouldn't still be reading at this point.

1 The Talent

We are: *Considering strengths and abilities you may have. Drawing connections between your talents and a range of opportunities in the working world. Showing you that lack of ideas, lack of contacts or lack of time need not be impossible barriers when it comes to getting your work out there and making money. Giving you some exercises to help you identify the best routes to getting a break.*

So it is time to think about your own strengths and weaknesses as a writer. We will start with a brief look at what it means to be creative, and then think about how your own skills and talents fit into the world of creativity.

The first thing to note about being creative is that definitions vary. 'Creative' is about as useful a description as 'beautiful.' In other words; deciding who is creative is often in the eye, or ear, of the beholder. There have been attempts to make sense of creativity and psychologists continue to research the area. Arguably, the most serious and important work in this area started in the 1950s and one of the major studies was carried out by J P Guilford. He identified several traits of highly creative people, and his study was based on a large sample of people doing creative jobs, his subjects being advertising professionals, journalists, artists and others employed to use their creative talents. His work is still available if you want to hunt online. A very simple summary of some of his findings suggests that creative people display a range of talents. Many creative people succeed because they concentrate their efforts in one or two areas of strengths. Typical strengths of creative people include:

- The ability to generate ideas around a theme.
- The ability to think laterally and flexibly.
- The ability to develop, embellish and conceive of the outcome of an idea
- The ability to focus and organize an idea.

One weakness in any study of creative people is that the studies tend to concentrate on people who have already become established in their working lives. These are the only people who can be identified as successful. So these studies are good at identifying what people do and how they do it. They are less effective at predicting how these skills will help you in the future. In the last few decades new areas of creativity have emerged with work in web design, cutting edge animation and other developing technologies. These require some of the traditional strengths, like focus and organization, but often demand very particular technical skills.

Alongside studies of creative people there have been attempts to define what 'creativity' means. Dictionary definitions often talk about the ability to 'invent' and show imagination or originality. This leaves us with the problem of trying to work out what imagination or originality might mean. This research is certainly useful but it is only a guide. For a general idea of what we might agree on as creativity we could look at some of the definitions presented by two researchers called Besemer and Treffinger in 1981.

- Novelty: The newness of an idea in terms of process, techniques and application.
- Resolution: The extent to which an idea resolves a situation.
- Synthesis: The extent to which an idea combines elements which are unalike into a coherent whole.

This is a really simple run through the main points. Before we go any further, it is worth remembering a very important point often overlooked by researchers. Most professionally creative people, including writers, got to their positions without making a study of creativity. They achieved most of their success by getting on with their work and applying their talents.

For many years there was a problem in the creative industries; many intelligent and ambitious people wanted work in areas like advertising, but the people able to offer the jobs often struggled to tell the suitable candidates apart from the other applicants. The problem was that qualifications and experience didn't always give a good indication of what the people chasing the jobs could actually do. A graduate with a good degree could apply for a job in advertising and be interviewed on the same day as someone else who had spent a few years selling fruit from a market stall. Both would have skills and knowledge useful for an advertising career but finding the right skills for the right job often proved very hard. To deal with this problem advertising agencies used their own research tool. Often known as 'The Copy Test' it formed part of an interview, and often meant leaving the applicant alone with a sheet of paper covered in questions before coming back after a set time to collect the answers. There was never one test done by everyone, most agencies had their own version of the test and most agencies would vary the questions depending on the kind of person they wanted to employ. Copy testing fell out of favour at the end of the twentieth century, mainly because most agencies no longer needed such an activity for interviews. By this point university courses, like the one I run, and other courses had produced thousands of students with portfolios full of work showing what they could do. Most of these courses had also coached their students in interview technique and had supported them with careers advice, so matching the right applicant to the right kind of position had become a much more predictable process.

A copy test is still useful on writing courses, or in the first chapter of a book like this, because it helps you identify your own skills. And it draws on the all research about traits of creative people, and what creativity might be, but keeps it all in an area where the results are practical and useful.

Despite the variety in copy tests there were certain types of question that kept recurring. The test below is something like a Greatest Hits collection of copy test problems. It asks you to produce novelty, synthesis and resolution and expects you to show particular traits to deal with each separate question.

Attempt all the questions but DO NOT get nervous and DO NOT think you are failing if you find any question difficult. Many creative careers have been built by people who could only perform well on one of the questions below. If the ability to answer one question well can pay a mortgage, feed children and keep a car on the road, that is something to celebrate. The point of the test is to help you find your own strengths. You DO NOT have to be good at everything all the time. If any question completely confuses you, there is a review of possible answers to help.

Copy Test

Take as long as you like but answer EVERY question.

1. Describe toast to a Martian in a maximum of 50 words.

2. You have two £5 notes; persuade someone to buy the note in your left hand.

3. You have no money, no mobile phone & no credit cards. Describe how you will spend a day in Belgium.

4. Describe the colour red to a blind person.

5. Write a notice asking members of a country club to shower before using the swimming pool.

6. Create an advert for a pair of indestructible socks OR a car that runs on air OR a brand of chewing gum that cures blood pressure problems.

7. Describe your face to someone who will never see it.

8. Write a poem of any length that scans perfectly but contains no rhymes.

Copy Test discussion

Toast

This is about generating ideas around a theme. It also tests your ability to get 'novelty' into a message. If you found this easy and came up with a range of different approaches you may well have potential to work in any area demanding a high turnover of ideas. Somebody who does well on this question would – for example – probably cope with coming up with a stream of ideas for the adventures of a comic book character, or topics for a long-running television series. When teams of people come together to plan future adventures of fictional characters the work is known as 'storylining, or 'story lining.'

Advertisors used this question to test for people who could see familiar products and services in a new way. Over the years I've seen answers from students that describe toast as 'human fuel, simple and effective.' I've also seen clever scientific answers that talk about its food value, and others that link it to a time and place, normally explaining it as part of breakfast. If anyone ever chose to advertise toast, all of those ideas could be a good starting point.

Two £5 notes

This is about focus and organization. You have to create 'differentiation,' finding differences where none appear to exist. Someone who delights in this question is often very good at planning creatively. Such a person might work effectively writing or creating work for a well established market. A good journalist would probably cope well with this question because he or she might be writing a copy with enough of a personal touch to make it stand out in a crowded market. Useful answers to this question include selling the note in your left hand because you think it once belonged to a celebrity. You can also sell it with a personal endorsement; 'I love £5 notes, but I'm prepared to share this love by selling you one.' You could also sell its properties; 'I'll take your clunky change and swap it for this light, easily portable alternative.' This question tests the same skills that advertisers use to sell products in a market crowded with similarities. Nobody ever advertises a hatchback family car by saying: 'It's 4.6 metres long, offers the same number of paint and seat colour options as the competition and more or less matches their fuel consumption figures. If you shop around one other manufacturer is probably offering a better bargain than us at the moment.' But that is often the truth. Cars are made for markets and developing a new model is hugely expensive and risky, so manufacturers repeat successful ideas of the past, and then make an effort to advertise them in ways that suggest the new cars are new and different to what went before. Peugeot offer; 'The drive of your life.' The Fiat Punto was advertised with praise for its 'spirit' etc.

No money, mobile phone...

This is attempting to find something about your personality, and there really is no 'right' answer. There are, however, wrong answers. The wrong answer might involve an admission that you would panic, or you wouldn't know what to do. The right answer would depend on the circumstances in an agency setting the question. Sometimes I have seen inventive answers involving committing a small crime in the hope of getting deported back home. I have also seen people discuss busking for cash. Other solutions involve trying to find a means of making a free call; like heading for a police station to report your predicament.

The question is looking for synthesis and resolution. Your initial reaction to the question should give you some insight into how best your creative talents can be applied. People presenting 'small crime and I get deported' answers might well be maverick talents with good ideas, but they are probably not team players, and may well be good novelists, songwriters etc. By contrast, someone coming up with a practical solution like going to the police and being honest about their problem, might use the same skills if they were employed in an agency booking out talent, or if they worked in an area combining creativity and planning, like development production in television.

Red to a blind person

Any successful answer here needs focus and also the ability to think laterally (i.e. around a problem). Successful answers often revolve around being empathic with your blind audience, and finding some object or experience that has a similar association with red. I've seen people respond to this by suggesting you rub a blind person's cheek and say 'that's the red area.' I also once saw a response suggesting the blind person attempted to read a cheese grater as if it was Braille! If you find such a question easy or exciting it is likely you have the kind of creativity that sees things in terms of a big picture, or 'conceptually.' Pushed to its limits this ability can pay very well because it often helps you to see the potential of a huge idea, and how it can be aimed at a market. People involved in production management have the skills to answer this question well, but the danger of such a responsible job is that you lose touch with 'real' people and with it, the ability to channel ideas towards them. On a small scale people who do well on the red question can also work in areas, like music production, art direction and directing actors. There are plenty of opportunities for people who can focus an idea and find effective ways to communicate.

Country Club Notice

In all the years of using copy test questions with groups this question, or variations on it, have caused the most problems. Many people simply miss the reference to the country club and – with it – miss the creative challenge of the question. A right answer here depends totally on understanding your market, the people reading the notice have joined a country club. This will be expensive. For most of them this achievement means they see themselves as deserving of respect, and would expect the notice to open with words like; 'Would patrons kindly...'

This question is a test of a few creative skills but it focuses most tellingly on your ability to conceive of the outcome of your idea. You have to be able to get into the minds of those who will read the notice. It is also a test of organizational ability and attention to detail. In this respect it shows more clearly than any other question how someone who doesn't see him or herself as creative can play a crucial role in a creative team. The attention to detail here is vital to success in the same way good editing is vital to the success of an ambitious novel or complicated film script. The person with the ambitious or creative idea may well be talented, but may also lack that attention to detail.

Although the news media focus on the Oscar winners for acting, Best Director and Best Film there is a reason the other awards exist. Complicated works like feature films depend on quality in every department and good sound technicians, camera operators and script editors provide an input that supports the better known people involved in the work. It is likely that a good script or book editor could devise a dozen excellent answers to the country club notice question in the time it took a person burdened with massive ideas to devise one or two suitable replies. If you are that person: there are things to celebrate in your ability to give attention to detail. You have a marketable skill. This skill can get you employed, and probably keep you employed when others around you struggle to stay in work. For example; if you worked as an editor on a project – like a book – that was a spectacular flop, it is likely that the author would be the one taking most of the blame, whilst you went on to more editing work.

Indestructible socks, car that runs on air...

The key point here is that the world *has* changed. These impossible products would bring about a difference to most of our lives. A breakthrough in technology does sometimes change the world. For example; DNA profiling has brought about convictions for crimes the police thought they might never solve.

In terms of creative skills major changes in the world demand you take on board the novelty of the new product, produce work that synthesises the new information with the way we live, and think flexibly around the problem. In other words; the right answer here is one that shows clearly how the world has changed, but still remembers that we want to feel secure. Too much new science doesn't work, and pretending the world is just the same also doesn't work. Show people the difference, but make them feel like they understand it. To show how this might work on the copy test question I once came up with a storyboard for the indestructible socks. In my idea a young man in a suit shuffles into a room with bare walls and seats, another young man comes to meet him. They are obviously uncomfortable. They exchange a little conversation until it becomes obvious that one man is picking up the ashes of his grandfather from a crematorium. Having got the box of ashes, he turns to leave, only for the other man to hold up a pair of socks and ask; 'What do we do with these?'

People who enjoy questions like this are often those who can think in the abstract and find themselves happy with notions of change and difference. They are also people who can get things done because they can see the end of a process whilst they are still working on it. Such people are often useful in a team, whilst they tend not to make the best managers, editors or technical people, they do have the creative vision to drive a project forward. One place such skills truly come into their own is in a team writing scripts under pressure. Many comedies and series are written in some form of script factory, a process that usually involves writers coming together, finding out how an entire series will pan out, and then splitting to write their own work. In some cases, whole teams end up in the same room arguing out the final version of the work. The 'indestructible socks' skill matters in these circumstances because the scripts for comedy and drama series often veer into impossible territory when characters are killed off or other massive changes come on board. The ability to absorb these events and write them in a way that never leaves the audience struggling to believe what is going on is central to keeping shows like *Eastenders* at the top of the ratings.

Your face

This is a difficult act of synthesis. A right answer here needs some self-knowledge, some sign that you are able to see yourself the way others see you, and the ability to generate ideas around the theme. On top of all that it needs the kind of editing skills seen in the country club notice and the ability to be focused and not ramble on about yourself. Used by an advertising agency, this question would test the ability to think clearly about a difficult subject and would help the agency to identify someone who might progress to become an account handler. In other words, the kind of person who would spend part of their time explaining creative ideas to clients and then go back to the creative people in the agency and keep them focused on what the client wanted. Someone doing well on this question may well have the ability to see a problem clearly from two sides and could, therefore, find themselves working to manage a project. It is also likely that someone finding this question exciting or inspiring could go on to write personal and very detailed pieces of journalism. Novelists, and those working in the developing field of creative nonfiction, would probably perform well on this question.

Poem of any length that scans perfectly but contains no rhymes

This is a test of your sense of balance, timing and rhythm in writing. It demands creative skills and organizational ability, it also demands some intelligence. The usefulness of the question to advertising is obvious, catchy and memorable slogans get products and services noticed. The skill of summarizing a complicated idea in a few words, and also grabbing attention, can earn a writer good money. A number of famous writers have started a career in advertising. Some – like Fay Weldon – worked in the area for several years. One of the most famous former advertising copywriters is Salman Rushdie. Rushdie won the Booker Prize for his novel *Midnight's Children* and when the Booker Prize had produced 40 years of winners, Rushdie's novel was voted the best winner of all, a unique award. For all this success, it is likely the best known words he ever wrote are still the three that formed the slogan for a hugely successful advertising campaign for cream cakes: 'Naughty. But nice.'

People who cope well with this question could go on to a range of writing activities in which the sense of how the words sound is as important as the information they carry. Poets form one end of this group, using words to make complicated and emotional points. At the other end, sub-editors in the news media need a sense of rhythm to write attention grabbing headlines, or bulletins that will sound right when read on radio or television. Some people with these skills work effectively in jobs where they speak to groups of people. Teachers, trainers, comedians, radio and television presents all need to be able to invent phrases in the moment.

At the start of the chapter I said we would be: *Considering strengths and abilities you may have. Drawing connections between your talents and a range of opportunities in the working world. Showing you that lack of ideas, lack of contacts or lack of time need not be impossible barriers when it comes to getting your work out there and making money. Giving you some exercises to help you identify the best routes to getting a break.*

The copy test contains the exercises and each consideration of your answer tries to link the skills shown in answering the question with one or more areas of work for writers and people with creative ideas. It should be obvious by this stage that writing and working with creative ideas are part of a wide range of possibilities you could follow. It should also be obvious that some people without too many creative ideas of their own are still vitally important in the creative industries. The question on the country club notice asks for a kind of creativity we don't see celebrated too often in the media. But people who can organize, pay attention to detail and tinker with an idea are as valuable to some areas of creative work as people who bombard us with big ideas.

You might want to take some time to think about how easy or difficult you found each question, and what the analysis of the answers has taught you about your own skills. You might also want to flip ahead to the end of the book and chase up some of the resources on offer to help you understand more about the kind of work that might be out there waiting for you, or check out the glossary to find more about the work done by people in jobs like account handling and development production.

In the next chapter, we will look in more detail at the kind of work available to anyone intending to write for money.

2 The Job

This chapter is: *A detailed look at professional writing, taking into account the range of the work on offer. Discussion of pros and cons of different areas of work. Concluding statements about the nature of professional writing work at present and in the future. Consideration of likely earnings in the different areas of work.*

I'll also confess something about this chapter that doesn't appeal to me. This is probably the hardest chapter to write because I am attempting to describe a situation that is constantly changing. The best I can do is line up the main points and capture some recent examples to explain them. So – be warned – this is a long chapter by comparison to some of the others. With regard to 'the job,' and having spent over a decade running a university programme in Professional Writing, I can state three things with certainty:

1. The possibilities for paid writing work are as varied and bizarre as you can imagine. The constant changes brought about by lowering production costs linked to ever more powerful information technology mean that paid work is constantly being created in areas that previously offered little opportunity for profit. Most of this paid work produces small amounts of money, but it does allow people to build careers and develop contacts, and if you are looking to kick start a writing career it could be exactly where you need to concentrate your efforts.

2. The traditional jobs and career paths followed by writers have been adversely affected by the advance of the new technologies. A perfect example of this is the ongoing crisis in journalism. Local and national papers are struggling to cope profitably in a world offering internet news updates for free. Customers appear increasingly reluctant to pay for news, advertisers are not easily persuaded to pay for adverts in papers read by declining numbers of people. Most writers looking to start a career today will not be able to develop one set of skills and hone them in one career area. To be a writer these days is often to be someone with creative talent and contacts, and the ability to apply ideas to problems, and get paid for the effort you make. I apologise if that sounds vague, but that sentence is the most truthful statement I can make about the 'job' of being a writer in the 21st century. This chapter is an attempt to look at this complicated situation.

3. There are lots of great books on the market explaining how to write professionally. Some, like the annual 'handbook' tomes, are packed with good general advice and lots of contacts. Others set out to show you how to write and pitch a novel. These books are all designed to do their own job well, but very few of them deal directly with the difficulty of trying to get a break in a rapidly changing world. Most of the books on one aspect of writing, like producing books or journalism, concentrate on specific targets. Most aspiring writers have a better chance of getting a first break if they aim away from the traditional areas. I want to keep this book practical but I

> think a metaphor might be useful in this case. To put it bluntly, you have a better chance of a break if you aim for a moving target. It is true that moving targets are harder to hit, but the one thing about the moving targets in the writing world is that *everyone* struggles to hit them so the difference between a novice and an experienced writer counts for less. Another advantage is whilst they may be hard to hit, there are lots of them.

Because the situation is changing, the best I can do in this chapter is to explain the main points, illustrate these points with some varied examples, and show you ways of using the talents you identified in the first chapter to meet the needs of 'the job.' To me this chapter – despite its length – is short, because there is no way it can cover the diversity of 'the job' of writing and I'm conscious of the number of corners I have cut in completing it.

Defining the job of a professional writer isn't as easy as some people think. I spent years on the fringes of paranormal research, in particular UFO investigation. It struck me in preparing this chapter that UFO investigation is a little like trying to define professional writing. In both areas we have people who think they know what the term means, but mapping the whole area proves difficult. What we are faced with is evidence of something going on, many sightings fitting specific patterns but when added up, they never explain the whole phenomenon. Probably because we are trying to describe something that is being changed by our interest in it, and we struggle to separate our own ideas of what we are looking at from the evidence in front of us, so we often lack objectivity.

I am not alone in thinking like this and one report, published in 2007, set out to map the working world of the professional writer. As with the paranormal, the investigators had to go to the evidence they could find, and make the best guesses they could about what it told them about the whole picture. There are a number of organizations involved in monitoring and managing the working life of professional writers. Between them the The National Union of Journalists and National Council for the Training of Journalists look after the interests of journalists and work to ensure those going into the profession are well prepared. For book authors The Society of Authors does a similar job. The Writer's Guild, grew out of looking after creative writers working in skilled trade areas like scriptwriting and continues to look after many of the disparate talents in film, television and radio. The authors' and writers' organizations don't have such a strong training role and – technically speaking – The Society of Authors is not a trade union. Their membership is so varied that it would be hard to identify a great deal of common aims, or common working conditions, beyond the members' wish for better rates of pay and respect for the integrity of their work.

Some other organizations monitor earnings. The Authors' Licensing and Collecting Society deals with fees due from copying of copyrighted work. The Inland Revenue has figures on tax returns filed by those working in the creative industries. The 2007 survey went round some of the main organizations involved in working with 'authors' and tried to establish what they earned and how they earned their money. They managed to produce figures, based mainly on tax returns, though some of the conclusions drawn when the work was discussed in specialist journals and the press varied. Magazines like *The Author* – published by The Society of Authors – felt the conclusions matched the concerns of their members, papers like *The Guardian* discussed wider issues. Broadly the survey established the following, as of 2007:

- On average a British author earns around £4,000 per year.
- This figure has dropped from £6,333, a figure identified in a similar survey in 2001.
- Around 25,000 people in the UK file tax returns as authors.
- 10% of UK authors account for 50% of the money earned by all UK authors.
- 60% of UK professional writers need other sources of income to survive.

Income is being squeezed badly in some areas, notably in the way advances for literary, (i.e. ambitious and artistic), novels have stayed around the same figure for over a decade and the way that the increasing digitization of written work hasn't resulted in massive payments for those whose work has been made available in digital form. 85% of those involved in the survey reported having work available digitally for which they received no payment.

One thing this survey makes clear is the lack of any significant dividing line between 'authors' and 'professional writers' many people involved in selling their ideas and using words as their main means of producing work fall into both categories. The dispiritingly low figures in the survey don't take account of a few elements of good news, such as:

Some professional writers earn massive salaries but remain outside the survey because their work in areas like development production and advertising is taxed at source and they don't file independent tax returns for any freelance work.

Some of those earning small sums as professional writers do other jobs they love, teaching being a particularly popular main occupation for writers. Many of these people are quite happy with their sideline and the money they earn from it, and like the balance of a main salaried job with a second, more creative occupation.

Making complete sense of the survey would take us the length of this book but it does suggest a few things we need to take on board before we examine the range of things that make up 'the job' you might want to do.

I would also like to add a few points of my own to the confusing mass of statistics and ideas already presented. Firstly, I would like to remind you this is a book about *Getting a Break as a Writer* so when we devote the remainder of this chapter to considering the jobs available it is important we focus mainly on the accessible jobs you might be able to do, even if you are a complete novice. These jobs are closer to the £4,000 a year part-time working life of the professional writers who made up most of the survey outlined above. Yes, it is true that a few people out there earn vast sums, and a few of the very highest earners got their first massive pay cheque by reaching the right agent or publisher. But, statistically speaking, the breaks enjoyed by J K Rowling and the like are very hard to come by. In fact, her success was so freakish nobody involved at the early stage of her career had a clue what they were dealing with. Once she had her publishing deal, her agent – Christopher Little – did the sensible thing and advised her not to give up the day job. The £1500 advance he had secured her was very welcome but neither he, nor his newly signed author, had high expectations that her earnings would allow her to give up teaching.

For most authors a four figure advance would be a result, even today. For many of those working hard to get their book noticed, such an advance remains a distant dream. If you are one such person I'd suggest you take on board the range and diversity of possible work that will soon follow in this chapter. One depressing element in my working life of interviewing potential undergraduate students and doing the odd bit of script and manuscript doctoring is the amount of work I see that has no hope of success in the form it is presented. I read an estimate from – I think – the Society of Authors once suggesting that one in every 2000 novels written goes on to get a publishing deal. At the time I wondered how they could ever know. Since then I have had some insight into this, sometimes because I am faced with an interview candidate who brings his/her novel to the interview. As a rule these people aren't that interested in the general training we offer. They are interested in the chance of me reading their entire book and giving them feedback for free, and some of them imagine the route to success is as simple as me suggesting one agent or publisher. I don't read the manuscripts in their entirety but I often skim them and typically find basic flaws that would stop them selling. So, for example, someone making a basic mistake with capital letters or possessive apostrophes on page 1 is likely to be repeating the same mistake on page 221. A film script in which characters spend the opening pages delivering chunks of plot in their speeches is likely to repeat the mistake to the very end. I'm sure this pattern is repeated many times, with people slogging away for hundreds of hours on ideas that contain terminal flaws, precluding any chance of success.

One route through the problem is to get help, often by paying for it. Another route which doesn't always occur to people is to get work, any kind of work, involving developing words and ideas for an audience. It is no accident that those already in writing based trades, like journalism and advertising, are often well-represented amongst the hot new novelists in any given year.

Something I think it worth considering if your ultimate aim is to sell a big idea, like a novel, is honing your skills elsewhere. You stand to gain two things. One obvious gain is the sharpening of your ability to communicate with an audience. Another benefit that often eludes those focused on novels, scripts and the like, is the chance to find something else you are good at. Finding something else you are good at really matters in terms of getting a break as a writer. Firstly, because the range of skills you develop can help with any major writing ambitions you have. For example; if you want to be a novelist, it helps to have done live events earlier in your career because the performance skills developed at this point can help with promoting your novel. Secondly, finding other things you are good at matters because it may be that your writing ambitions will change as a result. It is – frankly – naive to assume that getting one major work, like a novel or script, accepted will 'sort out' your life. The fairly normal people behind the vast tonnage of published books mentioned in the last chapter are proof of that. Many people who think they will find satisfaction and respect from writing creative works like novels, eventually find both of those things in other areas of work, using the same skills.

What follows in this chapter is a round up of different professional writing activities, varied jobs with varying rewards in terms of money and personal satisfaction. We'll start with work that may pay little or nothing, but does allow you to put achievements on your CV. We'll also start by assuming you know nobody in the writing world capable of opening a door for you. So we're starting at the very bottom, I'm assuming only that you have enough ambition and focus to have read this far in this book. I'll also take the trouble to 'start' this series of examples twice. In the first section of examples we will look at 'creative writing,' in other words the arty end of the market containing a lot of poetry, short stories and the like. Then we'll begin again, looking more at the 'real world' options of simply getting stuck in and writing for others with a foothold in the industry. So, where – exactly – do we start?

We could start with a girl I met in her final year of GCSE studies. Rachel Jones came from a local grammar school and – as she would remind me four years later – turned up for her interview in a hoodie, and mentioned her favourite music. The fact we got onto discussing Slipknot (as in the US band of that name), was apparently central to her decision to leave school and start a BTEC National Diploma. From my point of view she appeared to have the arty qualities, intelligence and deep thinking nature that marked her out right away as a writer. I often come back from such interviews and tell one of my colleagues, 'that one was definitely one of ours.' I probably said something similar after meeting Rachel. Two years later she moved up to our Foundation Degree course. By this time she was well-known in the department. Anyone new to teaching her would be told something like; 'you know the one, dresses in black, writes poetry.'

The poetry was central to Rachel's decision to join the Professional Writing course, and in her first term she was faced with an assignment she could only pass if she produced proof she had arranged to work for 'an identified employer of writers.' Poetry remained her first love, so much so that the easier routes through the assignment – like completing a week of work experience in a press agency – never looked likely. In the end the evidence that got her through the first assignment fell into my email inbox when a local network of writers decided to stage a live 'Word-Slam' event. I put Rachel in touch with them and she was quickly added to the bill. Her 'evidence' for the assignment came in the form of the emails confirming her scheduled appearance. Low ticket sales led to the cancellation of the event but we had – at least – the consolation of finding an avenue that saw Rachel through two years of assignments requiring evidence she was making things happen for herself. At the end of her first term I took her group to the National Portrait Gallery, at the end of the visit she set off down Charing Cross Road whilst most of the others set off for a pub. Her destination was Covent Garden, and The Poetry Café, where she managed to talk herself into appearing at live nights. In less than a year I went to

Gravesend Library and watched Rachel topping the bill at a live event celebrating National Poetry Day. She was worth the headlining slot because she had managed to put more bodies into the crowd than the other act that night. Most of this had been achieved with a combination of a very unique talent, and common sense. Rachel obviously had faith in her work and the ability to produce a varied catalogue of poems, but the other thing getting her through her assignments, and creating new opportunities was the pragmatic quality she applied to developing her career. If opportunities came my way, as with an internet radio station contacting me, I would pass them on to her and Rachel got a few short poems broadcast online. Because the recordings were very short they made a perfect means of ensuring the station's timing ran exactly to schedule because a 45 second poem could easily be slotted in if a play or audio book ran short. For every break I passed on to Rachel she made a few of her own. She soon addressed the obvious things, like a Facebook page and MySpace page. Less obvious moves included changing her name, performing briefly as 'Ryoko' (distinctive and not a name generally associated with poets from Kent). By the end of her course she was performing in the end of year show, billed as 'Rae Louise' and closing her set by playing a poem set to music and available as a download.

From my point of view I saw an ambitious and intelligent writer grow in confidence and I knew she could be relied on to cope with every challenge, and use the assignment targets to focus her in producing a varied catalogue of work. At the start of her Professional Writing course Rae had work written at home. By the end she had evidence of networking and the beginnings of a writer's CV. She had achieved both by looking for opportunities, taking on board constructive suggestions, and building on the successes that came her way. Frankly, this is common sense. Rachel is in this book because she impressed her tutors and made things happen. The means by which she did this could easily be adapted by anyone with writing ambitions.

Rae has her own take on her fledgling writing career.

Rae Louise Jones

1. What to you are the best things about performing and writing poetry?

For me, it has been the fact that it gives me the opportunity to write whatever I want, and however I feel, without any restrictions or boundaries. I feel the best poetry is that which is written following no rules other than the individual poet's own. I haven't had the easiest of a past or a home life, and when I was younger I had little self-esteem, so writing my thoughts and emotions, and then turning them into poetry, has always been the easiest way for me to express myself.

The best thing about performing poetry is that it really makes the poems come alive; for some people, who may not really be fans of poetry at all, performing your poem may be the only way to encourage them to enjoy the experience. Giving them a copy to read may not have any kind of impact, but turning the piece into a performance really draws people in. On a final note, there is nothing more exhilarating than performing your work to an audience. It's as simple as that.

2. Have there been nervous and off-putting times in developing your contacts and trying to a break as a poet?
In the beginning, I would have said that the most off-putting thing was people dismissing your poetry simply because it's just that, a poem, and not a lot of people seem to "get" poetry. Nowadays, I'd say the most off-putting thing for me is the regular experience of attending a certain open mic night (which shall remain anonymous). It is probably the biggest exposure I get as an unknown, as it is a very popular weekly open mic night, and I will continue to attend it for that reason. However, I have never felt completely welcomed by the regulars and the other poets; it's almost as if there is an exclusive clique for the more established poets and people in the area, and if you're a newbie or simply not from around there, it's almost as if they will tolerate you, but never fully accept you. That, for me, has always been an awkward obstacle to overcome, and I wouldn't be surprised if other poets attending open mic nights didn't experience it themselves at some point.

3. Where do you want the progress made to date to take you in the future?
I would like to be able to perform my poetry to bigger audiences, not just at small open mic nights, and I hope to get more poems published in the future. What I would also like to do, which may seem ambitious right now, is to form a band in which I could be the vocalist and lyricist, perhaps even re-write some of my poems to be more like song lyrics. I already have the experience and confidence to get up on a stage and perform, I just need to find some musicians. Watch this space!

4. How much does earning money for your poetry matter to you?
It actually does matter quite a bit to me, precisely because it's hard to earn money from writing poetry alone. I've never actually earned any money at all from my poetry, if anything I've enabled others to earn money, from paying to enter poetry competitions,

to paying small fees to perform at the open mic nights. Being a cash-strapped student, I look forward to the day when I can start earning money from my writing, not just so that I have money to speak of, but also because I would love to earn a living from doing something that is very close to my heart. Be it from poetry readings or performing with a future band, I think the most money to be earned, in my case at least, will be from live performances.

5. Have you identified any positive role models for your future writing career? If so, who are they and what do they teach you?

My biggest influences have always been lyricists and songwriters, rather than authentic poets. The person who is currently having an increasing amount of influence over my writing is the Japanese singer-songwriter Ayumi Hamasaki. Many will not be familiar with her, but in Japan and Asia she is one of the most successful artists of all time, the aspect of her artistry most popular with fans and respected by critics being her lyrics, all her own. What her work has taught me is that poetry can be presented and sold in a more accessible form than mere publishing or reading aloud, and yet still be completely honest and heartfelt. Reading the English translations of her lyrics, many would be surprised at how unashamedly honest and introspective they are, seemingly more suited to an underground, "alternative" artist than one as successful as her. While I am by no means trying to emulate the heights Hamasaki has reached, I will freely admit that I am trying to follow in her footsteps in keeping my poetry/lyrics as truthful and honest as can be, at all times, but if it means experimenting with music in order to try and attract even bigger audiences for my writing, then so be it.

6. If your present day self could walk into the room and speak to your GCSE student self in the hoodie, what would you tell her now? Would you tell her to do anything differently to the way you did it?

All I would say to her is to not do anything differently, in terms of taking up different opportunities. I would tell her to stick to more or less the same path that I've so far followed, because on the whole it has been a very rewarding one, and I dread to think how much less I may have achieved had I done anything different. The only thing I would encourage her to do differently is to try everything younger. At twenty, I already sometimes feel "old" when noticing the amount of people around the same age as me, who are already starting to make a name for themselves in the varied world of the creative arts. Creativity and willingness to take chances, I believe, are more fruitful and potent during a person's younger years, and so I would tell my GCSE student self to start attending open mic nights and trying to form a band immediately, rather than wait to the ages of eighteen and twenty, respectively.

7. If your thirty year old self were to walk in on you answering these questions, what would she be like and what would she say if she had to introduce herself to a stranger in a couple of sentences?

I hope she would be happy and content, in other words, not having been disillusioned by the limited success of poetry and be still working a part-time (or dare I say it, full-time) job in retail. I hope she would have made a name for herself either as a writer, or as a singer in a band plus performance poet. The latter is what I really would love aspire to right now, and I hope my future self would represent as close to those aspirations as possible.

Introducing herself to a stranger in a few sentences, I'd like her to say:

"Hi! I'm Rae. I work as a singer, lyricist, and performance poet. I live in Camden, not far from the High Street. It's great; the band has a following but on the whole we can still go shopping for groceries in peace. You should go to my next reading; it'll be small and cosy, and the atmosphere is very laid-back and warm, the regulars are lovely guys. For my holidays? Oh, I'm going to Tokyo with some friends. Yes, I am very happy."

Rae Louise Jones and many like her are most likely to make money from live performance, a point she identifies in answering the questions. For many poets and others involved in the creative side of writing, live events and arts 'festival' type events are the best chance of a regular income from their writing. Even established writers find themselves doing such work. Financing poetry events and groups is often the responsibility of local authorities and finding regular income for writers is always a headache, especially in times of national recession. Some organizations, like schools and colleges do have budgets for guest lecturers. These budgets, whilst seldom generous, do mean writers can earn anywhere from a few dozen to a few hundred pounds depending on the size of the group they meet, the length of time they are expected to stay etc.

Sourcing money and supporting such events isn't easy. In many towns and cities it is the responsibility of the Borough Arts Officer to finance, support and co-ordinate arts events. Being innovative as he or she does all of this is also expected. In the course of compiling this book I spoke to Sarah Robson, an Arts Development Officer for Maidstone Borough Council. She discussed the problems, pitfalls and positives of her work. I approached her in a time of tough financial conditions, though if you talk to Borough Arts Officers in general, at any time, all of them will tell you that there are *always* financial restrictions. For all that, Sarah Robson was able to identify some positives and some strategic moves that can still produce results.

The Borough Council's Cultural Grants ceased to run in 2008. There are no other forms of funding for arts available from the Council. We usually sign post people to Arts Council England or the Kent Investment Fund. We have supported writing events and workshops in the past. Most of these look to supporting literacy and promoting positive mental health in young people. We work with the Maidstone Youth Forum to help guide our education programme – they choose the type of workshops they would like delivered in their area. Between 2005-2008, we ran an Artist Newsletter which encouraged local writers, an editor and artists to showcase their work. The project was funded by Arts Council England. One of the commonest mistakes most people make in any funding application form is not to read the application criteria first to check whether they are eligible or what is required from the applicant. I see the Adult Education service, who deliver writing workshops, becoming more of a key player in promoting writing and literacy.

Nobody promised it would be easy to get a break as a writer, but Sarah Robson's comments do – at least – show routes to results. Above all, they indicate that as one door is closed, resourceful people in positions of responsibility have to redefine what they are doing and think carefully about how to source money and help. It's never easy, but even in very hard times, it is still possible.

I should have taken more time to consult the local Arts Development Officer before embarking on *Dreams Wander On*. I'll confess the following example was my own idea, it is included here to show how it is possible to create a book without involving an agent, editor or commercial publisher. I have gone on from this work to start an operation with my students involving us offering copywriting services to create books for charities and voluntary organizations. Both these areas of work will appear later in this book when we consider ways of getting a book published yourself. However, at this point we need to consider the basic problem of making something happen.

The truth about the book that started me on this journey is that its origins were far from honourable. I had a good friend who owned a coffee bar and we would often talk about our working lives. He was interested in writing, and together we concocted an idea to start a writers' group in his coffee bar. I wanted a relatively easy job in which I could use a lot of the exercises from my undergraduate classes, without the added baggage of managing students to a qualification. My friend wanted a chance to keep his coffee bar open into the evening with a paying crowd inside. We both wanted some money to subsidise the whole operation, and this was where we ran into trouble. The local borough council and the National Lottery both turned us down and we soon realized two able-bodied, reasonably well-off men trying to snag funds for a writing group were likely to struggle. Had we taken on board the kind of advice provided earlier in this chapter, things might have gone differently. There was a grimly funny conversation over a couple of beers one night as we started to list everyone in a minority group we knew. My friend had access to a few lesbians, mainly because they seemed to frequent his coffee bar. I knew a few disabled people… we didn't seriously consider taking the idea in those directions, but I'm sure you see where it could have gone. Avoiding that level of cynicism and deciding to ditch the project was probably the most honourable decision we made.

I did, however, take on board my wife's suggestion that I approach the local hospice with the same idea. This led to a successful bid for charity money and a one year programme involving me managing a writers' group and editing a book. The project I had originally suggested involved publishing a book to be sold to raise funds for the hospice. We called the book *Dreams Wander On* a reference to the work the writers were leaving behind, since most of the group were fighting terminal illness. The title also came from my favourite poem, the last haiku written by the Japanese master poet, Basho.

> Sick on a journey -
> over parched fields
> dreams wander on.[1]

The juxtaposition of the poet's dying body, with the knowledge that his life would continue to have resonance for others seemed the perfect focus for the project we had planned. The rewards of the project were a long way from the somewhat cynical way my friend and I had started thinking about a group in his coffee bar. Yes, I was paid and I managed a book project. But I also got involved in a very emotional journey, and the group managed to achieve things none of us believed possible at the start. One member of the group even privileged me with the difficult task of helping her write letters for her children to open after her death.

We had put aside money for a book launch event and – finally – my friend's coffee bar got involved. One moment that will

1 Translation from *On Love and Barley: Haiku of Basho* – Penguin 1985
Other translations of the final haiku vary.

stay with me forever is over-hearing Dave – a man who had spent his working life in railway engineering – mumbling; 'I never thought I'd do this,' as he signed a copy of the book to which he had contributed. Dave was signing the book about an hour after we had left the local Waterstone's, having just broken the house record for the largest crowd at a book launch, and also managed the largest number of books sold in the store at an author event. The record for sales of books had been relatively easy to break. The production costs of the book had been under-written by our grant so we didn't have any money to recoup. On that basis we marked the book at the low price of £3 and offered Waterstone's 50% of the cover price, meaning they got a lot more money per copy than on most of their best selling titles, and had an item cheaper than most of the low-price gift books on their counter. The hospice enjoyed much goodwill in the community. Many books sold on the night went to people who wanted to buy them simply to support the hospice. Some people bought a handful.

The writing group was about making the most of limited life expectancy, it was never about book sales and representing it in this way doesn't do justice to the whole project. However, in the context of this book on *Getting a Break as a Writer* there are important lessons here. With the right idea it is possible to get involved in writing projects, and produce books that allow you to achieve things as a writer. More importantly, such projects can open up experiences and insights into the world that will challenge you both as a writer and a person. They need thinking about, carefully, and I am not suggesting that you start spamming every worthy organization in your local *Yellow Pages* until you can get a book deal. I am – however – pointing out that some lateral thinking on your part could identify a project you could deliver. Money might well be available if you find the right project, and the rewards on offer go much further than the money. Typically a project like this would pay a few thousand pounds, slightly more than you might get as an advance on a first book from a commercial publisher. It is worth comparing such a project with a commercial book. Both approaches could help you become a published author. Managing a small local project could get you involved in all stages of book production, particularly useful if you have no prior experience of this and – crucially – if you do your preparation work properly you have a better chance of seeing the work through to final success than you do if you start writing a book for a commercial publisher.

So far we have considered examples starting with unpaid live work and gone on to more structured one-off projects. Most of the focus has been on the creative side of writing. Writers wishing to stay in this area often need some regular income to support them through periods when books, poems and the like are paying very little. The work on offer can be very varied. A few writers have written entertainingly about the pros and cons of such a life. I would thoroughly recommend Martin Millar's novel *Love and Peace With Melody Paradise.* The story concerns a writer's involvement with a group of new age travelers, the organization of a festival and the disastrous literary event he runs as part of the festival. Chaotic planning, incessant rain and his inability to work out exactly what he is supposed to be doing all contribute to a cautionary tale. I approached Martin Millar for comments on the events of the novel and he insisted the whole work is fictional. However, the chaos and confusion he describes does resemble many horror stories professional writers tell about the worst gig or event they ever experienced. Even household names involved in creative writing can struggle to say exactly what it is they do for a living. Simon Armitage's collection of writings on the north of England *All Points North* includes two short fragments both called 'Directory Enquiries.' In the first he is phoned at home by Direct Line Insurance who check he has ceased working as a probation officer and become a poet. In 'Directory Enquiries II' they inform him his life insurance premium has been increased as a result of his career change. When he asks why his new job is higher rated than the previous employment he is told the danger is 'nutters and that.'[2] He obviously wishes to protest but the caller from Direct Line points out he can only do this if he tells them 'exactly what it is you do for a living.' Armitage is stuck for an answer, and ends up paying the higher premium.

Both of the stories above are cautionary tales, told with self-depreciating humour, but they make a serious point. Creative writers in search of a steady income often struggle to hold down one consistent line of employment. In these

2 – The increase in life insurance moving from probation officer to poet isn't as implausible as it sounds, though the risk isn't 'nutters and that.' For insurance purposes allied occupations are often lumped together by companies and probation officers, as local government workers, can be ranked alongside tax officials and other office bound employees. The few professional poets seeking life insurance tend to be classed as entertainers, a group who accrue a higher risk because entertaining involves travel. Much travel by entertainers is late at night, many entertainers earn so little they are obliged to drive themselves to and from live performances. Tiredness, drink and stress further complicate the situation and, predictably, entertainers run higher risks than many others in the population from transport accidents and the early onset of life threatening illness. Despite the famous cases – like John Lennon – few entertainers experience death by nutter.

circumstances their careers move from one project to another, often with some steady part-time work alongside. If you are focused on a creative career, in other words a career with your own individual writing – like poems or novels – as a central part of the work, it is likely you face similar choices to Simon Armitage. There are up and down sides to this career path. The positives include keeping your own creative vision central to your career, often finding things out about your abilities you didn't suspect to be true. You also get to do things that others envy. The down sides include inconsistent levels of income and the attached problems that brings. It is – for example – hard to negotiate a mortgage if you are a freelance writer. Harder, generally, than it would be for a self-employed hairdresser or builder. The hairdresser's arguments about his or her income can take into account the previous years and there is a reasonable degree of expectation that a hairdresser consistently earning a good living can sustain the success. In the case of a writer steady success can still precede a dip in earnings.

In the circumstances it is easy to understand why many people with an ambition to write novels, scripts, stage plays and the like opt for related trades, like teaching or lecturing in English. Those jobs, at least, form the basis of the negotiation of a mortgage. For those a little more adventurous there are other regular areas of work, projects that appear to have the ability to survive fluctuations in the economy. A range of writing activities, often linked to some branch of the public services, can offer a more challenging alternative to standard teaching and lecturing posts. One example of this work is run by the Writers in Prison network. Part of the Arts in Prison Network, the writers network dates back to 1998 when it was appointed to administer existing work for writers in prison. The previous programme had been founded in 1992. Writers in prison deal directly with inmates, often responding to individual needs and combining writing work with activities designed to build self-esteem and help prisoners rehabilitate. There is also scope for the writers to develop their own individual work and when the Writers in Prison Network website offers up job vacancies writers are generally encouraged to personalize applications with details of what they would bring to the posts. Like most such areas this is work that suits some, and would prove too challenging for others. A sense of the tensions and triumphs available comes in a comment posted by one writer in prison on the organization's website: "In this strange and sometimes harsh world, creativity flourishes..."

Clive Hopwood of the Writers in Prison Network answered the following questions

1. How long has WIPN been running?
After a couple of pioneer projects in the late 1980s/early 1990s the Scheme was launched in 1992 with eight residencies. The Writers in Prison Network (WIPN), formed in 1996, took over the running of the Scheme in 1997. Over 130 residencies have been delivered in the last 18 years.

2. Where, and in what proportion, do you draw down funds for your work?
Arts Council England provide approximately 50% of the annual funding for the core residency scheme, about £140,000+. Currently the other two major funders are the National Offender Management Service (NOMS) and the individual prisons where residencies are running – each provide about 25% of the funding.

Other funders in the past have included Prison Education Services, the Prisoners Learning & Skills Unit, the Offenders Learning & Skills Unit, the Business, Innovations & Skills Dept and the Office for Contracted Prisons.

Each residency costs £20K a year delivering 880 hours of work. A prison averages £47K p.a.. If we can turn one offender round that's £27K saved!

3. In times of recession how tight are your budgets?
We have always operated on tight budgets but we plan ahead and network well. Failing a major funder pulling out we see the scheme as surviving this current downturn.

4. Given there is no typical writer can you expand a little on age range, background of writers you have employed and the motivation of some of these writers in applying to WIPN?
The following could be said to hold true for the majority of our WIRs:

Strong track record in published/performed work in poetry, fiction, drama, television/radio/film, journalism or oral storytelling, and invariably in more than one of these areas

Wide experience of working with writers in groups (inc. running workshops) and as individuals (1-2-1s)

Work experience involved examples such as work in prisons, the mental health environment or writers with special needs etc.

Experience of having done writer's residencies before

Skills match against needs of the prison/ writer is willing to undertake training.

Keen understanding of the unique nature of working within a prison

5. What specific training do writers need to start with you, and does the training lead to some potential candidates deciding to duck out of the work?

All the new writers have a one week, residential Induction Course covering how a prison works, its security priorities, working with low literacy, the perspectives of offenders and officers and how to deliver the creative arts in a criminal justice setting. We cover everything from publishing to drama, oral storytelling to life stories, poetry and performance to magazine publishing, video to radio/audio production. Our training prepares writers to stretch themselves. No one, having undergone the training, has ever decided not to do the job. WIPN provides ongoing support and gathers all our writers for three conferences a year.

6. The briefs when advertised are quite general, can you expand a little on what 'writing' in prison might cover and how much individual choice about the work done lies with the writer.

WIPN works with each individual prison to devise a brief that meets their needs, they are all different and they need different briefs and different strategies from the writers. Some work is common. Everyone delivers workshops and 1-2-1 surgeries. Other work can include writing a newspaper, drama, producing DVDs to introduce people to prison, reading groups, adult literacy (overlapping with the education dept.), creating stories on CD for the prisoner's children etc. For a flavour of a 'typical' day we have the WRITERS BEHIND BARS leaflet on our website. Individual writers do have a lot of creative input, and we work with them to ensure this is used.

7. Are there any examples of innovation, good practice or impressive achieving of project aims you want to share?

Every year a new intake of highly creative and innovative artists join the Network and they are full of ideas. The number of innovatory ideas would take a volume. To name a few:

The **Pathways to Journalism** course was developed over several years with the National Union of Journalists, to support the publishing of quality prison magazines and to offer a national accreditation in journalism and graphic design.

Stories Connect started as an idea in the United States...a reading group programme focused around story and character rather than the quality of the writing, also piloted with probation services.

Storybook Dad/Mum – we didn't invent this but we have pioneered it. We use stories – original and found, written and recorded etc – to keep a connection between an offender and their children.

Prison Video – WIPN has pioneered video production in prisons since the mid-1990s covering a range of genres and continuing to diversify.

Books – WIPN is the largest producer of prison magazines, anthologies and collections. Using our own imprint we assist our writers to get offenders' (and staff) work into print. Again the genres and projects vary immensely.

8. What job satisfaction do writers report on completing a contract?

NOTE: WIPN responded with a range of comments amounting to 800 words, detailing varied areas of satisfaction from very personal satisfaction, to pride in work created and the knowledge that offenders' lives had been changed. Their web site also includes some of these comments.

9. How many writers do this work regularly?

20+ writers in residence at any one time. More when experienced writers are taken on to run concurrent special projects.

10. Other than writers using the work to provide income alongside their creative work, do some writers take new directions or use WIPN time on their CV to kick-start other similar projects after finishing with you?

A number of our writers are in their second or third residency with WIPN. There are numerous others who have gone on to other prison-related work. Prison can become 'addictive' and we continue to work in the field long after our residencies end, the work is so challenging and rewarding.

One writer at a young offenders institution with a background in the BBC Script Dept surprised herself by helping to produce three rap CDs in the space of a year; another who came from a non-fiction background now regularly uses drama and storytelling in his work; personally, without my prison residency I would probably never have got into screenwriting and video production. The majority of our ex-writers tell us that working as a WIR has increased their self-confidence, broadened their range of skills, honed their workshop and organizational skills and encouraged to explore a whole range of projects that they might not have considered before. All return to their writing, having been given a breathing space financially.

Former writers in prison, and others with a similar activity on their CV, often find further employment becomes easier to get. People respect the challenge faced and trust in the writer's ability to cope with other projects.

This book – of course – is about getting a break as a writer and the demanding nature of a writing residency in prison is only likely to be available to those with experience. There is – however – a serious point to placing this example in the current chapter. If we trace the examples from Rae Louise

Jones to the Writers in Prison Network it is obvious that a career path emerges. Vague and unpredictable for sure, but most certainly a path open to those who see themselves primarily as creative writers, focused on challenging ideas and their own unique use of words. If your vision is to write novels that gain respect and earn you a reputation, with an income to match, then the route carved out here allows you the chance to build that career. From the start of hustling your own slots at live literature events, through getting involved with a local network and kick-starting your own projects or joining the higher profile projects run by others you should always be somewhere within reach of contacts who can help you. Those around you should know something about sourcing money and should have experience(s) on which you can draw. More significantly working along the lines described in this series of examples gives you the chance to develop a highly individual portfolio, showing original work, not necessarily shaped by the needs of a market. It also allows you a series of jumping off points, should other opportunities arise.

If you currently have no experience but see yourself in the long run as a writer working on your own terms the obvious starting points are at live events, open mic nights, poetry slams, local literary events etc. If you lack the confidence to start at such events you can always begin online. Online work comes with a health warning. One danger of posting work on the internet is that you stay there, permanently. Whilst writers' websites have proven a useful meeting ground and a source of news and information for aspiring writers they also allow your more introspective and anti-social tendencies to come to the fore. There are business models that allow writers posting work online to make money, but these models tend to work best in writing territories on the margins of the mainstream. Some horror and pornographic writing sites have worked successfully by selling advertising and seeking writers to provide a steady stream of original material. The business model works because the sites keep tabs on how many hits they receive and how long those hitting the site tend to stay online. Writers are paid when they produce material that keeps readers online for a significant length of time. This model resembles the model used by phoneline services in the final years of the twentieth century, many of these lines offered lurid stories, some of them combining sex and humour, and most of them containing adverts for other recorded stories offered by the same company.

There are successful sites featuring creative writing, beginnings of unpublished novels poems, essays and other original material though very few of these sites pay writers directly. In some cases these sites ask writers to pay them, either directly to feature work or indirectly by entering work in competition. If you are prepared to pay for an online presence the best option is often to go to a site like writewords.org.uk, offering a range of services in exchange for an annual subscription. The best of these sites offer job adverts for a range of eclectic writing work, some paid, some to pay for. They also offer online meeting areas for people with shared interests and individual showcase pages for writers.

Later on in this book we will find out more about writewords.org.uk and hear directly from someone involved in running the site. For the moment; the point that needs to be made is that aspiring creative writers in search of a break can learn online and make contacts, but if you want to get that first break it still pays to get out of the house, meet people and do things. The change of environment, and challenge of face to face contact, matters if you are going to break out of your comfort zone to the point of being able to generate opportunities. This book is about getting a break, and you are more likely to do that if you push yourself to go out and network, or get involved in things that are happening. This chapter is about 'the job' and you are more likely to get 'the job' you want if you get out and make things happen.

Before we conclude the current section, looking mainly at creative writing type activities it is worth taking into account the way some writers involved in the highest levels of creative writing continue to network and present work in places usually associated with up and coming talent. In the course of researching this chapter I found an advert online for writers to contribute to a website: *thegoodearreview.com* The site was looking for monologues. I was interested in submitting something and looked over the site. Unlike many sites out there it was obvious from the start that this site had sourced good material from some exceptional writers, and had also given careful thought to what might work online. One thing I noticed immediately were the names of some writers, who had already built a reputation. Talking about itself on the site The Good Ear Review says:

The Good Ear Review is a dramatist's literary journal. It does exactly what it says on the tin.

We are dedicated to the publishing of original stand-alone monologues by quality writers of many lands. Monologues that are not only enjoyable to watch and/or listen to, but equally enjoyable to read. And read again.

Amongst the work I found there was a monologue by Daragh Carville, the site's write up on Daragh explains something of his impressive CV:

Daragh Carville is an award-winning Northern Irish playwright and screenwriter. His plays Language Roulette, Observatory, Family Plot, and This Other City have been produced in Ireland, Britain, Europe, and the U.S. His latest movie, Cherrybomb, was released in the U.K. in April 2010." That bio doesn't really do Daragh justice. He is also a hugely respected university lecturer in Creative Writing and his scripts have gathered considerable attention. Cherrybomb, a hard hitting drama set in Northern Ireland, boasts James Nesbitt and Rupert Grint amongst the stars and when it struggled to gain distribution after a screening at the 2009 Berlin Film Festival an online campaign mounted by Grint's considerable fan-base soon got to work to convince the industry there was an audience waiting to see it.

Regardless of his success, Daragh had contributed a monologue to a website. My apologies if the subject or language offends anyone. This is his work from *thegoodearreview*.

I'm a Good Man
by Daragh Carville
excerpt from the play *This Other City*

Setting: a hotel in Belfast, Northern Ireland
Time: present, night
Character: Patrick Hunter—age 40, well groomed, good suit

PATRICK
I'm a good man.

You have to know that, first of all, first and foremost, you have to understand that. I mean, I want you to know. This isn't—me.

Well, I mean, it is, I know that. But.

Look, I have a family. Let me tell you about my family. See, I have a daughter. Wee girl of my own. Orla. Well, I say wee girl. She's actually, I mean she's actually fifteen now. It's … But she's, she's such a great kid. I mean, I know all parents … But she is. She just is. She's smart, she's funny, she does well at school. She's—amazing. Sometimes I look at her and I just feel so much—I mean, this is embarrassing, but it's like I just feel so much love, it's like I can't breathe. And she'll catch me looking at her and she'll just smile. Her smile. And the way she smells. The top of her head. When she was wee.

And I'm a good man. Good father. I know I have to protect her. I mean, I know she's growing up and she's going to have to make her own way in the world, and the day will come when she has to go out there and, and stand on her own two feet. Out in the big bad world and. But I can't help it. It's like, that's my job. Y'know? I'm her dad and I have to protect her. From everything that's bad in the world. From all the bad people. Cos I know, I know what it's like out there. Believe you me. I've seen it all. The works.

Do you understand? Cos maybe your English …

It's just, I'm trying to explain this. Not because I have to, you understand. Because I want to.

I'm a good man. You understand me? I'm a good man.

Now come here. Come over here.
Because I want to fuck you in the skull.

I wondered what had motivated Daragh to send in a section of his acclaimed work. It is true that some writers with considerable reputations do still frequent websites and post work, though this isn't the case for all writers with a high critical standing. Because Daragh's reputation put him at the top of the career path I emailed some questions to Daragh.

1. Given the significant successes in your career what is it about online sites and competitions that still attract you?
In the case of this monologue, I was asked by a friend who runs the site and was happy to oblige. But in general I think it's just the way of the world: we all communicate more and more online, it's a great means of exchanging ideas and so it's natural that dramatists would want to be a part of that. And I've recently experienced the power of the internet myself, with the online support for *Cherrybomb*, which played a big part in securing distribution deals for the movie. As for competitions, they're still a great way into the professional world of writing. Something like Channel Four's 'Coming Up' scheme, for instance, offers new writers the chance for their work to be not only produced but also broadcast on national TV. That's an amazing opportunity, especially now, because since the credit crunch hit it's harder and harder for new writers to break into the industry, to get their voices heard.

2. Did you submit short pieces and other work to competitions as you built your career?
I did, yes. Poems, stories and so on. And I had the occasional small success, enough to keep spurring me on. But this was before the internet: this was back in the days of Stamped Addressed Envelopes and postal orders! Ancient history now.

3. Are there any specific sites/competitions you think

especially useful for an ambitious writer trying to have a career similar to your own?
The BBC's Writersroom website is an excellent resource. And one of the great things the internet has done is make available the screenplays of virtually any film you care to mention. A quick Google search and you can find pretty much any script you want to read. There are loads of sites dedicated to making scripts available. That kind of facility was never there before: it was very hard to find scripts when I started out. Even the rare few that were published - by Faber or whoever - tended to be incorrectly formatted and didn't really represent the script as written, more the finished film. So that's a brilliant learning resource for any would-be scriptwriter. Because of course a good writer is first and foremost a good reader. You need to read everything you can get your hands on.

4. If your present self could meet your unpublished/ undiscovered self what advice might he give the younger version?
Oh I'm sure my younger self wouldn't listen to a word I had to say. He'd just think 'who is this old fart? Who the hell does he think he is, giving me advice?' And he'd have a point. But I guess, if I had to, I'd just encourage him to keep at it, to keep the faith. But then, he knew that already.

Daragh's comments appear to confirm a lot of the points I've been driving at so far in this chapter. His success has come from sniping away at targets like competitions, and from building on any result he could gain. Born in 1969, as Daragh points out, his early attempts to win competitions go back to the days when entries went by post. It is a lot easier now, and the number of competitions has multiplied in recent years. His students now face the same challenges he once had to overcome, I agree totally with the advice he gives in his answers. Above all, I think the message here is to be discerning in your approaches, shop around to find the best online options, and get involved with opportunities wherever they arise. Daragh Carville's first significant breaks came with work for the stage, an area in which people have to come together and make things happen.

The distance between Rae Louise Jones and Daragh Carville is a distance many writers seek to travel in a career. A lot who try fail to go that distance. There are many reasons for writers not taking their ambitions to the point of seeing a complete stage play or film script turned into a production. This book is concerned with keeping the opportunities alive. If you want to make the whole journey we have already learned a lot of useful lessons. Most importantly, I think, the need to make and keep contacts. If you can't get your work accepted immediately by those in the creative arts, the least you can do is get involved, even in a supporting or helping capacity. That – at least – brings experience and the chance to network. It also gives you insights you would otherwise miss. This much was brought home to me quite a long way into my writing career. I had written a little for radio, mainly jokes for BBC Radio and hadn't really considered full-length radio drama. A mutual friend introduced me to a radio producer. The producer was struggling to find affordable work to turn into productions, mainly because the scripts he got involved huge casts, a lot of sound effects and a few other complications. Our mutual friend knew I had a pragmatic streak and tended to be able to produce work to clear guidelines. The meeting went well, I agreed to write a sample piece of script and a deal was done on the strength of the pages I produced. At this point I was faced with writing a full-length radio drama, having no experience of the form. I rang the producer and asked if I could add a small additional part, basically a character my age, with my accent. Part of the motivation was money, but a major part of the motivation was getting the chance to see what I was asking people to do. How – exactly – did actors in a radio play suddenly suffer an emotional breakdown, or kiss each other? My small role put me in the recording studio, or the control room, when all of this was going on. The kiss was easy; the actress with the line leading up to the kiss delivered her words, kissed the back of her hand a few inches from the microphone, and continued reading. The emotional breakdown was quicker, and simpler, than acting on television. In television dramas such scenes tend to be taken separately, the actor delivering the performance to one or two cameras with the other actors away from the set. In radio the production can be held up for a few seconds, the actor doing the emotional scene takes a breath or two and simply goes for it. Working like this was a new experience for me when it first happened, and it helped me write a series of radio plays. I could have chosen to be somewhere else on the day my first radio play was recorded, but deciding to get involved was crucial to being able to write more drama scripts that worked for radio.

So if a writer like Daragh Carville with an established reputation is still happy to provide work for a website and have it sit alongside the work of other hopeful writers, and if I can take the trouble to learn new working practices, you could surely make the effort to find something, anything, that is going on and get involved. You could trawl websites with adverts for all manner of creative writing opportunities and use the varied briefs on offer to focus your ideas. On sites like Writewords you will find some really strange opportunities, as I was researching this book I saw one advert for plays to be performed in pubs, another for plays lasting between one and three minutes, and the advert below:

BUGGED is a new project for UK writers in summer 2010

Summary: BUGGED is a new project for UK writers in summer 2010

Deadline: 15 August 2010

Date Posted: 01 June 2010

Details: BUGGED is a new project for UK writers in summer 2010. You write from a single happening on July 1st - we showcase the very best of the results. Here's how it works.

1 On July 1st 2010, go somewhere public - a train journey, a coffee shop, a library, the street - and just LISTEN for a little while. Eavesdrop. Make notes. If you like, you can send us a photo of your eavesdropping place or share overheard fragments here on Facebook - and send us links to help generate a buzzing writers' community.

2 Write a new piece based on what you've heard - a poem (< 60 lines), a short story (< 1000 words), a short script (< 5 minutes) or flash fiction (< 150 words). Make it good - we already have novelist Jenn Ashworth, travelogue writer Ian Marchant, poet Daljit Nagra and others on board.

3 Submit it via submit@bugged.org.uk before August 15th. Our blog www.buggedblog.wordpress.com will share the best of the incoming

material, chosen by editors Jo Bell (poet) and David Calcutt (playwright and novelist). The very best writing goes into a published anthology.

5 In October, join us at Manchester Literature Festival or Birmingham Book Festival for the twin launches of the book, including those top-name core writers alongside the best of the submitted work.

6 The anthology is print-on-demand. Buy one copy to read for pleasure - or if you made it into the book, buy many copies (at a reduced rate) to sell at readings. We aim to ensure that this is a high quality collection.

Email: submit@bugged.org.uk

The genius of the Bugged idea is fairly easy to see. The project uses the advantages of the internet and print-on-demand publishing, (something we'll discuss in detail in chapter eight), to bring the maximum amount of contributions to the largest possible audience at a low price. It helps to publicise the events in Manchester and Birmingham and the presence of some writers who have their work in the anthology helps to swell the attendance at the launch events. Whilst it is easy to be cynical, it is also worth considering the benefits of being able to pull out a book containing your own work and read from it at a live event. In 2009 I completed a smaller and similar project, getting a group of first year undergraduates to write a book called *Now That's What I Call Tuneful Tales*. The collection was themed around stories taking their titles from songs, the contents varied enormously but at the end of year show for these students a few of the group read from the collection, and it was the best seller of the nine books produced by the writing based students I taught that year. Its sales owed a lot to the number of different authors involved. For every aspiring writer that looks at opportunities like Bugged and decides the competition may be too fierce, or the theme doesn't appeal, there is another writer looking at it and thinking; 'I could do that and it might be helpful in putting something on the CV.' One thing I like about these projects, and one reason I'm always posting them online for my students, is the way they provide a more equal opportunity than short story competitions or competitions for longer works, like the opening chapter of a novel. When it comes to Bugged and similar opportunities one insightful idea, one good decision about when and where to listen in or one totally off-the-wall attempt to push yourself out of the usual comfort zone could pay off. And if it doesn't get a result, you will probably learn something useful about your writing and what you are capable of achieving. So for the cost of a little time and effort, I am always suggesting to my students that such opportunities are worthwhile.

I stated at the start of this chapter that we would discuss money and we have touched on the subject in connection with creative writing as we have run through the last series of examples. Rae Louise Jones still wasn't earning cash as a poet when she finished her second year of undergraduate studies. She had – however – put her exceptional skills in spelling, punctuation and grammar to work as a paid proof-reader. If you managed a project like the one I handled in the hospice you might be looking at around £5000 over a year, for a little less than that

I turned up every other week, planned sessions, edited work, liaised with the publisher of *Dreams Wander On* and helped to plan the book launch in January 2006. The work took place over a calendar year. Residencies, like the Writers in Prison positions can easily pay twice this, sometimes such posts go up to significant living wages, but posts paying £30,000 or more are usually the province of people already gaining media attention and significant critical respect. One-off grants from organizations like your local borough council, by contrast, might amount to a few thousand, and during times of recession any such grants tend to be paid out for expenses on a project. Individual bursaries and other support for writers tend to come once you have gained a break somewhere. Working your way up through the levels of achievement can eventually pay exceptionally well. Daragh Carville's movie script will have earned a cash payment up front as part of the option purchase agreement that contracted his script to a production company. Such advances start around a few hundred pounds and go up into thousands, but the real money comes once the film budget has been raised. Script deals generally cut a writer in for anything from 1.5% to 5% of the overall budget, and the budget for even a cheap UK movie can top £1 million.

This chapter so far has discussed the testing route you might have to follow if you want to be a creative writer. 'Creative' writing is a more troublesome term than it might appear. When used in the context of education it generally refers to courses focusing on the craft of writing and developing the abilities of the students to express ideas, greatly improve their skills and sustain their efforts as they produce complicated works. Some of the post-graduate programmes in Creative

Writing expect students to produce a complete novel. 'Creative' writing is generally understood to cover areas like poetry, fiction, essay writing and some elements of drama. This isn't exclusive and it is worth noting that many people join Creative Writing courses at university with the intention of following very pragmatic writing careers. Former Creative Writing students work in areas like marketing, PR, research and journalism. So some of those who enjoy 'creative' writing in the form of poetry, flash fiction and the like never lose the focus that will allow them to move on to more traditionally structured careers offering promotion through the ranks, yearly appraisals and a pension scheme.

In terms of education and training there are other courses focused on specific areas like Journalism and Marketing. There are also other more general courses working under a number of different names. I started the UK's first full-time higher education course in 'Professional Writing' in 1999. The name was an attempt to capture under one banner the notion that we were in the business of developing individual talents and helping them access opportunities in a range of professional areas. Other course titles available in UK education currently include Creative Industries and Media Writing. In general it is safe to assume that most Creative Writing students wish to develop their craft and most of those on the more professional options are interested in combining their creative work with training in the workings of the industries likely to offer them employment. This isn't always the case and – of course – some people change their minds as they learn, others make university decisions based on the location of a university, the cost of a course or other domestic factors.

What I think this proves is that there is a section of the writing community who see themselves primarily as creative individuals, others for whom the motivation is success and money based on using creative skills, and a group – probably the majority – to whom both ends of the equation appeal, and for whom the tension between creating work that gives them personal satisfaction and earning acceptable amounts of money never truly goes away. Sometimes this tension can be a positive thing, forcing the writers concerned into action. At other times it can be paralyzing, leaving them unable to decide between very different alternatives.

So, as I warned at the beginning of the chapter, we are now going to back to the start again. This time we'll veer away from the areas usually branded as 'creative' and get stuck in to the opportunities people target if they want the shortest route to money for words, and regular paid employment.

If you are looking for a break as a writer and at least part of your motivation is just to get yourself into a good working environment then the options are probably simpler than those outlined so far in this chapter. You will probably need two publications to get started properly. Both come in various forms but if we keep it as simple as possible here I suggest we follow the yellow route. Specifically the *Yellow Pages* and *The Writers & Artists' Yearbook*. Of course, alternative versions of their services are available[3]. There is no substitute for simply

3. In the UK there have traditionaly been three main publications covering this market. The oldest in terms of years published is *The Writers' and Artists' Yearbook*. Originally conceived as a guide and information source for those in both visual and verbal creative areas this publication still leads the pack

getting stuck in and trying to snag a work placement, almost any kind of work placement, to improve your knowledge and sharpen your skills. I've heard the argument from students for years that placements aren't available and opportunities don't present themselves. Bear in mind, I'm hearing these arguments in north west Kent, the nearest railway station offers travel times of around forty minutes to central London where the bulk of the UK media industry is located. It's a brutal argument but one worth pursuing that if you knew for a fact you would be shot dead one calendar year from today unless you could generate one good opportunity to move forward with your writing career, you would be almost certain to survive. The question isn't whether the opportunities exist, the question is how badly you – specifically YOU! – want them.

Let's start by destroying the argument that you need to know people and/or be living in the very biggest cities to get a break. It took me one cup of coffee and a flick through the magazines section of *The Writers' & Artists' Yearbook* to identify several national publications located well away from major centres of population. Working alphabetically we can deal with a handful

as far as photographers and artists are concerned. *The Writer's Handbook* was second into this market, pitching itself firmly at writers, note the different possessive apostrophe; because this book belongs to A WRITER whereas the *Writers' and Artists'* title suggests a general publication for all. Latterly *Writer's Market UK* has joined the best-selling collection. As each book stages an innovation – for example; having an information rich website and offering free membership with purchase of a book – the others tend to follow. I've used the *Writer's Handbook* as a set undergraduate tome for years, though – frankly – I doubt whether my students would have achieved significantly different results if we'd changed that decision at any time and gone for one of the others. *The Writers' Handbook* ceased publication with its 2011 issue, so we'll see if I'm right.

of examples. *Athletics Weekly* enjoys a circulation well into five figures and turns out a respected national magazine based in Peterborough. BBC Magazines – producing a range of high-profile titles – are located in Bristol. *Camping and Caravanning* magazine average over 200,000 sales of each magazine and they are based in Coventry. *Descent* a specialist magazine for those involved in caving is based in Abergavenny (population approx 14,000) in Wales. *Fast Car*, looks as slick as you would expect, attracts top of the range adverts and averages in excess of 50,000 sales per issue, and is based in Bath. Britain's most celebrated and durable publisher of comics, D.C. Thompson and co. has been established in its present form since 1905. The company has bases in London, Glasgow and Manchester but – as anyone who has passed the city centre statue of Desperate Dan will know – the company still thrives in its original home; Dundee. One of the most remarkable publications I found was *H&E* a celebrated naturist magazine. *H&E* boasts a publication history stretching back to 1898. What struck me as remarkable about *H&E* was the mention in its *Writer's Handbook* entry that it typically sources 90% of each issue from freelance contributors. Granted, this is a specialist magazine for naturists, so those articles had better deal with the philosophy and practice of living life without clothing, but – I wondered – did this magazine also offer work placements? A helpful and very pleasant voice on the end of the phone assured me they did but they couldn't consider anyone under 18 years old given the subject matter of the publication. Fair enough, but this ongoing publishing success, with an average sale around 20,000 copies, is located in Goole (population approx 17,500) just north of Doncaster in the East Riding of Yorkshire.

If you want an opportunity in the writing based industries you sometimes need to take this approach, flicking through lists of contacts, or looking them up on the internet. The point here is not to be too literal or picky. If you want to get a break as a writer, then the word to concentrate on is 'break.' It comes *before* writer in that sentence for a good reason. If you were based in the East Riding of Yorkshire you could sit back and think a naturist magazine had nothing to offer you because you weren't particularly interested in their lifestyle. But that isn't really what work placements, or getting involved, are about. All of the magazines listed in the paragraph above are specialist to some degree. Working for them, even in an unpaid capacity, would let you see how the industry that turns ideas into saleable product works. To stay alive magazines need to deliver an audience to their advertisers. The work that goes into this, the costs involved, the skills required to make things happen and the organization of all these different elements into an operation that keeps a magazine in business all require people who can remain focused on a task. If you had to work amongst them for a short time, you'd see what they do, and why the things they do matter. Getting a break as a writer might come from your ideas, and your skills, but without others around all doing their skilled jobs well, your efforts might not count for much.

The opportunities do exist all over the country. I grew up in rural Cumbria, a common observation amongst people being that 'nowt happens around here.' Googling advertising agencies in Cumbria recently I got 95 hits. To put this in context, Cumbria is England's second largest county in terms of square miles, but the population, including the occupants of Carlisle, its only city, doesn't reach half a million. That's very few people per square mile in comparison to most of the UK. There are more people in the city of Sheffield. Some of the advertising agencies I found are very small and most are located in centres of population. However, there will be others involved in media work in Cumbria who remain unlisted, mainly because they are freelance, solo operators. The point here is that creative work, requiring writing skills, is carried out everywhere in this country. Where there are people there is a need to communicate. Wherever you live there will be someone within reach who might just offer up a work placement, or some other chance to get involved. Experience and involvement counts on a CV and if you have no experience, you also stand to learn a lot once you get involved. If you approach getting experience with an open mind, you are more likely to get something useful from your efforts. A magazine with a subject of no interest to you can provide you with a placement that shows you how a company has to work to produce profits from a niche market. Working with an advertising agency handling a wide range of clients in the least promising media corner of the country might teach you useful lessons about the need to be determined and resourceful.

For years I have supported students to get work placements in high profile companies. One student wrote 119 letters before getting the placement she wanted on one of her favourite television shows, and then rang me in tears from inside the ladies toilets because the whole experience had proven a stressful disappointment. For all that, the student in question did well, and I wasn't surprised when the same tenacity that led her to 119 applications, and got her through a miserable week at work, eventually took her to a degree and a career in the media. I have visited others in placements at some of the UK's biggest selling publications, and best known media companies. For all this, I still think some of the most useful placements come at the other end completely. Someone hell-bent on a career in journalism might be blinded by the desire to find big stories and report them. If that person spends a week in a local free newspaper, and discovers the paper has more people in its offices selling advertising space than it does finding and reporting news, they might gain a respect for how the *business* of reporting the news works. If that would-be journalist joins a local press agency for a week he or she might also see that for every major transport disaster, or massive robbery on their doorstep there are other days when making money depends on squeezing any story out and hoping it makes a few pounds when picked up by a national paper. A student I knew once had a placement in a local press agency and within days the *Daily Star* ran a report on the students' canteen, as in the students' canteen she used most days, charging money for hot water to go into a Lemsip. It merited one small paragraph and the *Daily Star* was the only paper to run that story, but that student learned something valuable about the way press agencies dig out stories anywhere they can find them on a slow news day. You've probably worked the rest out for yourself but, if not, the whole story started when the agency found themselves with nothing to chase up and one of the regular journalists said to her; 'You know the course you're on… there must be something going on up there, right?'

And then there's always the internet, where sites like Gumtree and Craigslist have discreet sections offering work for writers.

There is a problem with these opportunities. I'm not against aspiring writers chasing opportunities online. In fact, I'd be a hypocrite if I was, since I've had an online football column for over a decade. The point I want to make about online opportunities is that they are more prone to being run by scammers and rip-off merchants than other areas of writing opportunity. It stands to reason; the internet allows you to work without meeting your employers, establishing any kind of friendship and – crucially – tends to operate in ways that leave no legally binding 'duty of care' obligation on your employer. The following advert isn't real. It is, however, paraphrased from a number I have seen online.

Soon we launching new networking site. We have need of a writer. This person involved in all sorts of communications with the people like messaging, email, blog and also with homepage. We are a fun bunch with loads of industry experience such as Amazon, Yahoo, etc.

We plan to offer equity and discuss payment as part of terms.

Adverts like this appear on the major sites, like Craigslist and Gumtree quite frequently. If you were desperate for work, you might be tempted to respond. I advise against that. There are a few obvious warning signs. 'Soon we launching...' and other grammatical howlers suggest either words translated by a software package from their original language, or people running the site with such little regard for their product that proofreading didn't occur to them. The job description is vague, suggesting you could be involved in anything. In fact, it's worse than that. Taken literally the description states you – as in you personally – could be involved in messaging, texting and blogging. So, technically speaking, if you send in your details and the people behind the advert make them publicly available, and earn money from forwarding your personal information to others, you were warned. The only evidence they are a 'fun bunch' is their own assertion of this, as a rule adverts like this are not easy to track down to a specific web site so you can't check out the person or company behind the offer before deciding if you will respond. Finally, they 'plan to offer equity...' Reading between the lines this could mean; 'we've got no money, we know we're scammers, if by any miracle this latest wheeze turns into sustainable cash; we'll pocket most of it and give you a little, maybe.'

I should point out right away; the above advert is my creation, and should not be confused with any other appearing on sites like Craigslist. But there are some chancers out there, you know it, and I know it, and some of these chancers will happily exploit writers they'll never meet. Be warned.

But also, be hopeful. Despite the many pitfalls there are opportunities for making money and building a portfolio to be found online. Most reputable media companies offering work to writers have online options for you to submit material. Some other operations are run almost entirely online, offering genuine opportunities, and as much security as a first-time freelance writer will find elsewhere. There are some obvious soft targets available if you simply want to get work out there and receive some feedback. Posting reviews on retail sites, like Amazon, allows others to state if the words were useful. As I mentioned earlier, writers sites, like Writewords, also have forums allowing for members to post and discuss work. Beyond this there are a host of 'lifestyle' sites concerned with live music, films and other events. Many of these make some money from advertising and pay limited, as in *very* small amounts for publishing work. The down side is that the work itself is almost carried out at slave labour rates if you include the traveling time to and from events. The up side is that many of these sites last long enough and have just enough of a reputation to get their writers on a guest list here and there. So, if the events you are reviewing include some up and coming band in a local club you could at least save yourself the ticket price. If you were likely to be going anyway, it probably pays to try and get some published work out of the event. A few sites do offer stable work, a lot of it unpaid, but some of it very useful.

One site typical of this approach is My Village; www.myvillage.com. My Village makes a virtue of the way the internet can reach a world wide audience, and also be useful to a very local audience. The site draws some fairly high profile advertising and divides itself into sections based around your 'village.' In other words, the site has pages set up for locations all over the UK, these pages contain information on forthcoming events, attractions and all the entertainment and activity on offer. An obvious attraction to advertisers is the chance to target a group of people actively looking for things to do in an area. Some of these people may be living in the area, others may be going there for a holiday or visit. The site draws contributions from a range of people and reviews almost anything within reason. So there are no age limits on who can post or where the posters live. A New Yorker seeking out family history in Hexham could post a review of a restaurant there, someone visiting an historic site in Inverness could post a review on the Inverness page and lots of people do post live music reviews, theatre reviews and the like every day, for towns and cities all over the UK.

My Village has a business model that works online. Posting, collecting your work in your portfolio, and practicing the art of cutting and editing words to fit someone else's editorial model is good for you if you haven't done anything like this before. There is a danger, even with the best online sites, that posting and checking how useful people find your comments to be can become addictive. When all is said and done My Village and its ilk will always have a high turnover of writers, the best ones will move on and get paid and published elsewhere. So the site is a great start, and if you have nothing, this is one of the best ways of proving you can write for an audience. But there are other ways of getting work out there and getting paid a little.

Two obvious things you can do both revolve around your local press. The local press in the UK is in crisis and has been for a few years. The basic problem is the availability of news online. To many local papers the biggest villains in the picture are the BBC. Local BBC news, updated throughout the day, is one reason that newspapers are struggling to convince people to pay for printed news. The problem is particularly seen amongst young people, a generation who have grown up with online news. Many of those 25 years old and under never got into the habit of reading a local newspaper. The problem isn't as simple as the BBC destroying part of an industry, and many media commentators have been predicting the demise of printed newspapers for a long time. At present it looks like printed newspapers have a future, but many of them might be forced into radical changes about what they print, and how they make money. For many local papers the last few years have involved redundancies amongst staff, limited pay rises at best and fewer opportunities for new recruits. Oddly, that is potentially very good news for first time writers. Obviously, if you want a career as a typical scoop-hungry reporter it is bad news. But if you just want to get published and show people you are employable as a writer, there are two obvious routes to take.

Firstly, find a story and file it. This isn't easy, editors want material they can use and in the current climate editors are very busy. Too busy by far to enter into lengthy discussions about how you might get involved. If you can get a work placement, you will probably learn a lot about what a paper wants and how they want it submitted. If not, you have to do your own work. A little common sense goes a long way here. Read the editorials in the paper to see what they think about events in the local area. Read the letters sent in by readers to see who really reads the paper and what they are worried about, and read the short 'filler' items they print, because filing items like these is your best chance of a result. Go to the paper's website, or their list of journalists if they print one, and get any information they give about how to file stories, and who to contact. The main reason aspiring writers get no joy from local papers is that work is submitted in a form the paper can't use. The standard mistakes include; too many grammatical errors, inappropriate subject matter and – most commonly – far too many words and far too much detail on a very minor story. If your local paper gives 70 words and a picture to the opening of a new village hall, and you want to file a story about the opening of some other building, then cut your story to 70 words, and a picture. Take care with the picture. If you point a camera and fire at a group of six people, you may have rendered the story useless for an inside page where six faces will be too many when they run a picture in a very small box. Pictures should tell stories, so if your friend is running a marathon for charity and you want to file a story. Get the friend, dressed in running gear, and one person from the charity. Get them to do something, even if it is only shaking hands to indicate the bond between them that has led to this gesture by your friend.

The rewards financially can be very slight indeed. I've filed stories in the 21st century for an agreed £10. Not great, but the point for me was helping a friend here and there to get some publicity. Local papers can't afford the network of correspondents they used to enjoy, they can sometimes pay very small sums for material that saves work for a journalist. Increasingly these days a paper will use a well-written story without changing the words. A short-staffed local paper still tries to cover the same breadth of subjects it used to cover with more people, so these days that can mean a greater acceptance for well-written copy sent in by an unknown writer. I can't stress strongly enough how important it is to keep a clear head and check carefully before submitting anything. I would also recommend that you try submitting material, even if you know for certain the paper can't pay anything. Experience is experience, particularly if you have no published work in your portfolio. Getting material in a local paper was a useful first-step to a lot of writers who went on to be successful. Despite the predictions of doom, local papers are still alive and kicking and some business models have proven successful in the face of the threats to the local news industry.

'Free-sheet' papers, delivered to local addresses and paid for by the advertisers have managed to withstand the decline in sales of local news. In the case of these publications their strength has often been their ability to keep the news local, and concentrate on things the internet can't match. The internet may provide up to the minute local news, but that often comes with problems. Some stories get pushed down the list and lost in a day or so. Local free-sheet papers can gather parish news, obituaries, details of local burglaries and other things likely to be discussed in local pubs and over garden fences. One success story in this area has been Maidstone's *Downs Mail*, the paper started with one local edition, reaching 13,000 homes, in the late nineties. It currently has four local editions, each hitting a different region of Maidstone, and a circulation of 88,000. If your local area has a similar publication, it might be a good place to submit material.

Another possibility in local news has already been alluded to as we discussed working for a local paper. If you can't report the news, you can always help someone else to make the news. Local papers, and specialist publications in general, are always looking for material to fill pages. This is a competitive and difficult business and getting a result is not usually easy. However, it is an area in which an aspiring writer can prove their talent. It is also an area that will test your creative abilities and – perhaps – show you skills you didn't realize you had.

Many businesses and services use local news stories as part of their marketing. This may involve staging stunts, bringing interesting and unusual stories to the attention of readers etc. During the period of writing this book I had a break down in my car and had to be towed to my friend's garage. A week or so later a press agency contacted me. They were linked to the GEM (Guild of Experienced Motorists), who have provided me with breakdown cover for years. The agency sent details of how to contact them with any story of an interesting or unusual breakdown. They also indicated that sums of up to £100 were available when such stories appeared in the press. Obviously they were looking for the 'My waters broke, then the car broke down……' kind of stories that cast the GEM in a good light as a trustable rescue service. My story wasn't any such thing. I learned that the staff of a chip shop were very kind and helpful, and my mate Rob was as reliable as I'd hoped when I knocked on his door late in the evening and told him my misfiring car had just been towed to his garage, but it wasn't news. However, this kind of press operation shows a strand of work that is open to the hopeful writer in search of a break. 'Spinning' stories is something you could seriously consider as a first step in generating a portfolio. If local newspapers are short of material you only need to make something interesting/unusual and – preferably – photogenic happen, and present it in the right way. The right presentation should involve a press release.

A press release is a short write up covering the main points of a story or event and including contact details and very precise information about **what** is happening, **when** it is happening and **where** everything is taking place. In the case of a strange or complex story you might also have to explain **why** this matters. There are lots of online resources designed to teach you how to write a press release and some sites – like Pressbox.co.uk – feature press releases. In fact, a useful exercise is to go to pressbox, look at their current crop of press releases, and ask yourself; 'If that story was happening in my local area and I had to get it into the local press, what pictures would I plan and how would I write it to fit the style of the best known local paper in my area?'

Consider the following examples. The first is one page release I wrote during the same week I was writing this chapter, the second is a release for a high-profile specialist client from a respected UK PR agency, Cream Communications. The second release is more wordy and less pre-occupied with the when/where details at the top because this version of the Galaxy Fireworks press release was produced specifically for internet distribution.

PRESS RELEASE

What: Nursery Manager Cycles 266 Miles in 1 Day for Charity

When: 1 June
Where: Pennies Day Nursery, Newnham Ct

Dominic Scotton, Operations Director of Pennies Day Nursery, Newnham Court, spent twelve hours in the saddle to raise money for two charities. His exercise bike marathon took place at Pennies Day Nursery, Newnham Court on 1 June. He was accompanied on two other bikes by staff from the nursery, taking turns to clock up additional miles. Dominic's slot stretched over thirteen hours, allowing him a five minute break every hour, making twelve hours in total. He covered 266 miles, the combined miles of the team reached 586.

Collection buckets on the day raised just under £200, flyers and information given out directed people to a Just Giving page for Pennies Peddlers - a team from the nursery who are raising money for the British Heart Foundation by completing the London-Brighton Cycle Ride on 20 June. In addition, Dominic Scotton has his own fundraising challenge to gather money for two charities helping his son, William.

William was born with cerebral palsy in 2007. Dominic is raising money for the National Institute of Conductive Education; helping children with cerebral palsy and Look; a charity helping the visually impaired. The 12 hour peddleathon is in addition to other completed activities; a half marathon, ascent of Scafell Pike and completing the London Marathon. Dominic will lead the Pennies team in the London to Brighton Cycle Ride.

He says: My son was given 48 hours to live and has battled through a lot, this is the least I can do to help him, and others like him.'

Contacts: Dominic Scotton; Operations Director - xxxxxx

Neil Nixon: Media Officer - xxxxxxx

http://www.justgiving.com/Dominic-Scotton - Just Giving page, detailing Dominic's fundraising challenge.

1st Galaxy Fireworks has reached the finals of the British Fireworks Championship 2010, one of only six companies in the UK.

The annual British Fireworks Championships is the pinnacle of the UK fireworks calendar for the industry, with 2010 marking the 14th time the competition has been held.

1st Galaxy Fireworks has, along with only five other companies, reached the final, due to be held in August at Plymouth Hoe. The competition is hosted by City of Plymouth Council and The Event Service Association (TESA). Spread over two evenings, and watched by an audience of approximately 200,000 on the shoreline, the finalists each have to choreograph and execute a 10-minute fireworks display), timed to the second. Precision is everything - points are added and deducted for every second either over or under the 10-minute mark.

This is the second time that 1st Galaxy has reached the final of the Championships - the last time was in 2007, when it came second. Lee Smith, Managing Director of 1st Galaxy said: "We are thrilled to have reached the finals of the British Fireworks Championships. It is a massive date in the fireworks calendar - everyone in the industry will be watching alongside the 200,000 spectators, and although there is a monetary prize, the real prize is the kudos that the winning company receives."

As well as the timing, the judges have a whole host of other criteria against which to mark the contestants including; rhythm, continuity, pattern, creation and the crowd-pleasing 'wow' factor.

He continued: "We are already well into planning our 10-minute show - it's amazing that just three minutes of a display can take up to two days to prepare! We are really excited as we are doing everything to ensure it will be spectacular."

An estimated 10 tonnes of explosives are set off in total, with the British Champions going on to represent Britain in an international competition. The event will take place on the 10th - 11th August 2010 with displays starting from 9.30pm.

About us:
1st Galaxy Fireworks is one of the UK's leading fireworks specialists, with expertise in providing displays for all sorts of events, including wedding

fireworks, corporate events, parties and celebrations. It also supplies high quality display fireworks through its retail shops and mail order. It is also possible to ensuring the very best firework collection is available for private celebrations nationwide.

In the case of the Pennies press release I am not claiming my work as special or significantly better than others involved in local PR. It matters here because it helps me to make some important points. A press release needs to announce itself clearly and the headline – one man had cycled 266 miles in a day for charity – does that. In fact, it's quite a complicated story beyond this. There are two separate areas of fundraising, the Pennies team in the London- Brighton event raising money specifically for the British Heart Foundation, and Dominic's own personal challenge to raise money for the charities helping his son. Given the complexity of the story it matters that the usual rules of writing a press release are followed clearly. The **when** and **where** angles are clearly established. The 'where' element is vital when sending material to local papers because many have regional editions and may mark a story up for one or two of these, before leaving it out of others. In general you should imagine the information in a press release as a triangle, and picture the triangle pointing down towards the bottom of the page. In other words, stack the main facts towards the top of the release and leave the fine details further down. In this case the main fact is the eye-catching achievement of the miles covered in one day, that's the hook to draw in the journalists. It worked because the local papers covered this story. One or two of them made minor mistakes with the smaller details but the story did get covered and the main points; that Dominic led a team on the day, and that a large amount of fundraising for good causes was going on at the nursery, were all covered well in the local press.

The point of the second release is to promote a successful company who have just achieved a significant result in a tough competition. Once again the main element of attention grabbing information is at the top. 1st Galaxy are in the top six of a national competition. The 'spin' here is the suggestion of the company's quality, although the release doesn't spell out how many others entered the competition. The release does do an excellent job of anchoring the story in facts; when and where the final will be, the rules of the competition, and also painting a picture in words, notably of the huge crowds expected to watch the two nights of competition. The paragraph about 1st Galaxy at the end is a piece of punchy PR spin, delivered after the news above it has established the quality and success of the company. This is a detailed press release, produced by Cream Communications who work as a communications agency, handling a range of PR, press and marketing. A press release from such a company, working alongside another company like Galaxy Fireworks, will often be part of an overall campaign taking in other things: like the production of marketing material.

If you are looking to get a break as a writer then making something happen, or spinning an existing event into the press, is a good way of establishing an item in your portfolio. As we've already discussed some people are attracted to writing for a living because they find generating ideas easy, and want to make money from a skill they enjoy using. Sometimes this skill is better employed in PR and marketing where generating words is often secondary to making things happen and getting attention. This is worth considering, whatever your future writing intentions. Even if you want to write highly respected and original works the ability to get out there and move the product is likely to help your career. On the way up the ladder to respect and substantial income you will almost certainly have to co-operate when others arrange marketing opportunities. So consider the following problem; if your life depended on getting a story about an event in the local paper sometime in the next month, what would you do?

I seriously suggest you give this a few minutes thought, preferably with a notepad and pen. If you have no idea at all, start by making a list of people you know who might be up to something newsworthy. Alternatively, consider the 266 mile exercise bike marathon above and think; 'what am I capable of physically or mentally that might get attention?' Local papers love charity stunts and these stunts reflect well on the people involved who come across as caring, giving sorts prepared to make sacrifices for others. Part of my work with the group of nursery schools who staged all the charity fundraising described in the press release is simply to get them attention. In our case the nursery is a top of the range brand. The downside of this is that our fees are too expensive for some with an interest. The upside of this work is that as an 'aspirational brand' needs to be talked about and needs a high profile, obliging us to continue to produce a range of eye-catching events for the local press. Aspirational brands in terms of nursery schools and other child related services are often those most talked about. Parents can be competitive and willing to outdo each other in terms of the sacrifices made for their children so for a nursery school to be seen to be doing the right things, and doing them in an innovative and eye-catching way, is good business. In such cases the press coverage is worth more than buying the same number of column inches in a local paper and filling them with an advert.

Consider the following stunt that earned us coverage in a few local papers and also drew a television news crew to the nursery. It concerns Dominic, again. He had amassed a stock of Bath Store blue rubber ducks, having been given them for use in a fete. We had sacks of these ducks stuck in a storeroom, nobody had counted them but we knew for a fact we had well over 1000, and summer was turning into autumn. We had no more fetes or live events at which we could give out the ducks, and so we hit on a way of making this liability work for us. The stunt we dreamed up had enough of the right angles for everyone. A very basic mathematical calculation helped us work out a means of creating the shape of a huge flying bird in our foyer. We drew this out and then filled the shape with just over 1000 ducks, creating a massive blue bird with its beak pointing south. We did this on the first day of autumn, having first prepared a press release and photo call sheet explaining to the local media that this massive and unusual sculpture would be visible on one day and would serve to teach our pre-school children, (aged four), about autumn and the migration of birds.

It worked well, we got newspaper coverage and the television crew who came to film the bird had fun. Since I'd spent time along with one of the nursery staff putting the vast majority of the blue ducks into place I'd seen a filming opportunity. All the ducks faced forward and the sight of 1000 pairs of blue rubber duck eyes all staring at you resembled something from a horror film. I suggested to the news cameraman he took one shot slowly tracking back from the beak along the bird's body and once he started filming I heard him chuckling to himself. In years of gathering local news this obviously stood out as one of the odder images he'd shot, and for a few fleeting seconds such images make eye-catching television. The very shots that will stop somebody in mid-sentence and get them staring at the television screen wondering: 'what is that all about?'

It's probably best to come clean about the accuracy of the press release we sent out. We didn't lie, but we certainly left out a few key facts. It was true – as we claimed – that the pre-school children had helped to make the bird shape. However, the literal truth was that Katie (who worked with us in marketing) and I had put down around 950 ducks and left a gap in the head, at which point a few selected pre-schoolers came and helped us with the final ducks. It was also true – as we claimed – that the bird was helping us explain the points of the compass, the start of autumn and bird migrations to the children. Though – once again – it was a few of the most able children who were involved, most of the younger children in the nursery simply stumbled past and looked at the whole thing in amazement. It was also true that by the time the press photographer and television crew arrived the children could tell north from south, but then all they had to do was point in the same direction as the bird's beak. Had you driven them home and stood them in their own gardens, finding south would have been beyond most of them.

Like most press stunts, this was a spun story with a serious purpose behind it. The nursery got its foyer photographed and filmed in a way that drew attention. The huge blue bird shape was truly a spectacle. We got our name in the local media and got a topical news story in for an event – the first day of autumn – that few other companies bother to mark. The implication of the story was also very positive for us, very young children were being taught facts that most of their age didn't know, and this teaching appeared inventive and memorable. Above all, the story reinforced the marketing of the Pennies' brand which uses the slogan; 'The very best in childcare, learning and fun.' The press got what they need every week, a good filler story, a picture that told part of the story, and some 'feel good' news.

Remember, the start of this useful press coverage was the identification of a problem. It started with a discussion in a meeting about what we were going to do with 'those bloody ducks in the storeroom.' If you think back briefly to the previous chapter there is a question in the copy test about describing toast to a Martian. The point of the question is to test your ability to generate ideas around a theme. That skill was at the heart of our team's decision to turn a few sacks full of largely useless rubber toys into a public spectacle that reinforced the brand identity of a service provider with a keen sense of its own place in a local market.

So, you could go out and find yourself 1000 rubber ducks…

Or, alternatively, you could use your own imagination, your own contacts, your own knowledge of the local media and set yourself the challenge of making something happen. If the target is to produce a simple press release, and a stunt or event fit to gain local media coverage, what will you do?

So far this chapter has covered some slightly convoluted and difficult ways around getting a first break and doing 'the job' of a writer. Before we consider the financial implications of all the things covered this far, we should look at the most straightforward means of getting a break and doing the job for the first time. Quite simply, get a copy of *The Writers' & Artists' Yearbook* or one of its competitors, go straight to the section on magazines, radio production companies, or television and film production companies. Follow up the information in your book with a visit to their website, gather all the information you can on what to submit and how to submit it, and have a go. The opportunities are very varied, half a dozen random discoveries I made doing this same exercise ahead of writing this chapter include:

- *Motor Caravan* magazine (*www.motorcaravanmagazine.co.uk*) pay £60 for a page filled by a freelancer, and they are interested in: 'features on touring, unusual motor homes, and activities people pursue whilst out and about in their van.' Obviously, an interest in motor home holidays, or experience of working in the campsite trade would be helpful, but not essential.

- The *New Writer* magazine pays £20 for articles, a small sum but it is a magazine available only on subscription and focused on; 'practical 'nuts and bolts' advice on creative writing.' So it clearly shares a readership with the target market for this book. I wrote an article for the magazine and waived the fee but agreed a free one-year subscription. It was worth it.

- *Church Music Quarterly* a publication from the Royal School of Church Music (*www.rscm.com*) wants articles, 2100 words maximum, on church music and related subjects. With a circulation of 14,000 it offers £60 per page.

- *Real People* sells well in supermarkets, is a shiny gossip magazine and offers £300 for a 'spread.' A spread being a story on intimate or bizarre elements of human relations. Like the other magazines racked alongside it in supermarkets, the magazine specializes in first-hand accounts of family and relationship issues. So, if your partner is 42 years your senior, your six year old child survived a drowning incident because his Mohican haircut allowed a lifeguard to pull him out..

  Clearly, sharing dirty family laundry and the like isn't to everyone's taste, and the issue of the magazine open on my desk as I type this has a spread, advertised on the cover, about a sexual relationship between a mother and son which started after they found each other years after she gave him up for adoption. On the other hand, anyone might approach such a magazine with a story of something personal and unusual so – for example – if you were forced by circumstances to give birth at 33,000 feet, why not recount a story you know well for a few pounds. Channel Four did an excellent documentary on the kind of stories run by these magazines and the routes by which the stories reach the editors called *My Daughter Grew Another Head*. If you can't find a copy of it, you can watch it in segments since the whole documentary is currently available, in separate pieces on YouTube.

- *This England* magazine, a quarterly billing itself as; 'Britain's loveliest magazine since 1968!' pays £25 per 1000 words.

- *The Guardian* pays £25 for much shorter pieces in the family section dealing with memories around a treasured family photograph, songs that mean something to members of your family, or 'we like to eat' features on recipes developed in your family.

Granted the money above isn't great but the point of this little round up is to show you achievable first targets if you simply need a break, with no experience. The examples above also help us to map out some basic patterns in the publishing industry. Magazines with circulations under 20,000 and a specialist market, like *Motor Caravan* and *Church Music Quarterly*, can be run by a small number of people, and – therefore – welcome submissions. Their margins are tight, hence the small payment. But if you want a result to start your portfolio it is worth remembering that the same paltry sums that might make you think twice, probably deter experienced professionals used to bigger payments. As a rule, a more experience writer may use specialist magazines to place material with some other benefit, like allowing them to plug a book, or an event. The other titles in the list above are general, within reason anyone could find a way of approaching them with something.

A case study of one approachable publication follows. As with the example of the Daragh Carville script earlier, my apologies if anything you might find at *Poot!* Comic's website; *www.pootcomic.com* offends you. *Poot!* is an 'adult humour' comic, full of toilet gags, characters that include a tampon and a toilet brush, and prose humour that savages every style from tabloid journalism to trade catalogues. One thing worth noting on their site is the appeal below:

Contribute to Poot!
We're seeking talented cartoonists and writers, so please send us your stuff. Obviously we'll only publish it if we love it, but even if we don't love it, we'll send you a nice email explaining what we liked and what we didn't so much like. For us to just look at it, you can send it in any format you like.

I wrote for *Poot!* in the 80s and 90s, and was surprised to see them back in print after 18 years of inactivity. In preparing this chapter I emailed some questions to Jim Whittaker, asking him to explain the history of *Poot!* and how a writer looking for a break might take advantage of that offer on their site.

Q - In three or four sentences can you give is a history of *Poot!*?
A – *Poot1* was launched in 1986 by a group of students at Birmingham University. At first, it was meant to be the Midlands' version of *Viz* Comic, but soon evolved and developed a style of its own. It ran for 5 years – during which time the print run increased from 500 to 150,000. We stopped it in 1991 when our distributor went bust (owing us a lot of cash). We re-launched it in 2009 because by then we had saved up enough money to bring it back!

Q - What was the thinking behind aiming for a couple

of new contributors per issue when *Poot!* re-launched?
A - We want to make *Poot!* as inclusive as possible - somewhere where amateur artists have a genuine chance of seeing their stuff in print. Plus it helps keep each issue fresh and different. This time round we were also worried that our work wouldn't appeal to the students of today, since we are all 40-something year olds. Students remain our firm target market.

Q - In three or four sentences; how would you advise an aspiring contributor to convince you his/her work is fit for *Poot!*?
A - As silly or as ridiculous as possible is what we're after - make the reader laugh out loud. Utterly original. We're prepared to risk something edgy and controversial.

Q - In the same number of words, can you summarise the most common mistakes aspiring contributors make?
A - they assume we're after Viz-style gags involving big tits, swear words, general crudity. We're trying hard not to be laddish and want to also appeal to female readers.

Q - Roughly, what would you pay for contributions for a first time *Poot!* writer?
A - We pay up to £100 per page, depending on how 'finished' the piece is. Helps us if we get a digital file that we can slot into the mag without any rework. We pay for everything we use and treat all contributors equally.

Q - What 'job satisfaction' elements most appeal to your contributors?
A - Most of the cartoonists we use simply draw for the passion of drawing and understand it's hard to make it a decent paying profession. They love seeing their stuff and name in print. We get the impression they are used to being shafted by publishers. We don't want to do that.

Q - What other observations/comments do you want to make about contributing to *Poot!* to be read by those hoping for a writing career?
A - It's harder for us to assess just a script. We get sent tons of stuff each week and it takes a long time to work through it. For writers I would advise to 'partner' yourself with a cartoonist and send us stuff already drawn (and preferably coloured).

When it comes to simply getting a break it is targets like those above who provide the most specific opportunities. For every editor and publication prepared to be transparent about payment there are dozens more indicating via their websites and entries in publications like *The Writers' & Artists' Yearbook* that;

- Payment is negotiable
- Approach by email/sae in the first instance
- Approach with ideas in writing
- Items are by commission only

Firstly, 'negotiable' generally means the people at the other end will try to pay you little, or nothing. You will probably want more than they are offering and from that point on 'negotiable' means you negotiate. If you simply need a break, any kind of break, then you are more likely to get it if you ask for nothing. On the other hand, repeatedly punting work out there for free isn't a way to build your self-esteem. Much as I'd love to type one sentence at this point that tells you exactly what to do in every possible circumstance, it simply isn't possible. It can be a cruel world, the best thing I can advise is to; do the best you can, and keep moving forward.

The targets I am discussing are easier to hit once you have experience and material in a portfolio but they are also approachable if you have very strong ideas, useful specialist knowledge or something so useful they would struggle to get it cheaper via another route. If, for example, you are in a position to get a celebrity interview via a mutual contact, or if you have a particularly gripping first-hand experience, a short email with a good one-liner title, making it clear what the publication/radio show etc might get in return for negotiating with you is probably worth a try. A select few places openly seek first hand accounts and material you can easily prepare if you have something worth developing into an item. The BBC Radio Four show *Saturday Live* goes out to an audience of a few million from 9-00 to 10-00am on Saturdays. It also features items on people who were eyewitnesses when history was made. These items are not restricted to people who *made* history and so if you, for example, almost collided your bicycle with the prime minister's car as he or she headed for an important engagement, *Saturday Live* might just be interested. They also offer the user-friendly facility of approaching them via the show's own page on the BBC Radio Four website, so formatting the first approach is made easier because their own email set up obliges you to put it into the most useful format for their editorial team.

We will consider the varied opportunities offered by the BBC later in this book. For the most part aspiring writers think television, film and radio are harder markets to crack. They are right, mainly because ideas and scripts sent to producers in these areas often have to go through complicated rewrites to fit the demands of broadcast, fit within budgets and fit the very specific talents of a range of people – like directors and actors – who may get involved. Despite all of this a handful of companies do retain the very agreeable habit of reading everything they get, so long as it is presented properly. One such is Pozzitive Television, *www.pozzitive.co.uk* the outfit behind hits like *Dinner Ladies*. They are specific about not wanting screenplays, novels and stage plays. They do – however – work with radio and television comedy and entertainment. So feature ideas, sketches, pilot scripts for radio and television comedy and the like will get read. Scripts should be posted and accompanied by a stamped addressed envelope. If you want to get into submitting your work regularly you'll have to get used to the stamped addressed envelopes. Many people in the media industry still want hard copy, because the wear and tear on their printers from endless submissions of huge documents simply isn't worth the time and expense it would take up. One other engaging aspect of Pozzitive Television's work is their willingness to take time to find out about the subject of this book and answer some questions. I didn't find too many of their competitors willing to respond to unsolicited emails suggesting they give up their time to help aspiring writers. David Tyler of Pozzitive told us:

1 - On average how many unsolicited submissions do you get every week?
12

2 - What are the main reasons that work gets rejected?
It's not funny. This is a massive and overwhelming thing and all we care about in the first instance. Plotting, characterisation, length, format; these are all things that can be tussled with over

successive drafts, but funniness is non-negotiable and unfakeable.

3 - If you were advising an aspiring writer about how to get noticed, and taken seriously at Pozzitive, what would you say?
Write a funny script. No more, no less. Oh, ok, if you needed a bit more, I'd say try and ensure it's a reasonable go at a form of scripted comedy that exists. i.e. write a half-hour radio sitcom or a TV non-audience sitcom or a one-hour blue collar colourful ITV comedy drama. Don't write a 48 x 17m spoof of 1930's Basque cinema set in the Tardis. Because that won't get on. But mind you, why would a cartoon about yellow people, one of whom has tall blue hair get on? Because it's overwhelmingly funny. So yes, all rules are rubbish - but if you're going to ignore rules and conventions, do make sure you're a genius. For the rest of us mortals, make sure it's the sort of thing that telly or radio presently does in form (not in content!)

4. Are there any conspicuous success stories you want to share involving writers who sent you material and went on to success?
When I read scripts for Hat Trick I received a bonkers messy unstructured spoof documentary about an Irish priest making a video diary as he roamed across rural island, where 80% of this half-script was just one scene where he was refusing a cup of tea from an old woman who answered his knock on the door. It was called "Irish Lives with Father Ted Crilly". It was outstandingly funny but a mess. I passed it upward to Geoffrey Perkins, and it became *Father Ted*.

5 - We know prices vary etc, but could you give some guide prices for the following sales:
1 line gag used in one of your shows, BBC Radio = £10
30-60 sec comedy sketch used in comedy show, late-night BBC 2. Maybe £100-£120 per minute?

A final option worth considering when we look at 'the job' of professional writing is the area of business to business work or B2B as it is often called. Bear in mind that many of those chasing a first publication, or good work placement will target the high profile operators, read the same handbooks as you and think it terms of creative work like scripts, or factual work on subjects they know well.

Years ago I used to teach students intent on careers in the music industry. Many of them were disappointed when they managed to get responses from the major record labels, like EMI and Sony BMG, indicating that the waiting list for work placements meant they couldn't be considered for several months. Many of these students, at my urging, then contacted companies that worked on behalf of record companies. Pluggers, concert promoters, PR agencies and others are less visible to the general public, but still working in the music industry and offering placements with the chance to learn a lot about the way a complicated creative industry works.

The same is true in writing. So some of the following approaches might be a useful; firstly, find a local publication that isn't conspicuous by its high profile. Newsletters, industrial work – for example material produced by the local Chamber of Commerce – and even parish newsletters are often desperate for help, and ideas. It's also worth looking for operations who stage big exhibitions and other one off events. One of the largest organizations in the UK is GB Networks, which has links all over the country and specializes in business based events. Operations like this take on staff for events. Some B2B work placements require you to work in all areas a professional writer might usefully cover; research, writing material for distribution, marketing and networking and the like. Many people keen to present their own ideas in writing, or work in more high-profile areas like television and radio don't consider going to exhibition companies, or trade fairs. But the experience on offer is as good as the higher profile areas. For example; many B2B events are filmed, some of the filming is scripted and people exhibiting often get a DVD after the event, or see themselves on the website of the event. It's all good portfolio material if you are involved. Getting started in this area means, probably, going through the local *Yellow Pages*, looking for media companies and trawling their websites to find those who specialize in corporate and business work. They get less approaches for work placements than – say – the local ITV newsroom and you might find yourself working with one or two people who run the whole company, and are glad of help when they have a contract to film a local exhibition. Such work is very hands on and will demand you use a range of creative skills, so it makes for good portfolio material once completed. If you start off contacting people who make creative work for the market and at the same time you contact people who do corporate work my guess is that the corporate people will get back to you first. That's been my experience watching students do the same thing.

Linked to corporate work, and also curiously under-used in terms of job opportunities, placements and a target for creative ideas, are companies involved in communication for business. Specialist services like making radio adverts are the bedrock of these companies, but their work isn't that simple. Radio commercial writing appears well off the radar for most of the hopeful writers I see, and yet one of our most successful former students went into that area on leaving us, and has forged a spectacular and satisfying career ever since. One of the biggest companies in the UK radio commercial sector is London Creative (*www.londoncreative.com*) the front page of their website regularly changes the high-profile clients in their care and if you've listened to commercial radio anywhere in the UK you may well have heard their work. Explaining the services on offer on their site the company states:

Our Services
We love working with companies large and small to examine their business and provide solutions that create extraordinary results. The thrill of providing bespoke solutions to difficult problems – and the excitement and passion of working with your business and creating strategic creative models that make it work even better. If you want to create more enquiries, create efficiency or create amazing results – we believe that you deserve the very best.

Whilst it is easy to be cynical about any company offering a service and suggesting they can greatly improve your life, or business, it is also worth considering what London Creative and their ilk actually do for profit. The notion of advertising agencies is somewhat out of date and many companies previously expert in that area are now in the business of managing communications for others. This means that companies like London Creative will go into a business and handle anything from setting up a regular newsletter by email, to producing a series of media adverts, like radio ads. I am banging on about radio adverts simply because I am aware they require a great many tricks, tightly written scripts and a lot of invention, packed into a very small amount of airtime. If you have these on your CV then at the very least you should have produced short scripts that any potential employer could read and digest very quickly and, probably, some mp3 files small enough to be emailed to anyone else willing to employ your talents. So, working in a company producing commercials, is a good way to produce commercials for your own talents.

Interview with Matt Buckle: Creative Director of London Creative

1 - In your opinion, how good a training ground for effective script-writing is available in writing radio commercials?

In my opinion there is very little academic training in how to write radio commercials. Unfortunately, it is still seen as TV's ugly sister and as a result gets passed over by eager students. In actual fact, radio is much harder to write than TV, press or online as you have no other avenues in which to hide. What you write is what there is. No glossy production values or cutting edge camera technology can make a bad radio script passable. Most of the trained people that I have met were trained on the job by the large radio groups such as Global. Although the training was useful in terms of craft, it is mostly based on generations of experience rather than academic works. Having said that, a foundation in radio is a bedrock for other copywriting. If you can make an idea work in radio, you can make it work on other media. The same cannot be said the other way round.

2 - If an aspiring writer wanted to get a break in writing radio commercials what would you suggest s/he does in terms of preparing material and approaching a potential employer?

Both the beauty and the curse of radio is that it's incredibly transparent. Anyone wanting to get in to radio copywriting needs to study the Radio Advertising Hall of Fame (available from the RAB). However, that doesn't mean it's easy. Listen to your favourite station and you'll see that advertisers fail time and again to get good ads made.

As well as learning from the masters, a good writer needs to also be a good marketer. As radio is so transparent, the writer needs to be able to distil a marketing message in to a single concept or sometimes even a single line that will cut through the clutter and stick in the mind of the listener. This is key when looking at CVs of potential copywriters. I look for an advertising brain that can write, not a poet that wants to have a multi-national pay for their indulgences.

3 - London Creative is well established, with some high-profile clients. Without naming names (unless you want to) could you give us some ideas about the following?

The man hours that go into a high-profile radio ad campaign.
The majority of the man hours go in to the preparation and writing. If that's done correctly then the production is fairly quick and straightforward. How long it takes comes down to the skill of the writer as a marketeer. If they can understand and explain the sales message effectively, the number of executions and potential concepts come flooding in. This process can take hours, it can take days, but if you're spending more than a couple of hours trying to get a concept to work then there's something wrong with the concept.

The production costs for a typical high-profile campaign.
These can vary massively depending on what production values you're going for. A one voice ad will, in most cases, be cheaper

than a two or three voice ad. If you're recording a music track, it'll cost more, if you're having multiple ads, your costs go up (although the cost per ad actually goes down). If you use celebrities or famous music tracks, the sky is the limit. We've written national campaigns from as little as 5k right up to 50k.

The costs of buying airtime for the work.
Airtime costs work on even more complex dynamics than production so I'm afraid there are too many variables to answer this question effectively. Some clients spend thousands, some hundreds of thousands.

4 - What are the biggest mistakes aspiring writers make once they get involved with companies like yours, and what qualities help you spot talent with a bright future?
The biggest mistake I see time and time again, and unfortunately it's not just from young aspiring writers, is that the creative leads the ad and the sales message is left to sit uncomfortably in the corner. Advertising is all about getting results. If it doesn't work, the advertising has failed and the client won't come back. If it's a work of art (if that's what you want to call it), then that's a happy accident. The sales message needs to be the key, not getting some incredibly "funny" or "clever" idea on to the airwaves.

It's the writers that can get the message right that really have the bright futures. Anyone can have a great idea, but very few can make it work.

Like many others interviewed for this book Matt Buckle is understandably reticent to be specific about the exact amounts of money involved in work. Since this book was written in a financially turbulent time the costs for a range of creative work were in a flux. More accurately, they varied very much with supply and demand. Some advertisers got fantastic deals because radio stations were desperate for work. Elsewhere prices held. To put this in context, a few weeks before writing this chapter I was shopping around for a quote on producing radio adverts and getting airtime on a local station with a loyal listenership. I would script the adverts, the station would help us by finding a sub-contractor who would source the actors, provide the studio and produce the work, before it was broadcast. The airtime for regular insertions of a thirty second commercial in daytime radio, daily for a fortnight was likely to cost us between £2500 and £3000 depending on exactly how many times the ad was run. Recording and producing were likely to add around £1500 more. I contacted a recording studio directly to discuss this amount. I would name names, but then I wouldn't be able to add the fact that the studio involved did have a conversation with us about a significant discount, assuming we paid in cash!

London Creative is a good example here because they also demonstrate another factor you need to consider if looking to get a break. A trawl of their website, or the website of any other large organization involved in similar work can sometimes leave you confused. This company provide communication solutions, so the thing you can easily miss when looking at their site is exactly what it is they do. Customers typically find an agency like this for one of two reasons; either they know someone who used them, or the customer has a pressing need for a new brochure, new advertising etc.

Many hopeful writers look at sites a different way, trawling them to try to find the companies offering the kind of work the writer wants to get involved in. The end result of this behaviour is sometimes that writers apply to small, specialist, companies or send in their work in the hope of being offered some freelance jobs. If you stop and think about it for a second you can see how many people throw away a good opportunity without even realizing what they are doing. A bigger company offering solutions to all communication problems is a company with a range of skilled staff, a broader range of clients and – quite possibly – exciting tools, like in-house production facilities. If you send in sample material to such an outfit, or chase a work placement, you could soon find yourself being asked to get involved as a member of a team to solve a series of communication problems. What you'll realize if this happens to you is that 'the job' we've spent this chapter discussing, is often a changeable thing. The job of writers is changing because technology, markets, and the working world keep changing. However, 'the job' also changes regularly because clients and creative companies, when negotiating work, often change each other's minds. Bigger companies like London Creative expect this to be part of any working agreement. If you as a writer in search of a break get involved in such work you stand to learn a lot of things you can take with you. And, of course, you can still approach a bigger company on the basis of wanting to work in one area; like writing radio commercials.

Consider the advantages of working in a bigger company providing 'solutions' to communication problems. For example; if your client was a jewellers and they had an idea to sell watches under the slogan; 'It's time for a change,' you might start off writing commercials using sounds of ticking, a ringing alarm and a one-line slogan promoting the jewellers. Someone else in the agency might suggest to the client that an animated projection, displaying a clock face in which the numbers fell into the middle and morphed into the slogan would work to attract attention in a busy shopping mall. When the client protested the idea was naff, you might hear your colleague explaining that children would be riveted, they would drag parents over to see it, and the parents would be obliged to stand around long enough to look at the stock whilst the child stood there amazed at the little animation. If you heard that argument and its eventual resolution between client and creative team you might learn a lot about the way creative ideas work best when they take into account human behaviour, the environment in which the work is seen, and the possibilities of doing something a little unusual. You might also find yourself back in their offices an hour after that meeting, knocking out a story-line for the projected animation, and then watching over the next couple of days as the in-house production facility created the animation to fit your vision.

The above example is hypothetical but a real-life example that struck me as very effective was the presence of a toy train in a shoe shop near where I live. The train has been known and loved by generations of children, who insisted on going there for shoes. The same shoe shop sold my youngest his first pair of shoes when he could barely toddle, and he loved watching the little train. They then sent him a birthday card every year until he was five. These are small 'communication solutions,' good little marketing tricks, but they work. Almost all his shoes up to and including his first school shoes came from that shop and he never complained about us taking him there everytime we needed to buy more.

The above example is complicated, but consider the main point. Getting a placement in a creative consultancy might be a good idea, because it is a dive into the deep end in terms of learning to work with creative skills. Even if you feel you can usefully work in a few areas covered by the consultancy, the chance to be rubbing shoulders with people who work in other areas – like animation design – could be very useful in the long term.

A final option you could consider is working in an area using communication and linked to business that many aspiring writers don't know about, let alone consider as first-step employment; mystery shopping. There are a number of organizations in the UK employing people who sample services, retail outlets, visitor attractions and other organizations dealing with the public. This example straddles this chapter and the next. In chapter three we will be looking at strategies to build up a writer's CV. Mystery shopping involves posing as a customer or service user, making detailed notes of your first-hand experience and feeding it back to the client. Mystery shopping companies are paid by clients for this work, and need a range of people to pose as shoppers. The work offers some benefits to aspiring writers, mainly because it involves writing, working to deadlines and being able to think creatively. At the very least you may have to imagine yourself as someone with more money to spend than you have, or think yourself into the role of someone really keen to use a product or service you wouldn't usually consider. A detailed case study of mystery shopping opens the next chapter, this little round up simply makes the point that not all the jobs that might provide a first opportunity for writers are obvious creative jobs with organizations who produce media material.

My apologies for the extremely long chapter. But there is a real positive in being able to write such a lengthy chapter when you consider what we are covering. This chapter is:

A detailed look at professional writing, taking into account the range of the work on offer. Discussion of pros and cons of different areas of work. Concluding statements about the nature of professional writing work at present and in the future. Consideration of likely earnings in the different areas of work.

So, we can start with the good news. We have barely scratched the surface, we have had a detailed look at a few examples, all of which give us ideas about many more things going on in the world of writing. So, for example, the only national newspaper to get a mention is *The Guardian* with its £25 fee for a short piece in the *Family* section each Saturday. If you bought every broadsheet paper on one Saturday, you would find other special sections and regular features asking for you to contribute. In fact, *The Guardian* pay considerably more for a regular piece in their magazine on a Saturday, recounting a strange or unusual experience. 'The range of work on offer' is infinitely more varied and voluminous than most people realize, most writers are ignorant of the workings of whole areas of paid work, I'll confess to being in this category. For starters, writing this book taught me a lot about mystery shopping.

In general, we have seen that the pros of a range of very varied 'creative writing' work including poetry, placements and projects of all kinds involves being able to realize a creative vision. The benefits also include the chance to establish yourself and your own unique voice in a way that will allow you to compete meaningfully for opportunities including writing literary novels and collections of poetry. The cons include the danger of generating a CV that looks inconsistent, remaining trapped at one level of income, utilizing a range of skills on sporadic projects when employing them on a more focused career might generate more income, and – not least – devoting a lot of time to making funding applications which are turned down. In terms of the more career orientated work we have seen that some of the situation for creative writers is reversed. Placements, and smart thinking about getting involved with particular companies, probably offer a better chance of a result than chasing grants for creative work, though writing regular small items for a specialist magazine is not the most creative work on offer. Some of this freelance work is more like craftsmanship than out and out creative writing, but at the bottom level there are opportunities. So far as most of the options in this chapter are concerned any 'consideration of likely earnings' has to come with a health warning. If you are looking for that first break it pays to allow for some work to go out there for no return. It also pays think in terms of payments for other work – like articles – as a bonus. If you reward yourself for successes by going out for a pizza, or buying a round of drinks you can at least plan to enjoy the money, even if there isn't much of it. That's where most of us start, and that is the proving ground.

Your first publication, successfully pitched idea or work

placement is unlikely to set you up financially for a whole day; it certainly won't set you up for life. But these are first-steps, and once you are involved in professional writing, you are in a position to build on your contacts, and sustain your success. Which is where we are going next, by way of a return to mystery shopping.

3 Get Yourself Connected

This chapter offers: *Practical strategies to build the gap between chapters one and two. Starting with a list of strategies for generating a 'writer's CV' and exploring several case studies down to the specifics of likely income, level of difficulty and the pros and cons of each strategy. Examples considered include bypassing normal routes and going directly to a company, aiming for the softest targets available: such as charities.*

The case studies start where the last chapter finished, with mystery shopping. The point of this chapter is to examine the way the examples set by some people show us all how we can build on a first break. The obvious thing to state at the start of this chapter is that anyone succeeding with the entry level examples in chapter two; like getting a place on an open mic night as a poet, or selling a short article to a magazine, should keep on trying to do the same things, and use the contacts on offer to help with the sales of other work. One article in one specialist magazine gives you credibility when you approach another. A comedy item sold to *Poot!* comic demonstrates you can be funny in other circumstances. The 'keep on keeping on' school of career development has worked for many successful writers, and will continue to work in the future. The changing technology used by writers, will not rule out the need to simply grind away.

We held over one example from the last chapter because it provides the best means of demonstrating how one first-step writing related job can provide a means of generating a writer's CV. The example of mystery shopping is complex, because it is one area of work that offers obvious opportunities to diversify and demonstrate a range of very useful skills for writers.

Mystery shoppers and mystery shopping companies come in many shapes and sizes. Some major operators count blue-chip clients like international airlines amongst their clients. One operation offering opportunities to a range of people from most walks of life, and accessible to the target market for this book is Shopper Anonymous (*www.shopperanonymous.co.uk*). Sue Ford, their Customer Relations Manager generously answered a range of questions on who they employ, and what these people do. This conversation followed a meeting I had with representatives of Shopper Anonymous at a trade fair. What strikes me about mystery shopping as a useful first-step for those intending to work in the creative industries is the way the skills required match those of successful people in the media. Mystery shopping demands a combination of creativity, focusing on the world around you and attention to detail. If you attempt to build a career purely on the basis of submitting freelance articles you might eventually face a job interview for a full-time position in a magazine and be asked questions about your team-working abilities and interfacing with managers. If you combine the freelance writing with something like mystery shopping, your answer to that question will be more convincing.

Most mystery shopping operations have their own unique take

on the business. Shopper Anonymous state on their home page:

By delivering the most comprehensive and tailored Mystery Shopping feedback in the world Shopper Anonymous can help increase your profitability by improving your customer service experience.

Our unique approach centres on our team of carefully chosen mystery shoppers who produce reports more detailed and factual than any other in the marketplace—providing your staff with the perfect motivational and coaching tool ...

In its simplest form this states the company work very closely with their clients, take a pride in the quality of the written feedback provided and aim to produce material that feeds directly into the way their clients manage staff. 'Carefully chosen' means they have a range of mystery shoppers, from professionals with high-profile careers to people who wouldn't stand out in a crowd, from teenagers to the elderly and from the most able bodied to people whose disability is central to their ability to be a mystery shopper. Mystery shoppers don't just shop, they visit zoos and football grounds, make phone enquiries, visit town centres and provide feedback on cleanliness. In fact, where somebody seeks to serve the public, there is an opportunity for someone else to check out this serving, and produce a report.

Sue Ford's opinion on the people she is looking for may cover almost all appearances, social classes and areas of interest, but some things are non-negotiable. Employees will need I.T. skills, the ability to write concise and focused copy and a great eye for detail. Most mystery shopping operations – including Shopper Anonymous – provide training, but some affinity with these areas of skill is probably useful ahead of being trained. Job satisfaction comes partly from the things you get to do, a free day out at a zoo with all food paid for would be welcome for most families of four. Sue Ford also pointed out to me that many of her mystery shoppers find satisfaction from knowing that people who are doing their jobs well will gain recognition, be happy when confronted with their report and may well get recognition and some additional rewards at work. The job can make mystery shoppers feel good, mainly because their work makes a positive difference in many cases. Mystery shoppers might also enjoy the 'mystery' element of the work, posing as someone else and thinking themselves into a different income bracket, for example. Sue told me of one person who got very into the role of shopping for a static mobile home with a price tag on the far side of £40,000.

A job like this isn't totally about creativity, but in presenting yourself, dealing with a range of situations and condensing complex written information into a formatted report your creative skills are tested. So mystery shopping, like a few other possibilities we will examine in this chapter, is a useful option for you because it presents evidence of creativity being applied to a situation. In the case of Shopper Anonymous the situations vary from a single phone call to a full-scale visit to a public event or site catering to the public. Other companies provide mystery shopping up to and including testing the top end services of international corporations. Part-time work like this makes for an interesting item on a CV and suits almost anyone. Elderly and disabled people – for example – are used by mystery shopping companies to test facilities and access to buildings for people with their needs and problems. Few areas of employment discriminate quite so positively in favour of marginalized groups as mystery shopping.

Sue Ford's advice to anyone interested in getting involved is typical of the advice you see repeatedly from people in the media industry. It matters that you research a mystery shopping company before applying to them. A familiarity with who they are and what they do goes a long way when you submit an email and CV. Many mystery shopping organizations get applications from people who start by telling them they love shopping; which isn't really the point. One thing that surprises many is the range of people involved in mystery shopping. The business has a level of job satisfaction that keeps people involved for years, and the part-time nature of the work suits many people who continue mystery shopping as their careers develop. Like other such companies Shopper Anonymous are usually on the look-out for good recruits. Their current staff includes a doctor, a dentist and several people running their own businesses. At the other end of the scale I spoke to one girl, 16 years old and six feet tall, who was looking at getting involved in mystery shopping. She was savvy to the point she knew that her first assignments would be likely to include making herself up to look as old as possible and attempting to buy alcohol. This girl was unsure about her future career but clear on two things. Firstly, she would work in the media, possibly in music journalism but hopefully in event management linked to music. Secondly, that the mystery shopping work would be an intriguing part of her CV and she would use it to argue to future employers that she could present herself differently to meet the demands of a situation and muster the confidence to deal with a challenging situation. This example could have been slotted into the previous chapter, after all; I am presenting it as another example of 'the job' of being a writer. Like most of the examples that made up the second half of chapter two mystery shopping can be used as a work opportunity in which you can get in quickly, get some experience, and move on. It matters in this chapter because – to my mind at least – work like this exists on a borderline between grabbing at opportunities and sustaining strategies that will help you get the breaks you need.

To put this crudely, if we are talking about *How to Get a Break as a Writer* then we have done the job already. Chapters one and two allow you to look objectively at your talents and identify ways they can be made to work. Deal with those areas and you can get a break. That is A (as in singular), break. Most writers who get a break want more opportunities to follow. If you're still reading in chapter three, I assume your staying power means you'll want more than one sale in your writing career. So, let's be honest, the A break title of this book makes commercial sense. **From this point on, we're discussing how to keep yourself employed as a writer.** Mystery shopping is the perfect watershed to leave behind A break and move forward into sustaining your breaks because it provides the perfect model for how to do it. Long-term mystery shoppers take their creative talents, eye for detail and experience of their craft into a range of different situations. The core of what they do may stay the same, but the scenery changes constantly. The mystery shopping doctor and dentist are typical of such progress, having started their work in mystery shopping as students and stuck with it despite developing successful careers in another realm.

I could simply say at this stage that sustained employment as a writer comes because you keep on wanting it, keep on trying and use all the contacts you make to develop more opportunities. For almost everyone holding down long-term employment in this area, that is true. However, it is also a simplistic overview when what we really need at this point are insights into how you keep things going. If we are starting with 'a list of strategies to generate a writer's CV' then this matters. Basically, common sense goes a long way here. Writing, like plumbing, teaching people to drive, and running a bakery, is a job. Plumbers and the rest can use the same basic approaches as writers, so the 'list of strategies' should start with the obvious points.

There is no shortage of general careers advice, or people willing to offer you everything from life coaching to job hunting, usually for a fairly hefty fee. If you have the money, the time and the open mind then this could benefit you as a writer. Apart from anything else, the organizations and individuals offering this work may well make available much more complex diagnostic tools than the copy test in the opening chapter, and provide you with some detailed breakdown of the cognitive skills you show. All of which might well be helpful. Many aspiring writers don't think about seeking careers advice, paid for or bought in by way of a book. But it is worth considering, if only because it tends to focus on general principals and force you away from the typical writers' trap of obsessing about ideas and pet projects.

A list of strategies is just that. It is not a list of things you have half completed. So, 'Complete that short story and send it off to *People's Friend* magazine is NOT a strategy. 'Use *The Writers' and Artists' Yearbook* to identify short story markets, list in terms of money on offer per 1000 published words, and identify email addresses for specific editors,' IS a strategy.

CV building strategies should be general, objective, considered and – hopefully – proven to work in circumstances similar to your own. So a good way to think about building your writer's CV is to immerse yourself in the kind of literature or online advice available to anyone looking to boost their career prospects or move from one area to another. The down side of this is that you gather general advice, that doesn't really discuss the details down to the unfinished pieces of writing on your computer. The upside of this is that you focus on general issues, and get away from individual ideas. To use an old cliché; you see the wood instead of the trees. And that gets you round one massive obstacle the halts the careers of many hopeful writers.

General 'sort your life out' career advice focuses on a mix of facts about the working world, and personal details about yourself. What follows is a digest of material I gathered from wading through a great many sites and self-help careers books gathered at work.

Since we are talking strategies here let's start with a major and very important point: **It Pays to be Pro-active, or proactive** (people still use both forms of the word). What follows is either a round up of good practice, or a rant against being lazy and complacent. It really depends on your point of view. As with the sentence with bold type above I will highlight key points as we go through this collection of strategies to provide you with a hit list of useful strategies. Not all of these strategies apply to every hopeful author, so **make intelligent decisions about which strategies apply to you.**

We'll start with positives. If you're going to develop a writer's CV you might as well start by listing things you think you'd like to do. Football writing, music writing, having access to politicians and other apparent 'glamour' jobs may well motivate you. Motivation makes a hell of a difference, especially early in your writing career when you will have to fight to prove yourself. The important thing in terms of developing a CV as a writer is to be able to **find some directions that will work.** Apart from anything else, it matters that you examine a range of possibilities, use some basic research techniques and get stuck in to making contacts, speaking to people, swapping emails and engaging in a dialogue. Like many others I know who write, I have had work simply because I found myself sitting around the office, bored, and thought; 'I should make something happen.' That – more or less – is how the story of a student canteen charging for hot water made it to the *Daily Star* but it is also the story of how many major pieces of work, like film scripts, got started.

Back this work up with **an honest audit of what you do well.** The best way of finding this out is gathering any material you already have – like references from former employers, feedback sheets from teachers or lecturers etc and identifying the skills they see in you. You can also support this through discussions with others who know you well. If I were imposing a rule at this stage I would ban such discussions with close blood relatives and/or people you are currently sleeping with, though that isn't an absolute rule, just a useful guideline to remind you that objectivity is important. One thing worth taking into account if you do take on board the suggestions of these people is that the verbal broadsides they've hurled at you in anger may well be the most useful insights on offer. If the twentieth argument in a month with your mother about the state of your bedroom has just finished, why not think about it? If you're that disorganised then an objective route to making the best move as a writer might be to list places you can get work experience. Those places will invariably be better organised than your room, or your life, and your own fear of messing up on a work placement might well keep you focussed on doing a good job. So you'll do well in the work placement, even if you're going home to sleep in a bedroom that looks like it's been bombed. Those arranging your work placement won't see you fishing out the week old underwear from under the bed and making it last another day. More to the point, if your mother is driven to despair by your bedroom it may well be because she cares and thinks you can do a better job of sorting yourself out. So, the pair of you organising who to approach for that work placement, and how to contact them, might be a useful bonding experience. Anyway, it's an idea. What matters in this idea is that you take on board the evidence of what you can do, and make it count for something.

And if you are prepared to do research on yourself, **do research into what is on offer out there.** We have already touched on this, so banging on much more is – I think

– pointless at this stage. But consider the examples in the previous chapter. The best chances may well come if you dig deep enough to find areas of professional writing and developing ideas that others don't consider. Lots of people look to get jobs with television companies, or submit ideas directly to channels and individual film and television directors. Fewer people take the trouble to submit ideas to development production companies. Even fewer people think about getting work experience with development production companies and using it to learn about how ideas are submitted, and the main reasons some succeed and some fail. The irony here is that many people who get steady rejections are devoting hundreds of hours to sitting down and hammering out work, whilst some others are getting a break on many fewer hours of work, because they devote some of these hours to trawling websites, carefully reading information sources like *Writer's Market, The Writers' & Artists' Yearbook* etc. I wouldn't suggest you take it too literally, but I would recommend you try to see a British Movie called *Being Considered.* I won't spoil the plot too much in case you do take the trouble to see it, but I think it worth pointing out that the story concerns a desperately serious screenwriter who gets rejections. A thief takes his car, laptop and –crucially – his copy of *The Writer's Journey* (a seminal book on mythical structure in story, and a work well-known on degree courses in Film Studies and the like). Whilst our hero's life unravels the thief sets to work rewriting a script he finds on the lap-top, taking on board the sound advice in *The Writer's Journey.* At which point, I think, you can see where this is all leading. The serious point is that research, and making the effort to find out how things really are, counts for a lot if you are trying to build a CV from scratch.

Apart from anything else you might find out about the worst aspects of a job you find attractive, and change your mind. I can't name names here but for years I have been telling my students a story about a work placement I had in radio many years ago and one particular incident involving a member of the technical staff, a serious curry the previous night and a group of us waiting whilst this bloke queued for the only toilet at a live event, holding us all up, stressing us and leaving us breaking sweat to return to the studio and file a report on time. The moral of the story is that the attractive elements of a job often come with downsides you wouldn't necessarily consider. The reality of the story is that it explains why I didn't follow through on one career ambition when I was at university. So, make sure you find out the worst things about an area of work before making a commitment. That way, you develop a CV with fewer dead-ends.

A few other points are worth making with regard to strategy for building a CV. If we are talking about **internet searches, it pays to do them repeatedly.** An obvious thing to do is to join some writers' network – like Writewords – where a regularly updated series of job adverts is on offer, along with forum discussions on different areas of writing. If you don't want to pay a subscription, there are always the likes of Craigslist and Gumtree, with adverts for writing jobs that will – at least – allow you to use a little common sense and use email addresses on adverts to work out likely website addresses, and investigate a range of employers of writers. In terms of regular searching **it also pays to vary the things you type in ahead of a search.** So – for example – 'Award winning advertising agencies in Edinburgh' tends to throw up different contacts and possibilities to 'copywriting + Edinburgh.' If you are looking to get a break, the sheer volume of information you will gather this way should eventually prove helpful, at least because it will allow you to demonstrate a wide knowledge of an area that appeals to you. The best possible combination when you do such a search is often to find the employers who don't appear to be using the internet to attract work placement enquiries or original material, and then approach them with either. These people are often intolerant of time wasters, and some of them are just plain intolerant. But, a handful of those who have developed an aversion to being spammed by idiots react well when someone who has done proper research makes an intelligent and constructive approach.

It also pays to widen your trawling to **take in work that appears both above and below your ability level.** As I'll show you later on, sometimes approaching those who appear well out of your reach is the best means of securing a work placement, a chance to have your writing idea taken seriously or the chance to network effectively.

By the same token, **look for very unconventional places to get a break.** At this point we will divert into some stories from my own working life that show the potential value of this. Though, so far, the best stories I can tell in this area haven't netted me a fortune and the best two stories I can tell have netted me nothing, they still show the potential of the unconventional approach.

A few years ago I saw an advert for creative work in the media and the advert asked for something unusual, even by the standards of creative writing applications. Applicants were invited to apply, by letter, in the style of a deposed world leader. I've always had a love of off-the-wall projects and so that was an irresistible opportunity. I duly wrote one sheet of A4 claiming to be Idi Amin (former tyrant in charge of Uganda and best known these days from his portrayal in the movie The Last King of Scotland). This happened so long ago that Amin was still alive. I thought nothing more about it until my wife took a phone call at home one day, told the caller they obviously had a wrong number and hung up. When the same caller rang back and insisted they had the right number for 'Idi' my wife soon realised it must be a call for me. What transpired taught me a useful lesson. I found myself talking to a training and event management company. They had a massive programme to roll out nationally and had been advertising for confident people to learn the programme and front high-profile events in major UK cities. These people were clearly not the people I'd applied to in the advert, but they thought the sheer front of my application suggested I had what they wanted. We met and had a positive interview but nothing came of it because they were offering contracts of a few months duration, with lots of travel, and I had a mortgage, a family and a liking of being at home a little more often than their job would allow.

What matters at this point is how I ended up in that interview. It happened by mistake. I'd lovingly crafted a plea for a career break on behalf of Idi Amin, stuck it in an envelope and duly scribbled down the address from the newspaper advert. But I'd written the wrong address. I'd copied out the address in a neighbouring advert. The people I met hadn't wanted such an application. In fact, they had been looking for CVs and typical application letters from people with a background in education and training, and some creative flair. They received a letter that looked so over the top it stood out from everything else, made them laugh out loud, and intrigued them to the point they were prepared to make a phone call. Had I been ten years younger, single or unemployed, I'd have jumped at the chance they were offering. The money was great, the people booking in to receive the training included some high-profile companies and the chance to network and generate job opportunities when the training contract ended after a few months was obvious.

I generated another similar opportunity for myself around the same time. The following story is covered by a couple of confidentiality clauses so I can't be specific. My young son and I loved playing with a range of toys we bought in a major high-street retailer. I made up stories about the toys and told them to him. It struck me that publishing these stories could generate a lot of money but the copyright on the toys in terms of their name, image rights and the rest meant I couldn't simply write something and look for a deal. I did some research and found that the store selling them had exclusive rights. So I found the number for their head office and rang it. Within a few minutes I was talking to someone with national responsibility for stocking the toys and maintaining control over product range in a whole department of the national stores. I explained my idea, was told to put it in writing and started a short dialogue with this person. The pitch was fairly simple. I would write the material, the store would publish it and distribute it directly into their own high street outlets, a great many middle men would be cut out and the potential for us both to earn more than would usually be the case with such a product range was obvious. The store had done a basic costing exercise on making the material when a major problem emerged. The sales of the toys were in decline and it was obvious the product range was nearing the end of its shelf life. My idea came to nothing because other market forces were against us. But – as with Idi Amin's ill-fated attempt to become a trainer and writer for businesses – the whole exercise showed the value of an unconventional approach to an unlikely partner in a writing venture. The common language in our discussions involved the business potential and – in particular – the money we might make. Very recently, I have started a similar negotiation on an entirely different project linked to another merchandise range. It is too early to tell how this will go, but the same approach, of ringing head office and pitching the whole project directly, generated the same response. I found a national Director of Merchandise replying, taking the suggestion seriously, and initiating a look at the store's own data to see how profitable my idea might be.

Assuming you get replies and interest, **make sure there is material online to back up your claims about your abilities.** It is well documented that employers often use internet searches ahead of offering interviews and jobs so it pays to have things out there that do you justice. It also pays to produce this material and have others check it out, before you use it to land work for yourself. Rae Louise Jones – who appears in Chapter Two – has had a Facebook page devoted to her poetry since she was a student. She is also on MySpace. Her presence on these sites leaves her rubbing shoulders with bands in search of a record deal, aspiring film directors and the rest. What matters for the purposes of this argument is that her presence is appropriate. She doesn't claim to be better than Ted Hughes, but she doesn't hide either. Social networking sites are a mixed blessing. In terms of shifting material to a niche market they can be very useful. If you have written the definitive history of Dagenham and Redbridge FC then their Facebook page, their fan page and any pages dedicated to Dagenham history and Dagenham life would be useful places to post a link once the book appears on Amazon. Apart from anything else, you'll alert the exiled Dagenham fan who lives in San Diego, California and he (trust me; it will be a bloke), will buy your book because exiled fans exist on the back of merchandise and online contact with their fellow addicts.

The problem with social networking, and the internet in general, comes when your presence in cyberspace clashes with the image you are trying to cultivate. So, you might think having an email name like mentalgingerbastard#1 is funny.[4] It doesn't always impress creative employers; even those you think might find it funny.

If you are looking to create a good impression with online work the general rule is that less is more. This doesn't mean you should limit your online work to a few items, but it does mean you should make sure that someone seeking

4. I tried contacting mentalgingerbastard#1 on a few of the major email providers. He or she appears not to exist, hence me using the example. If you are now, or subsequently intend to be, mentalgingerbastard#1 no offence is intended. Go well!

you out online finds a handful of examples showcasing the skills they would most like to see. So, you can post the stomach churning stunts much loved by your regular Youtube followers under a nickname, and use the name on your birth certificate for the innovative ideas posted on the forum page of a writers' site that might – just – earn you a chance to put one of them onstage. If you are producing video, audio or document files it also pays to use standard formats. If you have a CV available for download, make sure it could be pasted into a Word Document, use mp3 files for audio etc. It stands to reason that someone in search of a break as a writer is likely to be reaching out to people who see themselves as busy and successful. Give them something user-friendly and save them time and you are more likely to generate an opportunity for yourself. You might assume your work online is user-friendly but it is worth getting someone whose opinion you trust to double check this. Let them surf and search to find you, and listen to their account of what they found and how it looked. As with other reality checks, it is better if you are asking someone you would trust to write you a reference, not necessarily someone you care about passionately. Objectivity is important in this area.

It is also useful to **keep your online presence up to date.** So – for example – show updated news items or similar, even if they only relate to reading your poetry in an open mic night in a pub. This is something of a difficult area to cultivate for aspiring writers but a useful rule would be to avoid using blogs or a similar networking presence as the main means of updating the news. The personal material like blogs can smack of self-indulgence and do you little justice. Short updates based more on fact look more focused and suggest a drive to achieve things. Of course, this isn't an absolute rule and there are documented examples of people who have used blogging as a direct route to major success, notably Dr Brooke Magnanti. For all her success as a research scientist, earning a PhD and going on to work on cutting edge research on the exposure of the unborn foetus to specific pesticides, Brooke Magnanti only made national news when her other life as the blogger and author of the memoirs of a London prostitute *Belle de Jour* became public knowledge. She worked as a prostitute during her PhD studies because she had run out of money and had successfully avoided being outed despite the high-profile success of her books. The story of how she eventually became identified for her writing is instructive in terms of you trying to get a break as a writer. Please understand; I'm not advocating a job in the sex industry as a career move for a writer. Two things make Brooke Magnanti's case worth mentioning here. Firstly; the anonymity she achieved and sustained. Her books and blog were hugely successful and still her agent didn't know her real identity. Moreover, because she had a literary agent and her work was praised for its quality of prose, infectious humour and its balance and understanding of all those working in the industry there were many – including respected journalists and literary reviewers – who considered the whole thing a literary hoax. A handful of suspects – including journalist Toby Young – were suggested as the likely author. Press coverage in 2009 when she finally outed herself made clear that a number of factors had finally led to her going public including her simply being fed up of the fuss her work had created and – as *The Times* reported – 'an ex-boyfriend with a big mouth lurking in the background.' The second notable point about her blog and book is that all the rumours about her started because the writing was simply so good.

If you intend to use a blog or other regular online presence as a means of making yourself a successful writer the only strategy that makes sense is to **make your blog, or regular web presence so stunningly good it demands to be noticed.** In fact, a more likely route from blog to book deal is that enjoyed by Judith O'Reilly, author of *Wife in the North* and a blogger under the same title. She was already an accomplished writer before her husband moved the family to the north east of England. Her blog explains:

"Moving to Northumberland from London was not my idea. My husband was in fact the only one terribly keen on the move. When I asked my younger son what he thought, he confided: "Bears might eat me". "There are no bears," I told him as I looked into the darkness and the growling started."

The sense of a person out of place, and humour being the best medicine runs through the blog and the highly popular *Wife in the North* blog site now takes advertising from a range of local tourist attractions, local producers and the like near Judith O'Reilly's home. Her book sold well too, even amongst those she gently mocks in her writing.

Brooke Magnanti and Judith O'Reilly succeeded as bloggers for the same reasons many writers succeed in other areas; they had things to say and their writing was exceptionally good from the start. Their route to writing success might have been peculiar to the 21st century; their skills and professional approach were very old fashioned. The one thing any aspiring writer could replicate from their work is **becoming an expert in some field, and sharing that expertise with the world.** One piece of common ground between Brooke Magnanti and Judith O'Reilly is their position of living a life that others might speculate upon, but couldn't know so well. That quality of explaining with insight and humour an area of life that has some passing fascination for others has been part of many successful first books, notably in the case of expose writing by anonymous authors. Francis Gilbert's first book *I'm A Teacher, Get me out of Here* used pseudonyms but still told a grim and – occasionally – hopeful tale of a working life in England's worst school. The same approach – more or less – informs *Wasting Police Time*, an insider's look at the day to day realities of being a front-line police officer. *Wasting Police Time* was a very unlikely success. Credited to PC David Copperfield it was – in reality – written by Stuart Davidson, a British police officer who had started writing about gardening, switched to police matters when his mention of his main job attracted more attention that his gardening writing and became a book author after a series of events that started with items from his blog being lifted without permission and printed in the national press. One thing any hopeful writer can learn from this is the value of having a solid factual basis to online writing. In the end Stuart Davidson was in the enviable position of being wanted by newspapers and publishers, and not having to chase them too hard.

Having ranted a little against using close friends and family as arbiters of talent I think it is worth redressing the balance. The one place their uncritical love of you and your work will come in handy is in helping you get contacts. A useful part of any strategy for getting and sustaining a break as a writer is **using friends, family and – indeed – anyone you know willing to help you secure contact with influential people**. As with some other elements of this strategy this is not an exact science. For example; someone too indulgent of you might unwittingly do you no favours if he or she puts your less than competent work in front of a film director. The honest feedback that results might fracture your relationship with the person who set out to help you and devastate your confidence as a writer. We'll assume for the purposes of this discussion that your work is fit to be seen and the people helping you have enough grasp of the quality of the work to know this. In reality, many people who might advance your cause will have to know how good your work is because helping you secure contacts is also a test of their reputation. However, mistakes are made and I trust that you are wise to the potential for this strategy to go wrong.

At the same time, don't assume an introduction, direct line phone number or personal email address is the end of the search. **Have material prepared in the event of some influential person being prepared to entertain you or your ideas.** A useful guide for this material can be found by looking in detail at the websites of leading literary agents, film production companies and similar. If they are specific as to how they want work submitted; the least you can do is take their suggestions on board. If you are simply trying to get a useful introduction ahead of a work placement then the best you can do is research likely career progression in your chosen area. Sites like Skillset lay out most of the important information you will need to know about creative career areas. Careers analysts and counselors often use an Americanism, referring to the need to prepare an 'elevator speech.' In other words; a short verbal outline of who you are and where you are going career-wise, or a clear presentation explaining an idea.

One of the most common failings of elevator speeches by writers is the way they focus entirely on the writer making the speech, or his/her work. So **make sure any short pitch you prepare is adapted to the needs of each audience you face.** For example; if you have a chance to meet another writer who can't produce your work, but can help you to reach others with that ability, don't just explain your idea and insist it is a work of genius. Tweak your pitch to make sure the writer to whom you are talking sees the passion and talent in your and – hopefully – identifies with it to the point that he or she is prepared to help. There are many places online and many sections in books on how to prepare and pitch major works, like novels. Most of these focus on the importance of opening sentences in submissions, strap-lines and thumbnail sketches in a film script etc. In other words, most of the standard guides on how to make it as a screenwriter or novelist suggest that you have succinct summaries to hand when presenting your work. Take this suggestion on board and rehearse your arguments ahead of dealing directly with anyone you wish to impress. Good places to find guidance on summarizing big ideas include forums for pitching full-length films. I've often suggested my students look carefully at the Rocliffe Forum, organized by BAFTA. The Rocliffe Forums encourage new talent into the film industry and have always offered options for writers. When they look for new writing talent BAFTA, via the Rocliffe Forums have the agreeable habit of getting the message out very widely and being very specific about what they want in terms of submissions. Their guidance for writers tends to insist on very short summaries of ideas, samples of script etc. I have often heard the argument from students that these short, sharp items won't do justice to their ideas. The point I make in return is that the Rocliffe Forums are a superb opportunity for aspiring writers and lots of people take advantage of this opportunity every year. For everyone thinking the targets too demanding there are others breaking sweat to meet the demands. Most of these people fail to get the break they want, but they do benefit from the discipline imposed by the targets, and most of them emerge with their complex ideas presented in a form resembling an elevator speech, making them more saleable than they were in their original form.

Finally, to sum up this section on strategies, it is worth stating the obvious. **It is a good idea to have answers prepared for standard interview questions like; 'Where do you see yourself in five years?'** Whilst these questions seem at first glance much more appropriate for a formal job interview with a salary and contract on offer they do also have a relevance to helping you get a break as a writer. In the case of your writing ambitions the point of having these answers prepared is that they may well form the basis of the first serious discussions you have with people in a position to help you. If you are aiming for a work placement or similar then the relevance of the questions is obvious. But even if you are pitching original work and ideas it pays to have these answers ready because the people looking at your original material may well want to know something about the person producing it. Without any serious prior knowledge of you they may fall back on these questions, because such questions are understood throughout a range of industries to be a key to understanding the seriousness of people trying to advance their careers. Beyond this, it is up to you to work out the answers. Your working out should take into account things you have discovered about where you might work, the opportunities you may find in the future etc. If you want to find yourself as a well-regarded novelist then appropriate responses might revolve around mentioning the right kind of companies to publish your work, other writers who have achieved a measure of independent success and the routes they took to get there. If you want to work in a well-paid position in the creative industries, like an advertising creative post, then investigating the job titles, salaries and range of work on offer in the industry is important and I suggest preparing useful answers to the questions below before reading any further.

1. Where do you see yourself in five years time?
2. What are your greatest strengths?
3. Can you give an example of something you did well, that helped you to understand more about your abilities?
4. What professional development do you think you would need in the next couple of years?
5. What experiences have helped to shape your present ambitions?

Beyond outlining the strategies above I think it vitally important to make one more point. **The strategies above are very helpful in getting you to build on any break as a writer, but they work best when you keep applying them, over and over again.** For example; if you have prepared material that proves useful in bringing you to the attention of someone influential, you are likely to keep on needing to prove yourself after that first break. So, it makes sense that we look at some people who have built creative careers using their writing skills, and other skills where appropriate. I make no apologies for the spread of eclectic examples that follows, you will see in their accounts some clear evidence of applying elements of the good practice highlighted so far. The writer and director of *Being Considered* was one person who replied to my requests for an interview via email. Jonathan Newman's replies were so comprehensive they make more sense at the end of the section on strategies than they do placed next to a brief discussion of his film. As with the other examples to follow, I have taken the liberty of highlighting key points in Jonathan's answers.

1 - How much of the *Being Considered* story of the ambitious writer with a brilliant idea getting knocked back is drawn from your life, or the life of others you know?

"Every time a friend of mine succeeds a little piece of me dies."
- Oscar Wilde

At the time I made *Being Considered* I was young, new to the film industry and not far out of film school. I was driven to make a movie and I had no script. I created an opportunity for myself by soliciting, amongst others, British Telecom who, remarkably, gave me £10,000 to make the film. This was in exchange for owning the VoD rights so they could test something called 'broadband"!

While at the time of writing the script, I didn't really have heaps of experience of the industry, I did have my fair share of rejections. In the beginning of my career I took rejection personally - as a slight to my ego and a slander to my ability to create. The thing is with our industry, or any form of art, is that you open yourself up to criticism. It is and exposed and vulnerable place to be.

Often I have found that writers often base their first script on something quite close and personal to them, because, I think, it is familiar to write about something you know. So my first screenplay was about film and a struggling writer trying to break into the industry. Having been around so many people who have been struggling for years in this industry, some with talent, others without, I have discovered that some people make it, some don't. It is the combination of talent, luck, experience and proactivity working in harmony that eventually lead to success. **Crucially, you have to be proactive. Because the more proactive you are, the more opportunities come your way, and your chances of being lucky increase.**

The idea for the script was born more out of an intellectual conversation on the nature of luck vs. talent, how increasingly talent has little to do with success, how sometimes luck has more to do with the unscientific formula that dictates success. Whatever the balance of the equation, I am convinced that it does, indeed, necessitate all three elements be present to make it (that is: action + talent +experience = success).

The screenplay for *Being Considered*, in a way, was catharsis for me. I was able to exercise all of my writing demons in that script - my neuroses. The prevailing attitude of a lot of creative people is 'why not me?" As if the world is conspiring against you. And I understand that, because it is easy to feel like your time will never come, and you deserve it. And perhaps you do.

2 - Without naming names; have you encountered any mediocre talents and chancers who used

screenwriting manuals and similar publications to shape half-baked ideas into saleable scripts?
No. That was just fabrication on my part. At the time I was really into Vogler's "Writer's Journey" and the book it was based on "The Hero with a Thousand Faces" - and I really used them in my writing. So I just thought it would be kind of a funny hook if a thief stole this guy's script and peddled it around town and it suddenly became the talk of the town, despite it being rubbished by the same people.

But I have met many mediocre talents, who have risen to the surface somehow. You can't begrudge them. Everyone deserves success, even those undeserving of it! Other people's success helps to highlight your own failures, and that insecurity is what caused bitterness. That is why successful people can be so generous - because when you are at the top of the food chain, there is nowhere else to go.

3 - In your opinion how much of a successfully pitched script is down to talent, and how much down to getting the approach right?
Pitching is an art form that can be learnt. It is a combination of both the concept and the presentation to spark the interest in the other person. After that, the script has to speak for itself. Pitches need to be concise. **The need to condense it in to one sellable logline is ultimately essential. I say this on the one hand, because you, as a writer, should be able to get to the crux of your story in one line. You should be able to deliver the heartbeat, and create an entire visual spectacle for your pitchee in just one line.** In other words, YOU should know what your film is about. And you shouldn't launch into detail, and endless descriptions of this and that. It's boring. No one wants to hear it. People have short attention spans - that's the other reason.

The best one line pitches contain four things.

1) Context
2) Characters
3) Location , and most crucially
4) A sense of irony.

If you want good examples of pitches, get Halliwell's film guide, which condenses every movie down to one line.

Here's a quick pitch for *ET*, which I pulled from IMDB

"A group of Earth children help a stranded alien botanist return home."

Notice is contains all four elements. Where this pitch would get unstuck is if it just read:

"An alien crash lands on earth"

Where is the irony?

It becomes interesting when you add the "and". "An alien lands on earth and is unable to return home... or befriends a 7 year old boy who helps him return home," Irony. That is the most important part of the pitch.

Or consider this pitch for *Pretty Woman.*
" A man in a legal but hurtful business needs an escort for some social events, and hires a beautiful prostitute he meets... only to fall in love."

It is the last bit that is really the most interesting bit... "only to fall in love". Because our minds, through association, create a visual framework for the entire film – a man hires a prostitute and falls in love. You can see the setting, and you can see, more importantly, the conflict.

The next part of the pitch is the presentation. **Effective pitches**

convey enthusiasm and passion and are clear and concise. If your eyes light up while delivering the pitch, this will get conveyed. If you are boring, flat and unsure in your delivery, than you can't expect the listener to be interested either. The idea is to enroll the listener, to actively take them on the fleeting journey with you.

If you have successfully engaged your listener, you can expect "Sounds interesting. I'd like to read it." That's really the best you can hope for, and then the rest depends on your script and how well the idea is executed.

If they don't like it, move on quickly to something else.

4 - Now you have your own company, and a track record of success, how many unsolicited approaches - from full-blown scripts to someone asking for work experience - do you get, and what singles out a successful approach from the others?
Like most people or companies that are listed somewhere, **I get loads of unsolicited submissions.** I do say on my website that I don't accept unsolicited submissions. People still send them. I don't blame anyone - I did the same thing in my youth (though I never send anything unsolicited anymore). Sending cold without any personal connection whatsoever results in one thing... "DELETE". It's just the nature of the beast. We get so much junk anyway filter into our email boxes, telling us we have won the lottery and the King of Nigeria wants to give us $5 million, the cold email from the desperate writer is just, sadly, another piece of spam mail I don't want. Cruel as it sounds, it's the truth. Think about it. You don't know that person. They don't know you. Why on earth should they entertain your rubbish idea? I received an email this week from a writer who said their script has the potential to win an Oscar. This just comes across as self-delusion and naivety and it quickly found its way into the trash bin.

Furthermore, **most people that work in the industry do not go about developing script and projects from random cold emails they receive from strangers. It just doesn't happen. It would be a crap shoot. It would be like trying to fund your feature film by buying lottery tickets** every week.

As for people asking for work experience, I get a lot of these too. This really depends on timing. If I am in pre-production, the timing is perfect, because we are crewing - so I will often forward the mail to my line producer and leave it in their hands. If I am not in production there is little I can do, so truthfully it will get deleted. Timing is everything.

5 - If your present day self could meet the version of you who hadn't sold a script or achieved a successful break, what would you tell him?
Build it and it will come. Do not give up the dream. Continue to take proactive action, create, make movies, take chances, don't take anything personally and it will come. Also, remember how important the script development process is. If you are shooting the first draft of your script you are more than likely not making the best film you can. Take time to develop the script. **Seek out constructive criticism, listen to those things that are being repeated by more than one person, because they might be right.**

Jonathan Newman is living proof that some of the strategies outlined in my write up above, and his answers beneath that, can work. So too is Erica Longdon, although her career route, taking in voice artist work and – currently – holistic/angel therapy, is very different from Jonathan's.

1 - Before you began working in the media did you think this was the right career area for you?
It was beyond my wildest dreams. I had no expectations of anything but a mundane, conventional life. And I hated the idea. I came from a conservative, with small and capital "C", small town in the Midlands and the careers advice I got centred around teaching, or how a 'gel' could use a job to marry well. I spotted an advert in *The Guardian* for a secretary to work on a television show in London. My future boss caught his coat on the way into the interview, swore and finally said:

"So what makes you think you'll do?"

Later, they asked me to describe the political differences between a major broadsheet and a tabloid, I was struck dumb. Lamely, I managed:

"Well, I like the Guardian because it has the best media jobs".

I thought I'd completely blown it, but the job offer arrived the next day. One day I asked them how on earth I got the job, what was it they had seen?

"You didn't know and you didn't try to bullshit.. But you were bright, keen to learn and very hungry for the opportunity. That's what we wanted, enthusiasm and a willingness to learn."

Motto: don't try to blag your way through an interview unless you really have the skills and knowledge to back it up. Just be yourself at the very best that you can be at that moment. I've sat on many an interview board since, and it was great advice.

2 - You spent years as a voice artist, can you describe this work and the variety of things you were expected to do?
Getting into the voice industry is extremely difficult. Rule

number one is get some experience and a demo disc. I started out on a magazine show for hospital radio. Many a well known broadcaster has started this way, and it's a great learning experience because of the range of skills you develop. After a subsequent course at The National Broadcasting School, I graduated with Honours and set out to work as a radio host. Invicta Radio in Kent was just starting and I agreed to work without pay for a month in return for a job as the producer on a music and chat show. Eventually I was given a show of my own on the "graveyard" shift. Then I swung through the hours to a weekend breakfast show, and finally graduated to my own prime-time three hour music and chat show. This used all the skills I'd ever accumulated as I was operating a full studio desk, playing in music, firing split commercials, with two different stacks playing at either end of the county and having to come back to music with split second timing. Plus I was bringing in telephone interviews and hosting live guests.

My next step was a return to television, I auditioned for a job as a Channel 4 announcer. Working as a "live" announcer for one of the main terrestrial channels means working long hours around a twenty-four hour shift system. Due to the great diversity of programmes on Channel 4 at that time, announcers were expected to view every programme they introduced, and to consult with a Commissioning Editor if you had any queries or couldn't get to grips with the content. So shifts were structured as time to view and write, and then the live announcing in the voice over booth. Scripts were anything from five to forty seconds long, and could vary from introducing comedy with Roseanne to a dissertation on the nature of history with Sir Karl Popper. Every television company has a Duty Officer's Log, and the public is very quick to let you know if they don't agree with what is said or feel that the grammar is incorrect. One of my colleagues once received a carpeting for a slip in which he said:

"There's more calculations on the way..."

He should, of course, have said: "There are more calculations…"

Another part of an announcer's job is often a weekly promo recording session. Nowadays, this is sometimes a specialist job, with a voice over booked specifically to suit a particular subject. I learned this craft at Channel 4. To voice a promo you must be able to spread or speed up the delivery of a line to fit into the picture gap. Inflection, tone and pitch are subject to the instructions of the director in charge. Sometimes your input is requested, but most of the time, you are the tool who must deliver what is requested of you, preferably in the fewest number of takes and delivering the director's exact requirements. Time is money in a studio. No matter how you feel that day, you must always be the consummate professional and do your best to comply. I did once have someone direct me with the description: "Yes…., that was almost it, but next time could you be more….erm….red.".

Patience and flexibility is most definitely required when voicing for a corporate client. You may well have the session director, the client and their PR agent in the box behind you, all with differing opinions. All of which stands you in good stead when you finally graduate to voicing over documentary programmes or educational series. You may well find by this point that you have an area of special expertise. Mine is medical documentaries. So while a previous voice over had fled in tears after a day of long Latin terminology, phrases such as: "glomerulo nephritis with subsequent hypertension" became my bread and butter.

3 - Given that you have had to write your own links for a range of situations, how much writing skill does such work take, and how hard did you have to try before perfecting your own links?

It might not seem, at first glance, that writing a script for television continuity or a promotion requires much thought. In general, the less time you have to get an idea across, the better a wordsmith you need to be. Also writing for a spoken piece is often the reverse of writing for a journalistic article. A journalist writes the: what, where, when, why and how; storytelling that follows a journey. By contrast a voiced introduction needs to be its own guide. The golden rule is to pick the one thing about the programme that grabs your attention. A startling fact, a shocking fact, a question. Rather like a tabloid headline you must get their attention.

I was trained with the principle: "Hey! Doreen!"

Doreen is a fictional lady, who has the radio on, is vaguely listening but also going about her daily tasks. If you want to attract her attention you'll have to give her an attention grabber. Having got her attention, you can then tell her where and when she can find the rest of the programme. Tell her you're going to tell her. Tell her. And then tell her you told her. Always put the time and date at the end. If you put it at the top, by the time she's decided that she'd like to listen; she hasn't taken note of when it is. Once you have this formula to hand, you can be as creative as you like to grab her attention. All you have to do then is fit it into the time slot.

4 - Can you tell us something about the range and diversity of other people doing voice artist work with you?

In London alone, there are scores of Voice Over Agents, with a diverse range of voices on their books. Some are very well known actors. There is a subconscious perception that you like the product if you identify with and like the voice. Some have cultural or regional accents. Many are classified by the "age" they can portray. Some do impressions, and they are very good at it. An ability to sing is also an advantage, and it shows an ear for pitch and timing. My particular niche markets are documentary reading, a native Brummie accent, and I am a medical specialist. Many of the "children" you hear on commercials are, in fact, adults. That said, there are also many children on the agents' books. Requirements for a voice over can also follow fashionable trends. When I started out, most work demanded a "received pronunciation" (in other words: accentless accent). Now there is more call for "estuary English" and regional voices.

5 - If you knew someone now who was attempting to follow your media career path, what advice would you give them?
Getting into the voice over circuit almost exclusively means you will need an agent. To be considered you will need to get a demo disc which has been professionally recorded. So this will require a financial outlay on your behalf. Before you set out on this path, go to all the voice agent sites you can find and listen to the voices on their books. The voice "cuts" will be short. Listen to the range of voices and accents in your age group. What can you offer that the agent doesn't already have? That's the prime question the agent will have in mind as they put your precious demo into their player. When you record your demo, be yourself. Record a variety of short pieces that you think will suit your voice. Now mail them to all the agents. Some may reply. Some may not. Be prepared for rejections. But, you only need one to like you.

6 - How transferrable have your media skills been into other areas of work?
I think that the skills from working as a voice over are very transferable and have been a very useful grounding in all areas of my life. Being a professional and successful voice artist requires dedication, a willingness to work long and difficult hours and self discipline. The latter is particularly apposite. Your agent may get you a job, but it is your personal responsibility to show up punctually, be personable and agreeable with studio technicians, directors and clients, no matter what is going on in your life or how you feel. If that sounds brutal, well there is a reason it's called a tough business

to be in. Now that I work as a therapist, it is paramount that I do not project my issues onto the client's problems.

7 - What role does creativity and the use of language play in your current work?

I now work as a holistic therapist with two clinics, and, I'm a psychic counselor for a premiere American site of 'phone advisors, 12Angel.com. As a bodywork therapist I need to listen carefully to my clients and choose my words carefully to guide them to talk and open up. Often they will reveal aspects of their lives that they had no idea might have a bearing on their physical problem. As a counselor on 12Angel, my "Brit" accent is a great asset and when I'm advising clients on the 'phone my ability to modulate the tone of my voice to show that I am listening and genuinely concentrating on their concerns is of paramount importance. I also do email readings via my website at Angelhandsheal.com, where again all the history of my writing skills is called into play. I am also very comfortable with giving talks and presenting workshops to promote my therapy business and running angel parties.

8 - You have stayed in touch with developments in the media industry for a long time, what changes have you seen in the opportunities available for hopeful writers in this period?

The industry used to be very controlled, and a union membership was necessary. This may have been restrictive, it also gave structure. Since the dissolution of this closed-shop, things have opened up to all comers. The intense competition this has ushered in has brought mixed fortunes. Yes there is great potential for newcomers. It also lends itself to nepotism. I think there is an underlying value to both. If you are creative and talented, keep trying and trust that you will be noticed.

9 - In general terms, are there any strategies for

getting and keeping work that have served you well consistently?
Be flexible. Be flexible. Be flexible. If you see yourself as only fitting into one mould, sooner or later someone will want a new model and you will find yourself out of work. The only constant in life is change and this applies not matter what industry you work in.

Don't hang onto a position until it is taken away from you. If you can see change coming, start preparing for something new before you hit crunch point. Always make sure that what you do you're passionate about and not doing it just for the money.

For me Erica's example proves beyond any question that it *is* possible to succeed in the hardest areas if you have the right approach and keep trying. The common denominators between radio hosting, voice-artist work and her current holistic therapy are her abilities as a skilled communicator, and the pragmatic dedication that has seen her develop a solid grounding in the right professional skills.

It is tempting to think that literature and art exist somewhere outside of the school of hard knocks and practical strategies to which we have dedicated this chapter. Tempting… but almost always wrong. Literate and critically applauded writers generally have to adopt the same tactics and strategic approaches as everyone else, the only significant difference between them and other types of writers and creative people is the work each produces. On the basis of his website, you might regard David Gaffney as a phenomenally creative artisan. You would be right, and it is worth investigating the vast and creative array of his output. The top of his 'about' page on the site reads:

David Gaffney comes from Cleator Moor in West Cumbria and now lives in Manchester. He is the author of Sawn Off Tales (2006), Aromabingo (2007), Never Never (2008), Buildings Crying Out, a story using lost cat posters (Lancaster litfest 2009), 23 Stops To Hull a set of short stories about every junction on the M62 (Humber Mouth festival 2009) Rivers Take Them a set of short operas with composer Ailis Ni Riain (BBC Radio Three 2008.) Destroy PowerPoint, stories in PowerPoint format for Edinburgh Festival in August 2009, the Poole Confessions stories told in a mobile confessional box (Poole Literature festival 2010) and his new collection of short stories, The Half Life of Songs, will be out in 2010.

David's journalism boasts both *The Guardian* and *The Financial Times* amongst the hit list, his completed projects show innovation and invention beyond the scope of many hopeful writers and some of his projects have a unique charm, notably the short stories produced as part of *Destroy PowerPoint* which exist as PowerPoint slides and his *23 Stops to Hull*, a creative commission based on visiting every junction of the M62 between Liverpool and Hull. He has also published two acclaimed books of flash fiction (ultra short stories) and one grimly funny novel, *Never Never*, which finds humour in an unlikely job (debt counselling) and shines a light on Cleator Moor, a Cumbrian town noted for the scarcity of lights shone upon it over the years. So, David's genius exists in the very places an aspiring writer might be advised to avoid, unlikely subjects, places, commissions and work. Yet, he has sustained a creative writing career.

1 - For want of a better word you are a 'creative' writer, in fact hugely creative and varied compared to many. Was this range and diversity always the plan for you?

No, I set out writing novels which somehow morphed into flash fiction, but it was when I began to get to know about all the peripheral activities around the publication of books – festivals, live appearances, commissions, participatory and community work, that I began to realise that there was more to writing than producing text for printed books. I realised that more people might see a piece of text in an art gallery for example than on the pages of an elegant slim volume in the little visited short story section of Waterstone's. Through my work for the Arts Council I also became more aware of developments in contemporary visual arts, public art, live art, performance and music, and I began to see how literature could be enhanced by linking up with other platforms and formats. So while producing a strong short story in a printed form is still my ultimate goal, I discovered I love to play with different ways of translating short stories for audiences. This means I am always trying to come up with writing projects that flex with the culture and push at boundaries. Different artistic formats can converge into exciting new products no-one has ever seen before; an example might be the recent project (not one of mine) linking car satellite navigation systems with stories about certain places, and the emerging iphone apps that use augmented reality to relate fictions about cities as we wander about and point the device at buildings. This way of working can mean coming up with really meaningful art form collaborations. I performed my PowerPoint stories project with a live free improvised music. All art forms are fair game for collaboration. Having said all of this, I value very highly a good quality printed product – something to hold and enjoys – which is why I enjoy the innovative design and graphic work of work of McSweeney's printed books, for example and also the work of graphic novelists like Daniel Clowes. In this world of transient digital ephemera people still want things they can touch and own and hold on to. And it's not all about digital, which is the mistake some people make when trying to force freshness onto a writing project. Too many new developments are just printed stories on websites.

2 - What strategic approaches have you had to adopt over the years to ensure funding for your own ideas?
I have found that festivals for example like a project that will get them some good quirky press coverage – preferably national – so when I produced my stories in a PowerPoint format, I had lots of press interest in this and spoke about it on Radio Four and wrote about it in *The Guardian*, which all helps, and my current project is set in a confessional box and will also get some interesting press I hope. I need to make sure what I am doing fits with the needs of arts funders like the Arts Council, whose main aim is to grow and build new audiences for high quality work. So keeping in mind the twin issue of high quality and expanding audiences, project can be designed which hopefully do both and satisfy the needs of lots of funders. For example local authority funders want engagement with as many people from their hard to reach communities as they can get, and as well this if your literature project can reduce crime, boost the economy, improve health, and clean chewing gum off the pavements at the same time, you are laughing. A writer will earn much more from projects, workshops, live appearances and commissions that he or she ever will from book sales in most cases, so one strategic approach is to make sure that the writing I am producing for my next print publication has another strand which is paid for by a live performance project or commission. For example my next book the half life of songs includes stories I performed for a show about motorway junctions on the M62, the PowerPoint stories commissioned by Wigan Literature Festival, and the stories I was commissioned to write about the renovation of a building in Lancaster. This way the work I am doing for my next collection is partly paid for by commissions and other project work.

3 - Which strategies have proven most successful for you and are most likely to be repeated?
See above?

4 - In your 'day job' for the Arts Council you must see many people applying for funds and support, what singles out those who succeed from those who don't?
Writers and literature programmers apply for Arts Council funding for a variety of things: festivals, digital projects, writers in residence, collaborations, and writers themselves sometimes apply for time to write. Time to write bids are basically income replacement streams so that you can you afford to have time off work. To be successful with these bids, writers need a good track record and some evidence of a demand and need for the work they are about to produce, such as commitment from a publisher. The amounts are never huge, and wouldn't really replace the income of a reasonably paid job. Around five thousand pounds and the average wage in this country is about twenty thousand a year, so this effectively buys you three months, which isn't really that long to write a book. Then there are always the sort of projects I do involving PowerPoint, confession boxes, and motorway junctions, and these can attract funding if you have the right funding partners in place – i.e. local authorities, festivals, and other arts organisations usually. Many writers apply for help to research books and if this is truly necessary to complete the book and you can prove so then there is sometimes help available.

I would avoid bids to the Arts Council which involve things like running away to write on a remote island, as it can look like you want the government to pay for your holiday. You'll need a very good reason to justify any additional costs for holing yourself away in the countryside or abroad; most interruptions to work are electronic and you always switch these things off. Family and caring responsibilities can of course prevent writers getting on with their books, but creative writing is work like all other work and demands concentration and time. You need to make arrangements so you can devote time to writing just as you would to academic study or paid work.

5 - How has support for the kind of work you do changed over the years, and how do you see the future of such work?

I see collaborative, cross art form work growing. Most people get their fiction fix from the screen – TV and film. The literary fiction audience comes from a very narrow demographic, mostly south east of England, mostly middle class, mostly female, and even genre fiction reading is still a minority pursuit compared to Film and TV. So the way we understand and receive stories has changed and the literature sector has to keep up with this. Audiences have become sophisticated in the way they read and understand texts. They pick up subtle nuances and complexity very quickly, and writers of fiction have to keep up with this. The fictional worlds of *The Wire* and *Madmen* are densely packed with information, often obtuse and obscure and sometimes difficult to understand, and it is all thrown at the 'reader' in a rapid fire, unforgiving way. Us book writers at the back have to keep up with this. Watch an episode of *The Wire* then go and see the average text based stage play and it is like watching something flattened out and in slow motion, with all the detail sucked out of it. So in short, yes - writers of books and short stories need to adapt and change if we are survive in this new world.

6 - Can you share any specific examples of things you attempted that succeeded beyond your wildest dreams, or crashed and burned, and tell us what you learned from these experiences?

I have two projects I am trying to get off the ground at the moment: One is a project for a festival called Preston Guild, a celebration of international trade in Preston which happens every twenty years. My project is a set of linked short stories by different writers commissioned throughout the whole period of twenty years between this festival and the next. Each year a high quality printed limited edition book is produced, in collaboration with a visual designer. So it's a long project which doesn't end until in 2032, so although it's not that expensive, getting the funding for a twenty years project is not that easy. My other project is a live performance by writers at a railway station. Six writers are linked up to a small audiences via wireless microphones and headphones, and performances take place in the station among the staff and passengers going about their normal business. This should happen in the spring of 2011 if we get the money we need.

7 - If your unpublished and uncommissioned self met you today, what would your present day self tell him?
I would say develop strong working relationships with artists from other arts forms, with people who can manage projects, and with digital designers. Small teams of people who work together regularly can really get things done quickly and well. Every project needs a visual element, a digital element and good project manager/producer.

Of course another obvious strategic route to a presence and portfolio likely to help you is to **make something happen yourself**. There are lots of obstacles if you want to become a producer, stager of events, editor or hold similar positions of responsibility. But there were lots of obstacles in the way for most people currently holding such positions, and they made it. The same strategic moves that made a success of the examples above can also apply to the two following examples. Both have created editorial/production jobs for an individual, and both required some initiative and focus. But beyond that, the main factor in achieving a measure of success was hard work.

For all the warnings you might see about creating a home for creative work on the internet there are examples of good practice and sites that make the most of the many advantages of the web. A notable strength of the internet is the way eclectic and very specific examples of creative work can find an audience. That notion is behind 433 Magazine, an online home for short pieces of recorded fiction. In compiling this chapter I chased down several adverts I'd found on sites like Gumtree and Craigslist, some of which sounded like scams, or half-baked notions likely to end in disaster. I picked 433 Magazine because the exchange of emails that followed my initial approach to them suggested they knew what they were doing. There are other sites online offering the chance to place recordings of your writing, and – in effect – enhance your portfolio. Many of these sites have a short shelf-life, some because they don't have the funds to sustain themselves and can't attract advertising, some because they never intended to run for long in the first place. Some sites might be little more than student projects. Some sites have a short shelf-life because they are badly run, badly conceived, or both.

433's online advertising suggested their plan to place short fiction recordings was always intended to last. If they, and I, are right in assuming they have a good idea and the skills to make it succeed, you should be able to find them online at the same time as you read the interview with their founder. Their site is located at: *www.fourthirtythree.com*. As before, I have added some highlights to the answers, to emphasise some points central to this chapter.

It started with the following advert:

fourthirtythree is a new audio magazine.
We'll be broadcasting and podcasting short stories of around five minutes (up to 1,000 words), written and read by top-notch contemporary writers.
We're looking for edgy, engaging stories about modern life – stories which work well when read aloud.
If you'd like to submit, or join our mailing list, or have any questions, or anything else really, just email us:
433mag@gmail.com

Michael Wendling, founder of fourthirtythree/433 answered some questions for this book.

1 - In four or five sentences can you explain your site and its main focus?
Fourthirtythree aims to bring cutting-edge fiction to ears around the world. We podcast, broadcast and stream short stories of around 1,000 words or less, mostly read by the authors themselves. It's a combination of technology and pure old-fashioned storytelling. In terms of the stories themselves, we're looking for modern themes and want to appeal to a somewhat younger audience than most literary magazines.

2 - What is your background and what skills are you bringing to running the site?
I'm a current affairs producer at the BBC, and I'm also a writer. For a while in 2009/10 I was working on the radio programme *From Our Own Correspondent* – dispatches from foreign reporters, each about five minutes long and told in the reporter's own voice without actuality (recorded sound or effects). It is very simple, very effective, much loved, and it also happens to be one of the BBC's longest-running programmes. So I basically nicked, fictionalised and adapted the idea for fourthirtythree.

3 - In business terms, how will the site work, and what do you see as the main chances for earning, and the main threats to long-term survival?
I'm hoping to get start-up costs covered by grants but will plough ahead even if that doesn't pan out. Running costs are very cheap and shoestringable. As I see it, the main opportunities for earning money lie first in building an audience by making everything free, and then at some point down the line venturing to see if our fans will pay for things like live events or premium downloads/CDs. I am not a huge fan of subscription charges or advertising, nor do I think it would be particularly lucrative for this project to go down either of those routes.

It's not a business as such, in that it won't make a profit; in fact I don't really plan to recoup anything I've put into it (in monetary terms, at least). Any money we make will go back into the project, and of course it would be great to get to the point where we could pay some writers, too.

4 - If as owner of 433 or as a working writer with BBC experience you were advising a hopeful radio drama writer on how to get a break, what would you tell them?
I've never had anything produced by the drama department at the BBC, so I might not be the right person to ask. However **I'm positive that the usual advice applies: try, try, and try again.** Listen to the Afternoon Play on Radio 4, and the other main drama slots, which will give you a good idea of what the producers are looking for. **Think laterally about where to place your writing and if you are compelled to, produce it yourself.** Local, community-based stations and alternatives such as Resonance FM are great places to start, even if you'll be donating your work. Unfortunately there are not masses of radio/audio drama outlets (a situation that in our own very tiny way fourthirtythree would like to improve). It is very easy to get discouraged after your ninth 45-minute play gets rejected yet again by the BBC. Don't.

5 - Roughly how much time, effort and money did it take to set up your site?
(I can give a more comprehensive and accurate answer once it's set up!)

I'm doing this in my spare time so by necessity it can't occupy my mind all the time: a few hours here and there. Money will be minimal: we could set this up for £200 at most, and a grant of say a couple of thousand pounds will open up floor-to-ceiling windows of opportunity. **In terms of the effort, if you are doing something you really like doing, you don't really notice the struggle.**

I would say this: the bottom line is that **(in business-speak) barriers to entry are just so low these days, if you have an idea about something, you are more or less required to do it!** Websites are almost free; it's easy to find technically minded people who will work on creative projects for nothing. Even print is easy; print-on-demand has got incredibly good in the past few years and eliminates the problems of printing too many or too few copies which gave publishers nightmares in the old days. We all know about new technology and dwindling distribution costs. Publicity and marketing, as always, is much better done cheap and creative than expensive and boring.

There are more quality writers and more sharp editors around than ever before; of course there is a big debate about what this means for the world of literature at large, however it's clear that if you want to get into publishing or broadcasting or the web, there's a supply-demand talent imbalance that works heavily in your favour.

And as a writer you're basically left with a choice between investing a very small amount of money and a bit more time in making something you believe in and have creative control over – or trying like hell for someone (a publisher, magazine editor, agent) to throw you a bone, usually on their own meagre terms. This is not a very hard decision to make.

6 - What level of response have you had from adverts like that on Writewords?
We've already had dozens of submissions through Writewords and other message boards, the 'gigs' section on Craigslist, the Arts Council jobs list and so forth. It is quite amazing that when presented with an email, brief hints of a website that doesn't yet exist, and the sketchiest of outlines in terms of what we're looking for, that writers have sent in their words and have trusted us to pass judgement. I expect that once we are actually up and running we will be absolutely bombarded, and as someone who loves stories and loves pulling apart words, thinking hard about writing and analyzing language, I can't wait.

7 - Is there anything else important you'd like to add about your site?
Only that it's free, so please check it out.

At the start of the chapter I stated we would examine: *aiming for the softest targets available: such as charities and free publications*. In terms of free publications, I think 433 or 'fourthirtythree' counts as a good example. We might have considered it strategically from the point of view of the person setting it up, but such examples do indicate a simple and effective point about building a strategy for success as a writer. **Being cash poor doesn't have to be a complete barrier to building your way to success.** The costings spelled out in the responses above shows that an entire website is being built for very little. There are more and more options online to use free software and website building programmes to set up your own operation and – at that point – you can find material from others to fill it, or use all of your own material. We will look later on at print-on-demand publishing, and one site that offers the chance to produce a complete book for free.

These cheap options and the use of print-on-demand are central to the next example of strategic building towards success and a presence as a writer. This is another project drawn from my own experience. I mention it here because the strategy we used to achieve success is one you could replicate over and over again without over-crowding the market. It is also a route to publication that would allow you as an aspiring writer to show a range of skills likely to boost your employability. Finally, it's a route that works for time-rich, cash-poor aspiring writers. This approach grew out of necessity, because of limited options.

A few years ago a course I delivered split into two pathways, one of which was based on 'Print.' We had an immediate and fairly substantial problem in that we had production facilities for video and some sound production facilities but virtually nothing of any quality in terms of producing print material. I was already aware of print-on-demand as a route to production and so using online options seemed the best route to go. We started getting students to work in groups on producing short books, usually around 20,000 words and it soon occurred to me that books around this length could be of use to clients. Soon I was cold calling local charities and voluntary organizations and working on arrangements with them.

We will deal with print-on-demand, self publishing and related areas later in the book. For the moment the point that really matters is that book publishing is becoming more accessible and cheaper as cheap information technology puts tools into the hands of many people who couldn't have considered doing such work a couple of decades ago. To take one example; I edited a book called 'Choices' in 2010. The client for this book was a charity called DGSMyourChoice. The 'DGSM' stands for Dartford, Swanley Gravesham Mencap; so the charity is a local branch of a national organization concerned with helping those with significant learning difficulties to live independent and fulfilling lives.

The project involved putting individual undergraduate students directly in touch with individuals helped by the charity, gathering the stories, presenting them in as a range of factual and fictionalized accounts and producing the whole collection as a book. Once the book had been published, gathered an ISBN (International Standard Book Number) and begun to appear online on sites like Amazon, we organized a launch event, invited the local press and began to generate publicity. We followed this by contacting the specialist national press associated with the area of learning difficulties and also got some national publicity in writers' magazines.

For the purposes of this chapter the thing that matters most is that all of the above was achieved by focusing on some of the strategic points found in the general run through of useful strategies that appeared much earlier in this chapter. The book came about because **we focused on things we could do well**, even when this was only to meet, interview and write up short pieces about the individuals helped by the charity. We also found an **unconventional place to get a break**, in that few people regard a charity helping those with severe learning difficulties as a likely source of a book. Finally, the project relied on **expertise in a very particular field**, although in this case the real expertise came from the charity and those running it, who guided us with the interviews. In the end we had a win/win situation, we handed over the copyright of the book to the charity, allowing them to buy in copies at an author price to stock in their own charity shop. The national publicity generated some specialist interest amongst similar charity operations up and down the country, all of whom could find the book on Amazon, and the resulting sales generated a few royalties for DGSMyourChoice. My undergraduate students got portfolio material and experience to help them with applying for jobs.

The cost of the operation, not including the time and effort which the students would have had to put into something to help them through their unit, was £249. That figure, and the low costs of print-on-demand publishing, will be central to some later discussions in this book. For the moment, it is worth comparing that figure with the minimal costs of the short story website 433 and wondering about whether, if you really want a break as a writer and you are prepared to work on the strategic points here, you should think about just making something happen yourself.

The last thing I would want to inspire is a mass cold calling of cash-strapped, over-worked charity offices. But if you really take on board the possibilities of the internet and print-on-demand publishing then it makes sense to look seriously at what you could do to produce work with a very specific niche market. If you provide the skills, the time and the effort you could be looking at creating work with a low cost base, generating publicity and producing something that does a useful job for others and provides good portfolio material for you.

In the case of the *Choices* book we were never trying to make significant money. The benefits were mainly in raising awareness of the work of the charity and – above all – in providing a positive experience for those in their care and also for my students. If you wanted to try similar projects using the same combination of factors I suggest reading carefully through the material on print-on-demand technology later in this book. I also suggest carefully thinking through the different elements of offering your writing skill and time to someone. But I hope the point is made. **You can make things happen for yourself at low cost and with virtually no contacts, and you could repeat that pattern a few times to improve your options and impress others who might offer you a more substantial break.**

Every once in a while my writing work has brought me into contact with people for whom this entire chapter would be a waste of time, because it would teach them nothing. There are people out there for whom being proactive and innovative is a way of life. In some cases it seems to be second nature for them. One such person is Kevin F Sutherland. Our paths first crossed when we both worked for the likes of *Viz Comic* and have continued to cross off and on ever since. The nearest thing to a 'normal' job Kevin currently possesses is as the principal artist for *The Bash Street Kids* and some other childrens' favourites in *The Beano*. Pretty much everything else that makes up Kevin's working life is work of his own invention, carried out with a combination of creativity and in your face delivery that puts others to shame.

His take on a strategic approach to getting breaks as a writer follows.

1 - Your working life seems to be based on being pro-active and innovative; how much of that approach is natural to you and how much did you have to work to achieve it?

The creative arts are competitive and often you have to go out and fight for work. In my case I've created work when there's none seemingly to be had. For example when most of the comics I'd been working for ceased to exist and work was drying up, I tried to do a comic books spin-off of the TV series *Gladiators*. I spoke to LWT and found what terms they'd ask for a licensed comic, then I spoke to a publisher I'd worked for before, contacted writers and artists, and brought the project together. Okay, it flopped after two issues and lost me money, but that's the sort of thing you have to do.

In another instance, when comics had again gone through a boom & bust cycle, I started producing the annual Comic Festival, something I'd never done before but that kept me in touch with my art form and the business until things looked up again.

2 - Looking at the unique ways you've got yourself out there - comic art masterclass, Scottish Falsetto Sock Puppet Theatre etc - can you talk us through

the process that turns these very individual ideas into income?

The mechanisms of most businesses are very simple. Make something you can sell, sell lots of them, and you're rich. **In the creative arts you have the choice of waiting until someone in a position of power recognises how good you are and pays you to do it (e.g. a publisher or a broadcaster), or alternatively do it yourself.** I have done a lot of both. In comics I have always made my money through the patronage of a publisher, be it DC Thomson and the Beano, or Marvel comics or whoever. I've convinced them I was good enough, made whatever changes or compromises they've demanded, and taken the money.

In comedy one tends to begin by making one's own work. Either by playing for free until you're good enough to get a paid gig, or staging your own shows. In the case of the Scottish Falsetto Sock Puppet Theatre I have to invest in my own shows, e.g. putting a show on at the Edinburgh Fringe which can cost £6000 so has to sell a lot of tickets to break even, but then I can get theatres to book my appearances later in the year and make guaranteed money that way. In comics I have tried self-publishing, which is increasingly popular and has made fortunes for some, but not yet for me.

3 - Are there any ideas, or attempts to develop ideas that finished unsuccessfully and taught you important lessons?

'The best laid plans of mice & men gang aft aglae.'[5] There are some people out there who can turn creative ideas into money, and succeed every time. I've not met any of them. **Most people I know have, at some point or other, had a flop.** In

5. Often quoted, especially in Scotland. The line comes from Robert Burns' poem 'To A Mouse, On Turning Her Up In Her Nest With The Plough' written in 1985.

comedy I took a sketch show called The Sitcom Trials up to the Edinburgh Fringe for three years, and every time it lost money (though it did get a short TV series, which was a great result). It was a well thought-through show, a genius format, and looked on paper like a surefire success. But it never was. Then, as a spin-off from that show, I started doing a little comedy act with some sock puppets with silly voices. That, The Scottish Falsetto Sock Puppet Theatre, has become the most successful comedy show I've ever been involved in and doubles its profits at Edinburgh every year. But on paper it probably still looks like a daft idea. Sometimes you just can't tell what will work. It's a good idea to Google the quote "in Hollywood, nobody knows anything."[6]

4 - What strategies in terms of getting and keeping the employment you want have been most useful to you over the years?
Expect the unexpected, and **remember the creative arts are probably the most consistently unreliable way of earning a living there has ever been.** There is a quantum jump between being the poorest person in the room and the richest. I know a great many comic artists; stand up comedians, actors, writers, and sculptors etc who have been in both positions at some point or the other. And it is not always the most talented who ends up the richest.

5 - What are the best elements of working so much on your own terms?
I have a degree of creative freedom that is envied by loads of people. And most of what I do is actually great fun while you're doing it. I get paid to make people laugh, which is fantastic. On

6 – If you Google it you'll find it attributed to William Goldman, screenwriter, producer and a man famous for his commentary and expose of Hollywood in works like *Adventures in the Screen Trade* (1983) and *Which Lie Did I Tell: More Adventures in the Screen Trade* (2000). Both highly recommended if you are seriously considering a career writing movie scripts.

the other side of the coin, boring accountants have big houses. You have a choice.

6 - And the worst elements of the same thing?
Did I mention the unreliability? By the end of the 1990s every comic I had ever worked for had ceased to exist. I phoned up one of my former editors to ask if there was any work going and he wasn't even in comics publishing any more, he was selling orthopaedic furniture. I worked for Marvel comics, the biggest comic publishers in the world, just as they filed for bankruptcy. I got the break of doing my first weekly strip for the second biggest music newspaper in the UK, *Sounds*. I was in the final issue of *Sounds*. I got my first big break in the brilliant British humour comic *Oink*. I was in the final issue of *Oink*. I went up in everyone's estimation when one of my strips made it into the legendary Brit comic *Warrior*. I was, as you possibly saw coming, in the final issue of *Warrior*. I really was hoping to be in the final issue of *The Beano*, and you never know, that could still happen.

The consolation is that, now there's a recession on, nobody has a secure job. Well hello everybody else, and welcome to the level of security freelance entertainers have always had.

7 - When you meet aspiring comic artists, comedy scriptwriters and the like, what advice do you give them?
If they're very young and don't realise they can do whatever they want for a living, **I like to keep them excited about the infinite possibilities that are out there.** If they're a bit older and in danger of stealing my work cos they're too talented I try and depress them so much they go into civil service.

8 - In terms of your Sitcom Trials, how much of the eventual success of any writer is down to talent, and how much down to working to achieve success?
In comedy writing you do actually have to be funny, that's hard

to get away without. But **hard work, perseverance, learning the ropes, making and exploiting the contacts, getting the breaks then not blowing them, these are all vital things on the road to success.**

9 - If the teenage Kevin encountered your present day self, what would each one say to the other?
Teenage me would be very disappointed with old me. He really thought I'd be living in a Manhattan penthouse making millions as a film director. Old me would tell teenage me to shut up and shave.

We are almost at the end of the chapter. The one thing we haven't covered in any specific detail is money. Understandably the friends and contacts who emailed in answers were less forthcoming about the exact contents of their bank accounts than they were about how they'd achieved their successes and survived their failures. In any case, their work is their work, the strategies highlighted in the section of the chapter that precedes the interviews are useful guidelines and so the main factor influencing any likely income for you as a hopeful writer will be your own work, and your own ability to turn all the helpful guidance here into money. If you want to write religious poetry and only religious poetry then you could spend your life turning the good advice here into success and still emerge with sums of cash that wouldn't withstand your ordering a takeaway pizza every other day. But then, I guess, if I have just described you the money would be secondary to the role the work played in your life. Realistically, the point of this chapter for a hopeful writer is to take the small sums – £20 here, £30 there – and turn them into *regular* small sums. If you copied out every highlighted point here, adopted them as a manifesto and worked hard over a period of months to turn them into income, I would still count yourself lucky to be clearing £150 a month in six months time, even if every spare moment was devoted to your writing and networking.

Real success here is getting regular work, contacts and a sense of direction and achievement as you see yourself moving forward. In terms of being offered more work. To put this crudely, if the point of chapter two was to get you a break and give you the novelty of a cheque or notification of payment, the point of chapter three is to get you *feeling* like a professional, creative, writing-based person and get you close enough to the whole thing that you can – metaphorically at least – smell and taste the job.

The case studies at the end are deliberately eclectic, there are much more 'regular' jobs, like journalism and copywriting out there. But then sites like Skillset (*www.skillset.org*) or Literaturetraining (*www.literaturetraining.com*) will give you a lot more guidance on those areas than this general book. I make no apologies for rounding up such varied examples as Kevin F Sutherland and Erica Longdon. Apart from anything else their lengthy and continuing use of their creative skills makes it obvious that anyone you meet who claims there are no opportunities and/or it is pointless to try and break barriers isn't telling it like it is. Nobody here has told you it is easy, but the people interviewed for this chapter continue to work, and earn, and that is the point as far as I am concerned.

Realistically it is people like Jonathan Newman who stand to earn the most. At his level of operation contracts offer up shares of the profits and percentages of the film budget. As a successful writer/director Jonathan could 'slum it' in jobs offering money and conditions some hopeful film makers will never see. I don't know how much he earns. I would guess he could have a conversation about 'rationalising' his earnings into different bank accounts and find himself discussing it with someone at the bank who worked hard to earn their position, but earned less than Jonathan. Potentially, Jonathan is one hit film away from millions in the bank, and he is in the position that many people held before producing just such a hit. But he is realistic enough to know there are no guarantees. So is Kevin F Sutherland. Kevin's car wasn't as big or new as mine the last time I booked him for a session with my students. But I think he owned his car, mine was leased. He also gets to see a lot of passable hotels and travel to places like Edinburgh where his developing brand of the Scottish Falsetto Sock Puppet Theatre brings in ever larger sums of money. Failure and financial loss are likely to be a regular feature of the working life of anyone willing to take as many risks as Kevin. But he is in a position to build on the good ideas, he stands to earn a reasonable living wage from the regular work for the likes of *Beano* and another regular living wage from his freelance work, add those together and you are looking at the kind of sum usually referred to as a 'professional salary.' So the jibe about civil servants in his answers is a good comparison, because the financial rewards for them, and him, might be quite similar. His freelance pension scheme isn't such a winner, but – crucially – Kevin *owns* most of his own genius ideas and should one of them take him to a major and long-lasting deal involving merchandising and world-wide rights, he may not need a pension in the sense that most people understand it.

David Gaffney is living proof that regular income and pushing the envelope on personal creativity can go hand in hand. Like Kevin, he is looking at a liveable income with the Arts Council work, his freelance work is probably less lucrative than Kevin's, but the pay off for David, along with the three figure sums he can pick up for the easier end of the work in terms of live appearances and lectures, is the chance to be paid for the kind of ideas that others would generate around a pub table and dismiss as having no potential. David gets to be himself in a way many writers envy, and he still earns enough to pay the mortgage on a home, keep his family fed and all the other mundane things. It is unlikely that Hollywood, or even Cricklewood will come offering David a film deal for his creative work covering the M62, or his project involving a mobile confessional box, but BBC4 and more marginal channels might well feature more regularly in his working life in the future, and his journalistic CV already packs credible names. Television claims to have no money but still offers a few thousand for projects to people like David, I guess he can measure his journalistic income in three figures sometimes, other journalistic jobs will pay less, but will generally be taken with other benefits of getting a plug for a book or project, or simply because they aren't that hard to do.

On the negative side, the skills shown by my interviewees could probably have earned greater sums of money if they had applied them to more regular career based jobs. Though I would struggle to see Kevin F Sutherland starting as a design assistant in a government department and climbing to the 'suit and commute' brigade as he finished his career as Chief Information Officer or something similar, with an income on a par with a League One footballer and a pension scheme guaranteeing him steady money for the rest of his life. On the positive side, these people have tried and succeeded in doing things that many aspiring writers desperately want to do. Every one of them has achieved lasting success on their own terms, and they are all still working. If they can do it…

This chapter set out to offer; *Practical strategies to build the gap between chapters one and two. Starting with a list of strategies for generating a 'writer's CV' and exploring several case studies down to the specifics of likely income, level of difficulty and the pros and cons of each strategy. Examples considered include bypassing normal routes and going directly to a company, aiming for the softest targets available: such as charities.*

I think we have spent long enough covering these issues in the chapter. You could usefully go away and think about ways of applying the highlighted points and lessons outlined by the examples in the interviews to your own life. The main points to consider are probably those around which of the strategic approaches covered here make the most sense to you. The danger with reading any book about writing for a living is that you reduce the things you have to do down to a list of good points, try them a few times, get a knock back and give up. That much I know from regular contacts I used to get on the back of writing a book on creative writing a few years ago. My *Pocket Essential: Creative Writing* is a short and punchy run over a lot of the main points and it became a mainstay of some Creative Writing courses, usually the one-term long variety run by places like adult education centres.

Having completed their courses a few of those buying the book found me online and emailed, telling me they'd finished studying my book and were stuck as to what to do next to get a break as a writer. A few asked if I'd read their novels before they went off to publishers and a few others asked my advice on a range of writing matters. The one thing this taught me is that many aspiring writers seem to have a model in their minds that they will work hard whilst others manage them to success. If you are thinking along those lines your best hope is to get a paid job using your writing, because that is about the only way you'll be managed to success with your talent.

If you want to sell original works, and keep more control over your creativity, you *have* to take responsibility for your own success. In fact, it's worth going over Kevin Sutherland's interview above, and taking on board just how assertive he is about the pros and pitfalls of his working life. Speaking of the pros and pitfalls; there were good and bad points in the contacts that followed people buying my book. I managed to help a few people though I DON'T read entire novels for free. On the other hand the adoption of the book by creative writing groups eventually killed off sales because Amazon became clogged with second hand copies trading around 1p a time. My guess is that most of these copies had been bought for courses, worked through over the 12 week duration and then ditched when the stories written on the courses failed to sell or the reader became disillusioned about writing in general.

That book has helpful exercises at the end of the chapters. Great if you are working your way through a course. Not so useful if you are serious about turning writing into a living.

The book you are now reading doesn't list a series of simple repetitive tasks at the end of each chapter. As you might have noticed, it keeps throwing the responsibility back in your direction. Which might seem harsh, but it *is* realistic. So when I say go away and think about this chapter, what I mean is take on board how hard it can be to earn your way into regular writing work, look at the bold sentences dealing with useful strategic ways of getting breaks and get stuck in. Short of knowing someone on the inside who owes you a monumental favour, this is how you'll work your way into earning part of your living in writing.

4 Are You Engaged?

In this chapter we will examine: *Case studies of how to build relationships with those offering opportunities for writers. Consideration of professional development, and building self-confidence as work develops.*

I should start with the good news. This chapter and the next are both considerably shorter than the lengthy slogs you have just survived. They are companion chapters in that some of the examples span both chapters, though each deals with a slightly different area of professional practice. I think at this stage we should also make an assumption: if you are still reading this book intently at chapter four then you must be dedicated enough to give professional writing a serious go. Taking that as read I also think it useful to look at what we are trying to achieve in the next two chapters.

'Engaged' in the context of this chapter simply means a feeling of consistent involvement, and a sense of belonging as a writer. All fairly vague sounding, but – like love – the kind of thing you tend to *know* 'in here' (at this point tap your chest).

Getting yourself 'engaged' in the writing world and preparing professional looking submissions means becoming a regular writer and preparing work that gets taken seriously on the basis of both its content and presentation. That sounds easy enough, though it is often extremely difficult. However, explaining the ins and outs of how to target potential employers and put work together professionally is only half the problem. What really matters in terms of keeping you active and ambitious as a writer is how you *feel* about the whole business. To that end I think we should establish two targets at the start of this chapter and return to them at the end of the next chapter. Both sound vague when written down but I would defend them on the grounds that these are targets concerned with being honest with yourself about how you are progressing and how you feel. Getting this right is the key to motivating yourself and seeing a purpose in your attempts to get a break as a writer. **Our targets are:**

1. **To be getting 'strokes' on your progress.**

2. **To be able to hold an intelligent conversation with anyone who asks how your writing is going and making it clear within this conversation that some of the power over what happens resides with you.**

Get the points above right, and you will be in a better position to build relationships within the writing world, achieve professional development and maintain self-confidence.

When it comes to the first of these points, getting some 'strokes' for yourself, I will confess that what follows is borrowed largely from a body of theory supporting Transactional Analysis, a branch of psychotherapy. I didn't just snatch this idea from the internet. I have worked with this material for a number of years, having become aware of it when my wife trained as a Transactional Analyst psychotherapist. She and her professional colleagues work much more intently with this and the first point I should make is I have no professional training in this area and what follows is not psychotherapy. What I have stolen is a key principle of Transactional Analysis (TA): the notion that someone in receipt of positive strokes is likely to experience positive mental health and feel more confident and capable as a result.

So – with the same combination of slight depth and serious brevity as Jennifer Aniston managed in her L'Oreal adverts – 'here comes the science bit.' A 'stroke' in Transactional Analysis (TA) terms can be defined as 'a unit of recognition.' A key figure in the development of the theory of such strokes is Eric Berne, who is also central to the development of TA as an area of practice. Berne noted that we develop a hunger for stimulation and recognition. Whilst Berne didn't specifically study writers in his work I think we can take it as central to the present book that getting a break as a writer means feeling we have been recognized for our efforts. So a 'stroke' is a transaction providing you with recognition or stimulation. TA theory has developed complicated models to look at the link between a range of strokes and the development of individual personalities. That is less important to us than the simple notion that becoming 'engaged' as a writer is really a process of getting recognition and stimulation fed to you by others whose attention you crave. Technically speaking, in stroke theory you can give yourself a positive stroke for a job well-done. However, if you are looking for a break as a writer an starting from a position of not being published the stro likely to make a crucial difference will be coming from o

TA identifies a range of different types of stroke. Some – like 'internal' strokes which take the form of self-praise, fantasies and the like – are useful to motivate you, but seldom guarantee you published work. We need to concern ourselves with 'external' strokes which come from others and 'conditional' strokes in which others single out some element for praise. Positive 'unconditional' strokes, like: 'You're a genius' may carry the most power to a hopeful writer. But they are also the hardest to achieve and this book aims for a pragmatic approach to the problems of writing for money.

Bearing in mind the target to be getting regular recognition, we can also aim for the ability to hold an intelligent conversation with some indication that you have power in your own writing career. In other words, if you can get your work to the point of entering into dialogue with others about being able to engage with them, you will also be able to talk about your writing in the same way others involved in a skilled trade discuss their work.

Crack these two targets and you begin to crack the all important issue of *feeling* like a writer. The perception of others matters when you are pitching your work, which is why I am starting chapter four in this way. So let's talk about strokes. Because strokes will motivate and focus you, and that will lead you to the position of being able to discuss your writing with
sense of having control over what you do. The best place
here we left off in the last chapter, with the key
d when we considered useful 'strategies' for
As I pointed out then, a strategy is a strategy
ly it repeatedly: *The strategies above are very helpful*

in getting you to build on any break as a writer, but they work best when you keep applying them, over and over again.

The strategies discussed for getting a break and highlighted have been cut and pasted below. Shorn of their context they look like a random series of jotted notes. To present the highlights as a list of bullet points I have added capital letters, and a few additional words, and turned the list into proper sentences. This is a road-map towards positive strokes and the ability to talk intelligently about your developing writing career. If I were delivering these words in a classroom a useful follow up would be to suggest you take the random list below, consider it for a week and come back prepared to make a ten minute PowerPoint presentation on how you would achieve these targets inside twelve months.

- It Pays to be Pro-active, or proactive (people still use both forms of the word).
- Make intelligent decisions about which strategies apply to you.
- Find some directions that will work.
- Complete an honest audit of what you do well.
- Do research into what is on offer out there.
- Internet searches; it pays to do them repeatedly.
- It also pays to vary the things you type in ahead of a search.
- Take in (i.e. search out and apply for) work that appears both above and below your ability level.

- Look for very unconventional places to get a break.
- Make sure there is material online to back up your claims about your abilities.
- If you are looking to create a good impression with online work the general rule is that less is more.
- Keep your online presence up to date.
- Make your blog or regular web presence so stunningly good it demands to be noticed.
- Become an expert in some field, and share that expertise with the world.
- Use friends, family and - indeed - anyone you know willing to help you secure contact with influential people.
- Have material prepared in the event of some influential person being prepared to entertain you or your ideas.
- Make sure any short pitch you prepare is adapted to the needs of each audience you face.
- Have answers prepared for standard interview questions like; 'Where do you see yourself in five years?'

Since the list is in a book I can only suggest you do the same.

Before you do, consider one example of conspicuous success that has little to do with your writing career. Consider David Beckham. Beckham is frequently referred to, without any sense of irony, with the words 'Brand Beckham.' When such references are made the subject may vary. In some cases the words refer to Beckham alone, sometimes to his wife, sometimes to the pair of them together, and sometimes not directly to them but to a product or event they have endorsed. As England's World Cup campaign of 2010 stuttered and sprawled along one conspicuous success was the presence of Beckham. He was passionate on the bench and suffering along with the fans, succinct and sympathetic in excusing the woeful performances of the highly paid players, and he was also involved directly when England officials rubbed shoulders with their counterparts at FIFA (the governing body of the world game). The latter mattered greatly. Before the World Cup Finals a few nations had presented their arguments for the right to stage the 2018 tournament. England's bid had – by general agreement – hit high points, (like our heritage as a football nation) and lows, (an ill-advised comment about corruption). One comment the normally tight-lipped FIFA officials let out to the world's press concerned their wish to see more of Beckham in the bidding process.

The world's best known footballer matters here because, I would like to suggest, he represents a successful life built on the ability to deliver well in all the areas outlined by the bullet points. Those who regularly slate Beckham for his lack of articulacy, supposed lack of intelligence and occasional lapses in his professional skills are – to my mind at least – missing the point on a large scale. Granted, Beckham's ability to deliver on some of the bullet points above – like updating his online presence – now depends on the PR skills of professionals, but he followed the path from phenomenal natural talent as a schoolboy to world icon so ubiquitous he *is* football so far as many with little interest in the game are concerned precisely because he worked at the targets, and achieved the results. And his career *does* show evidence of addressing *all* of the bullet points. Presentations are done, despite Beckham's obvious distaste for lengthy public speaking. They are often done on his terms, for example: with short interviews, simple questions and children on a Beckham brand soccer school playing in the background.

The use of a sports example here is also important because if you are truly going to become *engaged* to the point of getting positive strokes, and developing the confidence to discuss your own career, then sports provide a good comparison as to how you achieve that engagement. The difference between the strategies in the chapter on getting 'connected' and 'engaged' can usefully be measured in the time you spend doing something to further your writing career. And I mean time, not as in years gone by as you try this and that and hope for a result, but 'time' as in hours spent consistently working away.

Sports stars understand this, and they provide a useful benchmark for you. Sports coaches argue about exactly how to achieve success but one figure banded about regularly for a period of years suggests 10,000 hours devoted to regular practice will turn a natural talent into a an accomplished performer in most sports. Obviously, 10,000 hours spent jogging when your lifestyle includes regular pub sessions and 20 smokes a day doesn't count, so this is 10,000 hours of consistent, focused, repetitive practice. Sports coaches talk in terms of 'muscle memory' quite literally the co-ordination between brain and muscle that turns an action that has to be learned into a natural reflex. This might start with a natural talent, but *lots* of people have some natural talent. My guess is you went to school with some potential stars of sports or entertainment and not all of them turned their talents into paying careers. I would also guess that if anyone from your school did turn a natural talent for sports or entertainment into their main source of income it was not necessarily the person with the most obvious natural talent. That was certainly the case where I went to school.

My point is that improving your capacity as a writer is very like improving your ability as a sports performer. It's down to regular practice and accentuating the positives. Your equivalent of a crowd, certainly during the early stages of your writing career, is an audience giving you some positive response. In other words: providing the 'strokes' you need. There is no absolute winning formula but I would suggest that:

Engagement = Practice + Strokes + Intelligent Application.

In other words: you feel you *are* a writer when you've put in the work to generate the material, others are telling you it is good enough and you can see a way forward towards other opportunities. Strokes are vital here. Athletic coaches work to encourage muscle memory. Psychotherapy research suggests positive reinforcement over time leads to new neural pathways developing in the brain. These impact on mood, behaviour and capability. It isn't the job of this book to reprint reams of that research, which – in any case – is in its infancy and still open to debate. The fact that this happens is well attested, exactly how it happens and to what degree psychotherapy can contribute is the controversial area. There is – so far as I know – no definitive research mapping the neural pathways of an aspiring writer before and after a few thousand hours of consistent application at his or her craft. However, I do think it safe to assume that we can proceed on the basis that a writers' equivalent of muscle memory is development of natural reactions. These might include improved capacity to generate ideas around a theme, bouncing back very quickly from a rejection with a rapid reaction based around rethinking where the rejected work might next be offered, an increased concentration span, improved abilities to see two sides of a problem etc.

Your first step towards being engaged as a writer is to practice hard enough to develop some talents to the point that people around you will notice them. Most writers don't live around other writers and meet them all day at work. Aspiring writers in this position tend to be those in a very junior capacity in companies employing better paid writers. For example; those doing menial jobs in companies producing radio commercials, television programmes and the like. So the first people likely to notice your developing talents, and therefore noticing the degree to which you are becoming engaged as a writer, will be those people you see regularly. It is a really bad idea to set out deliberately to impress them. So if you are working in a media production firm a nightmare scenario between you and a person in a more senior position might involve you waiting until you are alone in the lift at which point you say: 'I can give you 30 uses of a house brick before the doors open again.' My guess is the pair of you would both remember the following minute for many years to come, and feel a cold sweat creeping on as you did.

A much better option is simply to let those around you discover your growing talents. For this the talent has to be growing and for it to grow you need to be working at it. The work involved will vary depending on your writing ambitions. For all that the house brick pitch in the lift is a bad idea, a really good idea with practicing writing and developing talent is to sit down and generate ideas around a theme. Take one product type for which the advertising seems predictable and try to re-invent the way it is presented. Before you do this make a study of the advertising out there, to be sure you haven't just assumed it is predictable. Also take some care to consider when and where this advertising is placed, giving you some idea of the likely budget. And then spend a few hours working really hard to come up with something that would make a difference, and make an impact, selling the same product. When I get students to tackle a similar problem, I get them working on marketing a brand of toilet paper. 'Toilet paper' and 'excitement' seldom appear in the same sentence.

An alternative, especially if you see yourself as a 'serious' writer of books or scripts based on your own ideas, is to set time aside and write consistently, setting targets and not stopping until they are reached. Lord Bragg of Wigton has enjoyed a stellar media career. But he was once the son of a couple who ran a pub in a small and largely ignored market town in Cumberland[7]. After a day at grammar school, well before he was accepted at Oxford University, he would write,

7. When I've told this story I have had people correcting me and saying I should use the word 'Cumbria.' Not so; Cumbria as a county only came into existence in 1974, combining parts of three existing counties. Melvyn Bragg (b 1939), spent his schooldays in Cumberland.

setting himself the target of producing 1000 words before he stopped. His approach is one that has served many successful writers. I single him out here because I wonder how far that hard work took him. He discussed this in an interview, and once directly with me, stating on both occasions that this work helped him to become a novelist, which was always an ambition of his. My guess is that those hours spent writing, reflecting, solving problems quickly in his head and considering the harder problems from more than one angle paid off in other ways. Obviously the Oxford degree helped but the biggest hits of Lord Bragg's considerable career, like his central role in shaping and presenting *The South Bank Show* have called for focus, creative imagination and the ability to communicate complicated ideas clearly to an audience. What is innate to him now was probably shaped in his bedroom over that Wigton pub in the fifties. And that consistent practice it is still an effective way to work today.

This is true whether you simply want to get a writing job of any description or whether you have strong artistic ambitions for very personal ideas. Beyond this point the routes to getting properly engaged will vary with your ambitions. Much as I would love to type a sentence pointing out the perfect route to success for you personally, I know that sentence could vary for every single reader. What matters for everyone are the words I added to the equation above…'**intelligent application.**'

Basically this means **channeling your efforts in the right direction, and being honest with yourself.** When areas of the working world want to be seen as 'professionals' there are several factors to develop. The highest ranked professions have their own regulatory bodies and codes of practice. Most areas aiming for professionalism lack those but do have some facility for people involved in the work to become involved in 'reflective practice,' quite literally: reviewing issues of their working lives in a situation designed to increase the effectiveness of the individual concerned. Creative Writing courses at undergraduate level and beyond often encourage reflective practice, both through tutorials and within group sessions. The point of this work is to take a writer out of his or her comfort zone and get those people to think constructively about strengths, weaknesses and progress in their writing. It is possible to do this alone although the temptation to delude yourself and avoid reality checks is stronger when you are alone.

Another general point worth taking on board here is that the consistent application is most effective when you push yourself. So locking yourself away, working endlessly over the same kind of writing and posting the results online where other like-minded individuals cherry pick their favourite points and give you praise is unlikely to help. Apologies for returning to the sports comparison one final time but if you ever had a games teacher who would gleefully tell you that sports were only doing you good when they hurt, he or she could probably say the same thing about your efforts to be a writer. Intelligent application sometimes means setting an ambitious target and not giving up until you have hit it. If you can be honest with yourself, fine. If not, it pays to be working with others who can provide that honesty. In short; no pain, no gain.

If we assume that the first part of being pro-active is committing the time and effort to work away at your writing consistently, then we can work out from this and look at how you get the strokes, and ability to talk intelligently about your writing. For this chapter and the next I set out to interview a few people for whom getting engaged meant hitting the hardest targets of all, getting a series of book contracts. With all due respects to salaried writers who work in areas like radio and television it is authors and solo scriptwriters, working away in isolation, who have it hardest when it comes to maintaining motivation, getting feedback, and being able to feel like writers when the knock-backs arrive. The complete interviews with the people I contacted appear at the end of the next chapter, but from this point on I will make fleeting references to them as we consider getting engaged as a writer.

Almost every writer I contacted for this book actually wanted a creative job when he or she was younger; most had tales of hard-work for little or no reward before they got a break. Taking into account the sports comparisons and the need to work hard I think it useful to consider the words of one of Britain's most inventive and individual novelists, Dan Rhodes: 'In a nutshell, the harder I worked the better I became at writing. I do feel that a lot of people who fancy themselves as writers aren't prepared to lock themselves away day in day out, year in year out, and wrestle with their work long enough or hard enough. To me it's like training to be an athlete – you aren't going to win races if you slob around.'

The ironic thing here is that many critics have praised the apparent effortlessness and lightness Dan Rhodes can bring to the craft of writing novels. His words make it obvious; it takes a lot of hard work before things look that easy.

In the last chapter, the points that followed the need to be proactive revolved around making intelligent decisions, finding the right directions and completing an honest audit of what you do well. We looked at ways to get connected. Going from connection to being engaged, i.e. regularly involved with some sense of belonging, is generally a case of sticking at any break you can get. However, one key difference between having the connection and having the sense of going somewhere with it is to **find one thing you can do well, and take some responsibility for it.** It is a fairly obvious strategy and one that depends entirely on circumstances but I have seen some good examples of this working in practice. The following list is based on things I have seen achieved by students, or other writers with whom I have crossed paths over the years. The point here is to move beyond the offer of a work placement to show you can be useful.

1. If you see yourself in marketing, PR, event management or anything similar: Make it your business to find ONE thing going on that is very likely to get some press coverage. Obvious things in this area might be a village fete, charity run etc. In these cases the organizers are often more concerned with the event than how the publicity will be handled. If you get involved, draft a press release, liaise with the press and also back up the whole thing by taking your own photographs and feeding last minute information to the press about any interesting/unusual thing that happened, you should be able to improve on the coverage the event would otherwise have had. More importantly, you will be able to generate a little pack showing what you did. At this point you can use the pack

generate more work for you. It might be worth targeting a few local businesses that don't get press coverage and offering to do ONE press job for them for free. I once offered to trade this service to a local paint company who had donated some free paint for a raft. I was part of the raft crew and the paint mattered in making us visible to spectators watching the raft race. On this basis you can generate some evidence of being able to work effectively in PR, you limit your commitment to any one company and you push yourself out of your comfort zone enough to get properly engaged. If you find that prospect daunting, you could try the same thing as a work-shadowing activity inside a PR company but ask them which press releases they find the least exciting and offer to draft them well-ahead of the deadline. At worst, your releases will be considered but replaced. At best, you will show initiative and skill, and produce work that looks good in a portfolio. If you repeat the work-shadowing in the same company, or others, you go beyond being connected to the point of feeling engaged.

2. Put aside a few hours a week and get involved over a period of months in the publicity and marketing of a local charity.
3. Take into account the money, and time you have available and either take a course in writing, or work directly with someone – like a professional editor – who can help you prepare one piece of work to be seen by professionals, (discussion of courses and professional help appears in chapter six of this book).
4. Contact local amateur dramatic groups and other theatre organizations until you find someone willing to take short

pieces from you and critique them. Work with them on a production or two to learn how good writing for performance is used by performers.

5. Find a niche in the local press, and milk it for a period of months. Local correspondents – i.e. those reporting on the most mundane meetings in a local area – are seldom paid much, and the turnover in their low paid ranks can often be rapid, meaning opportunities come up. Similarly, obituaries correspondents, those covering the lowest levels of local sport etc are either dedicated beyond all reason or looking to move on, so there may be opportunities in such areas.
6. If anyone local to you is involved in book publication, get a work-placement and agree some regular involvement over a period of months.
7. Surf the sites of literary agents (some details of agents and what they do are in chapter six), make notes on what they want and how they want it presented, set yourself the target of drafting one piece of work – like a book or script submission – and send it off following their guidelines. If it gets knocked back, take on board any feedback and keep repeating the process.
8. Join a writing site or two online and make it your business to master one short-form of writing (for example: flash fiction), also make it your business to study published criticism of such writing, and take on board some of the things you find in your own work. Post work on the site, snipe away at journals and other places likely to consider the work, and set yourself a period of months in which to construct a portfolio of your efforts.
9. Subscribe to the adult humour comics available in the

UK, surf websites taking jokes and use the BBC writersroom to find out how to format humour material and where the BBC are looking for new writing in this area. Set time aside anywhere to generate humour – some topical and some based on your own original ideas – keep up a steady flow of writing and submission for at least six months.

10. Take one thing on which you are an expert, produce a short-talk (around 45 minutes), produce good-looking material both online and on paper to promote your talk and start approaching everyone from the local Women's Institute to corporate clients, with the offer of speaking. If appropriate, produce a short published work using print-on-demand services (covered in chapter eight of this book), and offer copies of the book as part of the package of being booked.

The point of the list above is to focus your attention on getting 'engaged.' If you did one of the above, or something as demanding, you would almost certainly get into the zone of generating some feedback and having to network in a manner that would eventually give you some praise for your efforts. You would also be putting your work regularly into the public arena to the point that your skills would be likely to sharpen considerably. The regular collisions with the real world and the need for you get up to speed on someone else's agenda would also get you to the point of being able to hold intelligent discussions with others about your writing.

If you read the interviews I did for this chapter and the next you will notice one piece of common ground is the way each of the writers in question engaged directly with the real world. I chased a lot of people and – as should already be obvious – got answers from a broad range of writers for this book. I selected five interviews – Jenny Colgan, Jai Claire, Dan Rhodes, Tamsyn Murray and Sylvia Smith – for the end of chapter five because they provide a very varied range of responses, each has succeeded after working alone on material they cared about and each shows the value of getting reality checks. For Jenny Colgan it was simply observing those around her and instilling everything she did with a work ethic, Dan Rhodes benefitted from his fellow students and one of his lecturing staff, Sylvia Smith took on board the feedback received from an agent and used it to achieve success when she submitted her work for the second book she wrote.

If you look back inside this chapter and go to the list of strategies you will see the paragraphs above have left us having completed an audit of what you can do well, so the next point on the list is: **Do research into what is on offer out there.**

The one useful thing I can add to finish this chapter is that this point, and every subsequent point on the list is likely to change if you do something to get yourself 'engaged.' You might opt to ignore the ten suggestions I have made for getting yourself engaged in the writing world but if you are serious about writing I don't see any alternative to pushing out of your comfort zone, followed by consistent hard work and organizing all of your efforts in such a way as to ensure you make some contacts, all of this done with consistent reality checks on how well you are doing. If you are aiming to work in a salaried capacity – like working in advertising – this is your only option.

If you want to work primarily on your own material, like books, you still need the practical and pragmatic grounding you will get from working this way.
So, as you get stuck in and work hard you can go back to the list above, start with the point **'Do research'** in bold and look at all the subsequent points. Apply yourself properly and what you can do should change. As one opportunity opens up, your internet searching can adapt to take it on board, so can the 'elevator pitch' you prepare, etc.

Nobody said it would be easy, but you could skip ahead to the interviews at the end of the next chapter to find examples of very different people who all benefitted from applying themselves.

Put Up or Shut Up

This is a chapter devoted to: *the development and sale of big ideas – like book and film submissions – detailing what agents and producers look for, formats for submission and examples of successful, and unsuccessful, submissions.*

This chapter started life as an assignment for my second year students. The assignment has the same name as the chapter, the point I am making to my students is that successful writers tend to gain their success because they focus on something, and do it. An honest look at the other option suggests something writers should take on board and remember: **the world is full of people who can talk about what they are going to do!**

Bearing this in mind, I get my students to complete a lengthy assignment which starts with the demand they:

'Negotiate with your tutor to develop and present a fully realised submission for one of the following:

- *A script*
- *A book*
- *A collection of original items [for example poems]*
- *A series of articles or other non-fiction based work.'*

The assignment is user-friendly in that it allows a range of work to qualify as a **fully realized submission** but beyond that it is intended a crash course with the real world. The onus is on the students to research the market for their work, gather information on what those involved in publishing, agenting and producing television, film or radio want from them. I make no apologies for producing a daunting assignment, and repeating the approach in this chapter. Whatever your writing ambitions, the reality is that putting up, shutting up and letting your work gain you the breaks is likely to be the only option if you want success.

Having said that we can content ourselves with two bits of good news:

1. There is lots of help out there, if you are prepared to access it.
2. This is a mercifully short chapter.

This is a short chapter because, basically, all I need to do is point out why this stage of your work as a professional writer is so important, show you where the help exists, then get out of the way and let you devote your own time to seeking out the right kind of help and information.

'Help' in this case falls into two main categories, firstly very clear directions on what people want, secondly, some online examples to allow you to gauge the accuracy of your own attempts to hit the target.

My students generally start with research on what people want.

Most agents, publishers, producers and the rest have material online designed to help aspiring writers to produce the right kind of material. Most agents, publishers, producers and the rest regularly moan that they get inappropriate submissions from people who ignore this material. These inappropriate submissions are almost always disposed of with little or no ceremony and those providing the work get a brief 'thanks, no thanks, better luck somewhere else,' letter in return.

You can do better than that.

Most of the material online offering complete submissions is copyrighted and – therefore – not available for me to rip and paste here. But it is easily accessible, as are the details of what people want. Some examples of details from agents and publishers:

Firstly, some specialist publishers, accessible to writers without an agent:

The offers don't get much more user-friendly than **Jessica Kingsley Publishers** (JKP):

'Information for authors
We welcome ideas for new books in the areas in which we publish. Please email or write to us enclosing your curriculum vitae/résumé, and a completed copy of our New Book Proposals form (Word document).

If you are unable to download our New Book Proposals form, send your curriculum vitae/résumé, an outline of your proposal and a contents list.

Please email your submission...'

JKP is a US company with a UK arm, and they do source ideas for books from the UK. They are unusual in the degree to which they are user-friendly but – as with everything we will see in this chapter – there is solid commercial sense behind what they do. JKP are specialists in areas like writing about psychiatry, disabilities and education. JKP are world leaders in publications on subjects like autism, but their list combines works of profound research with first-hand insightful accounts of living with and coping with disability. For people who have lived with such issues at first, or second, hand and for professionals in the field, JKP are a well-loved publisher. Their list branches out into other areas like spirituality, fiction related to their favoured subjects etc. It ranges from authoritative to eclectic, a good example of the latter being: *Dasha's Journal, A Cat Reflects on Life, Catness and Autism* detailing the story of a cat and a child with autism, as told by the family, and Dasha the cat.

JKP aren't typical but they do show an approach to submissions offered by a range of specialist imprints. Ultimately they are looking for very few words up front in comparison to most other publishers, but they demand a clear argument about possible book and author. Being accepted as an author by JKP is a little like submitting an application for a vacancy. The same approach is seen in specialist publishers dealing with topics as varied as classic cars, cookery, and guides to fell-walking. Basically, these publishers want to know why your idea will work for them, and something akin to an elevator pitch, details of your career and a flawless and succinct outline of a book will go a long way. Obviously, as with an employer seeking a salaried person, a detailed knowledge of the company and its works is vital. Very specialized publishers, like Motor Racing Press, operate in this way because they tend to attract specialist authors.

A specialist company listed just after them – mph – is more specific, welcoming ideas but also mentioning a 'synopsis' on its website. I was told, though I can't verify this, that some would-be motor racing authors noticing mph listed just after Motor Racing Publications in places like *The Writers' and Artists Yearbook* have approached both. Since mph actually stands for 'Methodist Publishing House' and the publishing operation is an arm of the UK's Methodist churches, such submissions would be wasted. A helpful voice on the end of the phone at mph stated he hadn't seen such submissions but he wasn't sure how many speculative emails on such lines had arrived.

The truth is that most specialist book publishers and film companies do demand to see a substantial part of the work, if not the whole thing. Many book publishers and agents dealing with non-fiction would be happy with a three chapter sample, plus covering letter and synopsis of the whole book (including some clear evidence of your market knowledge). If you are pitching a non-fiction film script then the general rule is that you write the whole thing.

Even at the specialist end of the market it is fairly common for publishers and film companies to get totally inappropriate submissions. Around ten years ago a friend of mine – running a high-brow academic and literary list – once showed me a submitted book presenting a conspiracy theory on the murder of John Lennon. The book presented an interesting, if somewhat bizarre, argument. But perhaps a true indication of the level of solid research in the manuscript could be gathered when you looked at the detailed guide-lines on submitting to my friend's company, available in the standard writers' reference guides, looked at the Lennon manuscript, and realized it was totally inappropriate for the imprint. Such a slip is amusing for a second but if you consider the hundreds of man-hours (and yes; this author was male), poured into researching and writing the book, the wasting of that effort through lack of good research on the potential publishers borders on tragic. I've lost touch with my publishing friend over the years, but I searched for evidence that the Lennon book had found a publisher before writing this chapter, and it doesn't seem to be available anywhere.

We have – however – made the point that if you shop around in specialist areas there are people willing to start negotiations on the most complex works, like books, in response to relatively short pieces of approach writing. The deals will eventually be done on the back of more detailed discussions, but in these cases a 'fully realized submission' might not amount to many words. This applies only to non-fiction works. As a rule, fiction and poetry, in any form must be submitted as a complete work. So dramatic film scripts, and novels, tend to be complete before anyone with the ability to turn them into product is seriously involved. Options like the Rocliffe Forum, mentioned earlier, are the only realistic alternative to submitting a complete work, but if they generate a positive response the next thing you will be asked to produce is the complete manuscript.

Of course there are exceptions to all of the above. For example; Tango Books. Children's specialists, approachable directly and – since the manuscripts tend to be shy of 1000 words – Tango place more emphasis on an approach by letter, even for fictional ideas. Their specialist areas tend to be those avoided by many agents and larger publishers, Tango are behind some of the best known pop-up books, bath books and the like. If you approach a company with a specialist market, like Tango, you *have* to know that market well. You may be asked for less words up front, but you will probably have to present arguments about the whole package, including how your work will look, feel, how and where it will be used etc. Success in this area will often come down as to how you present yourself, as well as your idea. In the next chapter, dealing with agents, there is a detailed discussion of how the author Jake Arnott presented himself well, along with the first novel that earned him a substantial deal.

If you sift through film production companies and book publishers in a title like *The Writers' & Artists' Yearbook* you soon realize that there are still many operations out there founded on the personal interest of an individual, or group of individuals. Some such operations – like *Rough Guides* – have grown beyond the wildest dreams of their founders. But others – like Reardon Publishing – still maintain an eclectic mix. Reardon specialize in local interest books about the Cotswolds, but are also leading publishers of books about Antarctica. They have also diversified into related items, offering via their website DVDs on travel and some stylish clothing for travellers.

All of the examples to date prove there are still people out there with whom you can communicate directly, publishers and producers with a very personal interest in the work you might offer them.

Many agents, publishers and producers go to the trouble of spelling out exactly how to submit work. The US agency run by Irene Goodman is typical of many, presenting a page with easy to answer questions you should ask yourself before approaching them. Most agencies and publishers give you some guidance and there are books out there – notably Carole Blake's *From Pitch to Publication* (discussed in the next chapter) – which will give you a lot more detail. There are also companies out there willing to help you complete a submission document, for a fee, of course.

It would be tiresome and unnecessary to print a complete submission at this point in this book, but if you want to see examples they are out there. A lot of scriptwriting sites show examples of script formats and one of the most useful for UK writers is the BBC Writersroom. You can download or read online complete scripts from BBC productions including comedies, episodes of dramas – like *New Tricks* or *Holby City* – and a range of radio material.

When organizations make so much material available there is an implicit demand that anyone approaching them with a fully realized submission simply has to take on board the formatting and presentation of the professional work being shown. Pitching scripts to producers demands a lot more attention to detail than book submissions. In the case of books you need to ensure the work is clearly laid out, equipped with margins, properly formatted and – above all – the words do the job you claim and have the commercial potential to attract the publisher you want. The exact demands for book submissions vary a little but most book agents put some specific details on their sites, many preferring double spaced pages. Along with searching out the right book agent for the ideas you have, it matters that you check out any information on their site about how to submit. Once again, this is ground we will cover again in the next chapter.

Film and television scripts demand attention to detail with formatting, a working knowledge of the different elements (like the presentation of sound effects, screen directions, scene numbering etc). If you haven't attempted this and want to start, don't be too daunted by the prospect. There is a lot of software help out there and the BBC Writersroom identifies the Microsoft ScriptSmart packages as the ideal place to start laying out submissions to them. There is also software available to help aspiring novelists, non-fiction book authors and – indeed – most specialist areas of writing. I have heard book authors making adamant statements in favour of, and against, software packages designed to help prose writers. The common ground in both arguments being the fact that anyone already very familiar with standard word processing packages can probably produce a good looking submission without aid. When it comes to scriptwriting, university courses and other areas teaching the craft typically recommend you get a package and learn to use it. Some university lecturers will go as far as to specify a particular package.

There are two reasons I allow my students the option of

collecting a portfolio and presenting it within the confines of the 'Put Up or Shut Up' assignment. Firstly, by the time they reach this part of the course some of them want to work in event management, journalism or similar areas of regular employment so it is appropriate. Secondly, for some of those aiming to sell individual items – like scripts – the best route into achieving this ambition may be to work their way into it. Interviewed for the writers' site Writewords Philip Patterson of the Marjacq Agency pointed out that they find new writers through recommendations by other writers, publishers, writing competitions, writers' associations and direct approaches to people – mainly journalists and celebrities – who might be suitable authors. They also admit to having 'found a few writers on the unsolicited pile.'

In common with many other agencies, Marjacq also state openly how much they appreciate good presentation: 'I am not afraid of emailed submissions, but frankly they look ugly no matter what you do to them. Unless you live on the other side of the world, the best `in' is usually in print. There is nothing worse than getting an email with the writing sample in single-spaced script, cut and pasted underneath. They are usually the first ones to be deleted.' In common with a few other agencies in recent years Marjacq has moved into the area of computer games, widening their scope but obliging them to pay more attention to the submission of ideas in electronic format. Their site currently requests: 'Please do not send graphics (or any files larger than500Kb) without prior arrangement.' In this area Marjacq pretty much led the rest of the world, being the first agency to front electronic games as long ago as 1984.

So, whilst putting up and shutting up for my students means producing one assignment that hits a demanding target, for many writers the reality is that the grafting discussed up to this point in this book may well be important when they secure representation with an agency. The strokes I discussed in the previous chapter, and the ability to discuss your craft with some intelligence, might be the clincher in the deal for a book or script. If you read between the lines of Philip Patterson's answers above you can see how a writer with good ideas, who has grafted to a particular point and developed a good submission, might secure a place on the list of an agency by recommendation.

Agencies representing film directors and others involved in shaping ideas can find writers this way. A director might find him or herself working with someone who has produced a script. That writer might then be recommended directly to an agent, at which point the agent will see the submission, but also – probably – speak to the writer or exchange emails. If you are that writer then elevator pitch, ideas about where you'll be in five years and some reflections on your craft based on the things already achieved will come in very useful at that point.

The hypothetical example above has been played out in real life many times, usually over drinks, at parties etc. I have never found an agent this way but I have sold scripts through mutual contacts. One thing this reality teaches any aspiring writer is that **when it comes to putting up, you should always be working towards a result.** In the comedy movie *Throw Momma From the Train* Billy Crystal's character – a writer running a class on writing – has a motto for his students: 'A writer writes, always.' Intended as an insight into the sometimes facile philosophy he peddles as a teacher, the motto is still worth considering. For most writers 'putting up' for an agent, producer or publisher is likely to involve presenting an idea, and supporting it with some evidence from the writing career that preceded the presentation of this idea. If you are that writer you should always be writing, or at least you should have a track record that indicates you were always writing.

At the top end of deals secured in conversation are the legendary 'high concept pitch' stories of how major ideas were sold. A 'high-concept' pitch is the single sentence that distills the whole essence of a complete work. There are many stories of major ideas, particularly films, sold in this way. Most such stories are hard to verify, but it is generally accepted that some deals have been done in this way. One persistent rumour suggests the original *Alien* movie was sold on the high-concept pitch that the story was: '*Jaws* in space.' Websites like venturehacks.com continue to report this as fact.

Of course, if you are going to pitch a big idea this way, the ability to get 'face time' with those able to make it happen is crucial. High-concept pitching only works well when the party on the receiving end has some notion that those involved in pitching are capable of delivering good quality work. And to get that close to a producer or book publisher, you will probably need some notable work in your portfolio. The same approach as the high-concept pitch can work at a much lower level, if you approach someone involved in low-key book or film production. Whilst this might not represent a 'big idea' in market terms, it might still be a big idea to you. But it is rare for such pitching to work in any circumstances and in the context of a chapter on: what agents and producers look for, formats for submission and examples of successful, and unsuccessful, submissions.' It would be misleading to suggest you should work towards any kind of high-concept pitch and expect it to sort out your ambition to become a published novelist, filmed scriptwriter etc.

Usually there is no substitute to grafting, developing one idea with genuine potential, studying the market, studying the likely agents, publishers, film producers and the rest to find the right target, studying their online presence to get information on how to submit, and then delivering your idea, in the format they want.

The only realistic alternative – mainly relevant if you are a scriptwriter or someone who has strong ideas, but struggles to come up with a detailed script – is to find a development production company willing to work with you on pitching and presenting a script. We discussed development production earlier in the book, but approached it from the angle of the work on offer and why it might be a useful career move for an aspiring writer. In terms of signing your ideas and helping you to sell them development production offers some alternatives to direct approaches to producers and agents. It is something of a halfway house between both of those options. The good news about approaching development production companies is that most of them are honest enough on their websites about what they do and what they might consider from an unsolicited approach. The rest of the good news is that – if you are successful to the point of interesting such a company

– they will probably work with you to hone an idea and put it into its most effective form before fronting it to a television or radio producer.

Most of the potential bad news only applies if you are precious about your ideas and the control you maintain over these ideas. Development production as a sector deals in research and development of new material, mainly for television but also for radio and – occasionally – the film sector. If you are the kind of person who generates ideas around a theme, sees the saleable angles on the ideas but tends towards exploring the results rather than honing and developing one particular script then aiming to get your work accepted by a development production company is probably a good option. If you are lucky enough to place an idea with a development production company it is likely the creative minds within the company will want to shape it with you. It is also likely they will want to agree some sharing of revenue, and since their creative input will be greater than that of an agent, their cut may well also be greater than the typical 15% (book) 20% (script) taken by an agent.

It probably won't surprise you to know most of those involved in running development production companies have come from the industry and many have quite significant experience on staff with the best known production companies and broadcast organistations, like the BBC. In many cases their motivation for getting out and running their own operations is split into two main benefits; there is no upper limit to what they can earn if they sell a great idea, and there is more creative control for them in honing and developing an idea until *they* are happy before they pitch it. It matters you know this because most of those getting their work accepted by development production companies find themselves involved in a intense discussions about how the work should be developed before it is offered.

Development production companies don't take that much material from unsolicited approaches. In many cases those involved in running the companies are so well connected they end up working within a network of existing contacts, and finding new contacts through mutual friendships. So – once again – the best chance of placing your work with a development production company is to work your way up in the industry until your circle of contacts gets you into that league.

Of course, if you happen to develop a new format for a winning television show, i.e. an idea unique enough not to attract writs for copyright infringement from existing producers, and an idea attractive enough to sell around the world, linking with a development production company might be the logical next step, and a vast tonnage of cash might be the end result. Many aspiring writers are blinded by the wish to develop the one clever dramatic story for television that they dismiss ideas that seem to have novelty value. In financial terms this doesn't make sense. The real money in television writing comes from developing and selling formats. Noel Edmonds has been on the receiving end of much cruel joking and abuse, notably being set up by comedy satirist Chris Morris in his *Brass Eye* programme in the nineties. The gist of most of the jokes is that Edmonds is vacuous and lacking in talent. In reality he is conspicuously successful and someone who has mined one talent to the point of making himself exceptionally wealthy. Edmonds has earned a fortune through the consistent approach of developing new show ideas, suitable for selling as formats around the world. Years after a fatal accident involving a contestant foreshadowing the end of his *Late Late Breakfast Show* on BBC One, and the selling of t-shirts featuring Edmonds' face and the word 'Murderer' there were foreign versions of the same show running successfully. Edmonds surivived the furore and has gone on to present further shows, and forge a career in independent media production and theme parks.

It is easier to develop and pitch a format if you already work in the industry and have access to film and editing equipment that allows you to produce a polished pilot to demonstrate your idea. But the quality of cheap cameras and the availability of editing software that runs on home PCs and Macs continues to increase, putting the filming of such pilots within reach of most people within the UK.

Development production, independent production and production within major organizations like the BBC overlap with each other and – as with others chapters in this book – I would suggest you don't confuse yourself too much with pedantic definitions. Some independent production companies buy in ideas and develop them, working alongside the people who sent in the ideas. Big organizations have their own staff devoted to development production. Some companies exist primarily as development production operations, sharpening ideas before selling them off. Trying to figure out which is which can be confusing but one way of simplifying things from your own perspective is to visit a range of websites for independent companies and development production operations, familiarize yourself with what they do, check what they say about what to submit and how to present it, and accept that each of these operations has a good reason for the range of work it covers.

In the next chapter we will consider agents, and others capable of bringing about significant changes in your writing life. So the interviews specific to this chapter are limited to a couple of operators in the area of development production. Before we consider these interviews it is worth making one point about development production in general. Because development production is carried out by a range of organizations and companies and each tends to do its development work in its own way it is impossible to generalize about how you would be received and treated if you approached anyone involved in development production. When we come to agents in the next chapter we can make some general points about the likely percentages they might skim off the top of any money you earn. When it comes to development production we can't even be specific about likely financial splits if you sell an idea. Because I couldn't get a general answer about money and working conditions when I approached development production companies I rang The Writers' Guild of Great Britain. As the trade union for salaried and freelance writers involved in the media they are in the best position to know about the standard financial deals and contractual obligations involved in development production. They confirmed that there is no standard deal.

So, take the following interviews with development production operations for what they are, case studies from a very varied area of work employing writers.

There are very few high-profile independent producers of drama specializing in radio, but one such company is Fiction Factory, located in Greenwich. Although they have now branched out into video production and post-production, they remain heavily committed to radio. As their website explains: *Fiction Factory is a Sony Gold Award winner for radio drama and an ongoing supplier of programmes to the BBC. With a commitment to imagination and high production values, our primary purpose is to achieve successful outcomes for our clients and audiences.*

Their willingness to take unsolicited material has varied over the years, as this chapter was being finished their site indicated they were only willing to receive material from those with a strong track record, or an agent. However, they also indicated that writers outside of these categories could usefully call the company to discuss their ideas. Fiction Factory suggest writers use the services of a professional script reader, and are willing to facilitate contact between a reader with BBC experience and any writer interested in having work accepted by Fiction Factory.

John Taylor of Fiction Factory answered the following questions:

1 – In a few sentences can you tell us how Fiction Factory was established and how its areas of expertise became established?
By the early 1990s the BBC had been taking a limited amount of independent radio productions in certain areas. The

.independent sector was already well developed in television, of course, where the indie organisation PACT had negotiated a 25% quota for independent production companies. No such quota was established for radio production and there still isn't one, though the BBC does maintain that at least 10% of its radio programmes are made my indies. Fiction Factory was one of the first companies to produce drama for BBC radio, becoming established in 1993. Its creative director, John Taylor, had previously worked as a BBC staff producer of drama and, following that, as a freelance BBC drama producer.

2 – Your site makes clear the difficulty facing an aspiring writer. If a hopeful writer without a track record were looking to get work accepted by you, what would you want from that person?

The short answer to the question is: what I want from an aspiring writer is a great script. Seeking out writers, encouraging and developing them and working up proposals takes a large amount of time and effort and the BBC pay us nothing for this, whereas the in-house BBC producers are paid to do it as part of their salaried roles. However, rather than shutting the door completely to untried writers I try to gauge from their initial contact email something about their commitment, talent and grasp of the medium, and I then invite them to let me have a brief synopsis of the idea. From the way this is written I can generally tell whether I want to see a script.

3 – What are the most common mistakes made by writers submitting work for radio?

I'm not sure that "mistakes" is the right word for the most commonplace limitations which prevent a writer's work being taken further. Radio drama is an attractive option for someone who thinks they want to write. A Radio 4 afternoon play (the only option open to novitiates) is just over 8 thousand words, a lot easier to finish than a novel. But it's a craft with its own standards and constraints and I regularly find that aspiring writers are unacquainted with these. For example, I'm no longer surprised, because it happens so often, to find that writers aspiring to get their work onto BBC radio are almost completely ignorant about radio. They don't know what drama slots the BBC is running, they don't know which ones are open to them, they don't have a grasp of the range of genres which the BBC will consider suitable for the afternoon or those they consider unsuitable and, worst of all, they don't actually listen to radio drama. Let's be honest and say that a lot of afternoon plays on Radio 4 fall well short of the category of great drama, and hardly anybody would find them all to their taste, but it's essential for a writer to have a good grasp of the medium, to be in touch with the output, to appreciate the breadth of the range and to locate their own vision within it. So I suppose it would be a mistake for a writer not to listen ravenously to radio plays as a prelude to booting up the word processor.

4 – Is there any typical level of involvement from the writer as you develop his/her work for production?
The writer's job is to produce a script and once this has been commissioned he or she will be involved in a dialogue with the director to shape the script for production. This applies to top writers as well as beginners. A writer will also normally be present for the recording of the play and may be asked for rewrites as the recording progresses. Outside of this, any other involvement depends upon the writer's talents and the director's discretion. Some writers are also actors and may take a role, others may be established in the business and have ideas for casting which the director will consider, and there are occasions when the writer's experience will also enable him or her to direct the play.

5 – Can you give us one good example of work that arrived unsolicited and ended up as a successful Fiction Factory production?
It seems a little unfair to select one piece of work that made it

all the way, but I think INCOMMUNICADO, a play by the Canadian writer Stephanie Young is a good example of how something can develop. It was originally submitted as a fragment but Stephanie's talent for writing funny dialogue leapt off the page and over several weeks it evolved into a moving and original romantic comedy which had both bite and lyricism. It's important to say here that, statistically speaking, it is very difficult for an indie company to sell the BBC a play by a new writer. Much as I hate to say this, the fact is that as a new writer you have much more chance if an in-house producer picks you up because they have a guaranteed quota and any idea they propose - even if it's not as good as one proposed by an indie company - has a better chance of being bought. But the good news is that I think people with a serious talent for writing radio drama have an excellent chance of getting their work produced.

Note: At the time of answering these questions John Taylor also pointed out that Fiction Factory were in the process of changing some elements of their submission process. Since the changes were under discussion at the time of this book going to press I can only include the words John put in an email explaining the plans: *One change I intend to make is to offer the option of submission for new writers which enables me to reject their work without any written critical feedback. The reason for this is that I can often tell within a couple of pages whether a play has any merit, but at the same time I don't think there's much value for the writer in offering feedback of a judgement based on a short chunk. Obviously if I think the piece has merit I will then approach the writer.*

If you visit *www.fictionfactory.co.uk*, you will be able to check out their current submissions policy.

Development production in television also offers opportunities to new writers, though it is very hard to break into television by way of placing a big idea with a successful development

1 – In a few sentences can you tell us how NERD was established and how its areas of expertise became established?

JF - We had both ran development and production teams for some of the largest and most successful TV companies in the UK, including Tiger Aspect, Talkback Thames and Blink. With the backing of Charlie Parsons we are able to compete with companies significantly larger and yet retain total independence.

JL - We set up Nerd because we felt the industry needed a more collaborative and strategic approach to producing TV. We actively encourage writers, format designers and filmmakers to get in touch. We try and marry the perfect idea, with the right production partner and broadcaster. And we only work with someone where we can add real value.

2 – Your site makes clear that any aspiring writer looking to place work with NERD would have to be good. If a hopeful writer without a track record were looking to get work accepted by you, what – exactly - would you want from that person?

JL - for factual television the insatiable hunger is for authenticity of experience, emotion and character. If I were starting out now I'd concentrate a lot of firepower on finding extraordinary characters in ordinary world settings or the corollary, ordinary characters in extraordinary settings and building show propositions around those characters. We are always interested in such characters and keen to hear from people with access to them and ideas about them.

production company like NERD (New Entertainment Research and Design) who provided the answers that follow. John Farrar and Jago Lee from NERD answered a similar set of questions to those posed to Fiction Factory:

JF - An idea we've never heard of before is always a good start. Something bold and daring or a fresh spin on a familiar territory. You have just a couple of short lines to make us think, make us laugh and leave a mark. There was a time when a TV show could be commissioned off a paragraph, now commissioners want so much more. So anything that the creator has to make the idea more concrete helps - this could be a cracking piece of access to an institution, an estate, maybe life rights to someone extraordinary or a new piece of on or off-screen talent.

3 – What are the most common mistakes made by writers submitting work for TV?

JL - Too many people who are starting out are inevitably not familiar with what's already been done and end up pitching things that have already been made. While a great deal of TV is mildly derivative, producers and development writers need to get a nose for how formats and series develop subtly and what distinguishes a 'new idea' in TV terms. Now that online and multi-channel has turned every TV and computer into an infinite archive of material, commissioning editors are seeking originality and scale of ambition above all else.

JF - Ideas need to feel real, they need to jump off the page and be easy to grasp - it's amazing how often a new idea fails at the very first hurdle. Development writers need to write about what they know, but mustn't just write for themselves - it's a very, very fine line. Audience is hugely important though you can't be a slave to it.

4 – Is there any typical level of involvement from the writer as you develop his/her work for production?

JF - Depends on the idea. Often a freelance format creator will have no further involvement with the idea once it has been picked up, whereas a sitcom writer most definitely will. If the creative with the idea has relevant production skill then, in my experience, it is often invaluable to have them sit across the production.

JL - in scripted comedy and drama the writer is absolutely pivotal of course and remains involved from the first to last stage. In formatted entertainment and factual projects, whilst writing is still often key, but the terms are much more open and negotiable and the key is for creatives to find collaborative producers they really trust and enjoy working with.

5 – Can you give us one good example from your own career of work that arrived unsolicited and ended up as a successful television production?
JF - The School Boy Who Sailed the World, which we made for Channel 4, last year, began as an idea for a book. The writer, Kris Hollington, approached us with the story and the access and we then turned it into a 90' feature length documentary film.

JL - A Lion Called Christian - the book agent Alexandra Henderson called me and said her clients Ace Bourke and Jonathan Rendall were publishing a book in 6 weeks time that told the wonderful story of Christian, a lion cub from Harrods which they bought and brought up in the late 60s on the Kings Road in London. Because archive footage of the story was already a Youtube hit, we managed to make it in time to tie in with the publication - a personal record in a notoriously slow business! By tying in with the book we created a virtuous circle of publicity - the show rated extremely well on TV in both the UK and the US, and the book hit the bestseller lists both sides of the Atlantic.

The last two chapters are intended to work together so before we divert to a series of interviews with writers we should remind ourselves of the targets set at the beginning of the previous chapter:

1. To be getting 'strokes' on your progress.

2. To be able to hold an intelligent conversation with anyone who asks how your writing is going and making it clear within this conversation that some of the power over what happens resides with you.

Hopefully things are a lot clearer now. The strategies discussed and examples explored should give you some ideas of how to achieve strokes and feel engaged as a writer. The fine details should give you the basis of holding intelligent conversations on a whole range of writing related issues.

As we have seen, experiences of getting strokes and engaging directly with the writing world vary from writer to writer. In the course of interviewing people for this book I heard a lot of varying stories about how they had succeeded and the things that motivated them along the way. Since some of the interviews seemed to provide very useful insights into these areas I asked permission from those concerned to take their interviews out of specific discussions of points linked to writing, and group them in a separate section at the end of chapter five. These interviews focus on authors of books – mainly because this is probably the hardest area of writing in which to stay motivated – but beyond that similarity the work produced, the public response and the size of any royalty cheques involved will vary a great deal. I have lined these interviews up in alphabetical order.

Jai Claire inhabits the territory general referred to as 'literary' her work is intense, personal and sometimes extremely challenging. Her best known published work is the story collection *The Cusp of Something.* **Jenny Colgan** is generally referred to as a 'chick-lit' author and enjoys massive sales and a loyal following largely because she combines writing in a popular genre with a great deal of skill as a writer. **Tamsyn Murray** provided one of the most notable success stories of a breakthrough writer in recent years when she achieved major publisher deals for her work for adults, and also for her work for children, within a period of weeks. **Dan Rhodes** is another eclectic and highly unique talent and one who has succeeded with some career moves that fly in the face of all sensible advice. For example, his first published book – *Anthropology* – contains 101 stories, each exactly 101 words long! **Sylvia Smith** became an unlikely best-selling author in 2001 when her deadpan memoir *Misadventures* caused something of a sensation, sparking a range of rumours, including the story that it was the work of an established author masquerading as Smith. I can confirm she is the real deal, and continues with her work.

Regardless of their area of work, level of success and their own unique take on the problems of writing for a living all of those interviewed here have navigated the ground the covered in chapters four and five, and the questions focus on how they remained engaged with writing and how their acts of putting up their work led to success.

Interview: Jai Claire

1 - What first motivated you to take writing seriously?
When I started writing lyrics for a band. I moved onto poetry-which I had published in magazines and a chapbook when I was 21! Then that sort of dried up and I found that what I wanted to express no longer suited the poem format. It was bigger. So I moved onto to stories and writing a 'blockbuster' novel which nearly got taken by Headline but Aga Sagas had taken off by then and that's what they wanted!

2 - In three or four sentences; what experiences were central to honing your talent?
Joining an online workshop - in my case Zoetrope.com. Wonderful people even if some of the Americans were steadfastly literal! And reading widely of course. My MA helped a bit but teaching was more helpful!

3 - How important was recognition from others and what pieces of feedback most mattered when you were writing your first book?
Very important

4 - How hard was it to put together the submission for your first published work?
Not that bad. They wanted to focus on work that had previously been published and the book sort of grew an organic linked feel and I concentrated on what I considered my best pieces. I ignored some people's advice though! Then I put together a convincing cover letter.

5 - How many knock backs did you receive on the way to that first deal and how badly did these knock you back?
Well as it was a short story collection I didn't see the point in trying mainstream publishers! So Elastic it was or no one at the

time. I was convinced we were a good fit! And I was proved right!

6 - During the worst moments what motivated you to continue?
Sheer faith and will power!

7 - As clearly as you can remember, what was in the successful submission for *The Cusp of Something*?
I chose 3 stories as show cases and tried to show 3 very different styles to reflect the collection but he really didn't like one story at all and I had to convince him to let me send in another. That one worked! So I sent in my story Bone on Bone, The Land is Lighting and one other that I can't recall.

8 - Your writing has a very strong, dark, personal quality. The kind of thing that gets recognition from critics even when it doesn't make thousands of pounds. Are you ever motivated to go for the money, and change the style?
I'd love to but I can't. I have tried! But my heart's not in it. If I could. I am trying to write a thriller and if I can continue the way I have started I'd be happy.

9 - Your words will be read in a book about 'How to Get A Break as a Writer.' If your 21 year old self were reading that book what would you want her to know?
Get a skill other than writing or teaching! And write in part time and don't spend your life on your writing because they move the goalposts of what and what isn't wanted in terms of publishing so you can't write like that. Or the opposite - become a journalist and write anything that anyone would pay for. Don't mess about with art unless you have a private income! Live life more!

Interview: Jenny Colgan

1 - What first motivated you to take writing seriously?

I didn't really take it seriously, I'd been rejected from so many things I didn't really think writing was the one, no-one was more surprised than me when it came off (except, possibly, my mother). Although, of course, I wrote every single day and all that, I've always been disciplined towards work.

2 - In three or four sentences; what experiences were central to honing your talent?

The one thing I've noticed with every professional writer is that they're absolutely omnivorous readers, and I was and am the biggest bookworm imaginable. I hate having to own up to not having read something. Reading is everything; writing is just the next best thing to being able to read for a living.

3 - How important was recognition from others and what pieces of feedback most mattered when you were writing your first book?

I would say bollocks to recognition when you're starting out. People close to you have absolutely no idea and will either be gushing because they love you or hyper-critical because they feel they should be doing it. Edit and rewrite to the best of your abilities, then let the professionals decide.

4 - How hard was it to put together the submission for your first published work?

Actually not hard at all, because I was trying so many different things- stand up, poetry, and children's books- that I thought this would just be another thing I would be knocked back for. I wrote a very cheeky submission letter and sent three chapters (I don't think you can do that now) and I didn't bother with a synopsis because it made it sound so crap. Really, I wanted to be a strip cartoonist.

5 – How many knock backs did you receive on the way to that first deal and how badly did these knock you back?
I got knockbacks for sketch-writing, stand up, radio writing, poetry, children's stories and cartoons. Then I wrote a novel and it got taken on straight away and auctioned the following week. So it only goes to show: you never know, don't give up and don't take no for an answer.

6 – During the worst moments what motivated you to continue?
Well, there weren't worst moments as such, I was very young and living in London, and was surrounded by people failing to be actors or musicians or whatever, we were all in the same boat. I will say once we got to 30, about half of us had succeeded to an extent in our chosen careers, being creative, and about half hadn't and were stuck in jobs they didn't like and I will definitely tell you that the 50% who didn't make it were easily as talented and funny and good- often more so- than those of us who did, and the only difference, the sole difference, the only thing that made any difference at all, was work ethic, and when we were all down the pub every night, it was who was getting up the next morning and writing themselves a sitcom role or whatever. It's not just, or even nearly just, about talent.

7 – As clearly as you can remember, what was in the first successful book submission you wrote?
The first one I submitted. I didn't write a submission, just a letter with a one liner about what it was about, and the opening chapters.

8 – Your career has involved you treading a thin line, combining 'chick-lit' humour and critical respect. How much of this was pre-planned?
Hahahahahah. Hahaha. I may have to get back to you about the critical respect thing. I'm just happy to be working.

9 - You continue to thrive as a very individual author recognised for your talent and inventiveness that must be exciting but also hard to maintain. What do you do to remain motivated and confident in your work?
That's nice of you to say, but I'm not sure it's true. Anyway, motivation (I'm editing my thirteenth book now) is really that it's just my job. A job I love and a job that is great for choosing its own hours and so on, but it is just my job. And if I didn't do it, what would I do? You can't watch America's Top Model ALL day. Believe me, I know, I've tried.

10 - Your words will be read in a book about 'How to Get A Break as a Writer.' If your 21 year old self were reading that book what would you want her to know?
Well I was lucky because I stumbled on it by accident, but I can't overstate the case: there may be better writers out there than you. But are they working harder than you?

Interview: Tamsyn Murray

1 - What first motivated you to take writing seriously?
I'd toyed with writing since school but it wasn't until I picked up a 'How To' book on the subject that I decided to give it a go seriously. The author suggested writing short stories, something I'd never considered before. I sold my first story to a woman's magazine a few months later. It encouraged me to keep writing and I started my first novel shortly afterwards.

2 - In three or four sentences; what experiences were central to honing your talent?
Funnily enough, the rejections of my first short stories were the most useful experiences initially. When a story came back within a month, I knew I'd missed the mark completely. Later, the advice of my agent was vital in shaping my writing.

3 - How important was recognition from others and what pieces of feedback most mattered when you were writing your first book?
I entered the first thirty pages in a US YA competition and although it didn't make the shortlist, one of the three readers awarded me 138 out 140 points. Her comments made me realise I might just be onto something.

4 - How hard was it to put together the submission for your first published work?
Thankfully, it wasn't especially hard. The first agent I queried asked for the full MS and made suggestions on how to improve the story. I studied how to write a synopsis, which we then sent out to publishers and one of the first to see it offered me a publishing deal.

5 - How many knock backs did you receive on the way to that first deal and how badly did these knock you back?
I had quite a few rejections once the MS was with publishers and

there were times when I felt very low but it all melted away with the euphoria of that first deal.

6 - During the worst moments what motivated you to continue?
I think the encouragement of my agent was the best motivation - knowing she believed in me and the book made a massive difference.

7 - As clearly as you can remember, what was in the first successful book submission you wrote?
The initial query to my agent was a brief email outlining the very basic plot of the book. I made sure the style reflected the humorous nature of the book and kept it simple and polite. I also included a brief paragraph on my writing successes to date.

8 - Your career really took off when you got deals close together for books in different markets. Had you been planning to combine both areas of writing or was it more a case of sniping away in a number of areas and getting the two deals as a result?
I started the second book almost immediately after I'd submitted the first to my agent, to take my mind off waiting for her response as much as anything. Once I'd signed with the agency, my agent sent the second book out after I'd received my first deal and had interest from a number of publishers, before a four book offer came through. I've been very lucky to get publishing deals for all the books I've written so far.

9 - Your words will be read in a book about 'How to Get A Break as a Writer.' If your 21 year old self were reading that book what would you want her to know?
I'd want to tell the 21 year old me to know that reading is one of the most important things a wannabe writer can do - the more you read, the better you understand what makes a great book. I developed my own style from studying the way great writers did it.

Interview: Dan Rhodes

1 - What first motivated you to take writing seriously?
—It's just something I really wanted to do. I didn't ever see myself being particularly good at anything else, so I hurled myself at it. And of course I hoped it would get me a beautiful wife and a decent amount of money.

2 - In three or four sentences; what experiences were central to honing your talent?
In a nutshell, the harder I worked the better I became at writing. I do feel that a lot of people who fancy themselves as writers aren't prepared to lock themselves away day in day out, year in year out, and wrestle with their work long enough or hard enough. To me it's like training to be an athlete - you aren't going to win races if you slob around. You have to kick a lot out of your life to make a success of anything, and writing's no different.

3 - How important was recognition from others and what pieces of feedback most mattered when you were writing your first book?
Writing without an audience is tough. I was fortunate enough to find myself at the University of Glamorgan on a course with a Creative Writing option in the days before that wasn't ubiquitous. Being able to show my stuff to a room full of people gave me the impetus to keep writing and to try to get it right. Of course a lot of the things I wrote back then were ropey, some extremely so, and you can tell by people's faces when something's not going down well. But I got better as I went along, and they invited me back for the MA. Working closely with my MA tutor, Sheenagh Pugh, was a turning point. She was a superb reader, and had no qualms whatsoever in telling me when things were going off the rails. The key is finding people whose opinions you respect, and who are ready to be honest with you. It's a big ask, too -

particularly if you reader isn't being paid. It will be an ordeal for all concerned, and you have to think very carefully before you put another person through it.

4 - How hard was it to put together the submission for your first published work?

Very. The best advice I ever had when I was getting going came from Tony Curtis, the prof on the Creative Writing MA. He said you should never send anything out until you really feel it's ready. If you send something when it's undercooked you're just doing yourself a disservice. So for a long time I was battling my impatience - I was desperate to be published, but knew I wasn't ready, that I hadn't put in enough hours.

5 - How many knock backs did you receive on the way to that first deal and how badly did these knock you back?

By the time I felt my work was ready to be sent out I had a ferocious belief in it, and I knew that anyone who rejected it had serious taste issues. I sent some stories from Anthropology to The London Magazine, and had a letter back from a woman called Jane Rye [I still have it, so don't worry about being sued if you put her name in] who told me that "These really don't amount to stories in our view. There simply isn't anything to arouse the reader's interest. Best wishes..." Maybe I should have been crushed by this, but instead I just thought 'What a silly cow' and carried on regardless. No matter what you do, in any artistic field, there will be a queue of people waiting to lay into you. It's just the way it is, and you have to ignore them because ultimately you're writing for people who are going to like your stuff; they are the ones whose opinions count. I had many standard rejection letters, mainly from people who I suppose hadn't even read the work. I had one from Fourth Estate, who could have bought that book for virtually nothing, and a few months later, when I came to them via an agent, they entered a bidding war for it. Duh! The worst knockbacks came when I was already in the biz. When Fourth Estate told me they thought my third book, Timoleon Vieta Come Home, was 'unpublishable' it was pretty crushing, particularly as by that point my livelihood was tied up in the situation. But even so, I stuck to my guns, remained convinced that they were wrong and it ended up winning a bunch of prizes and selling a decent amount of copies. I spent a year in battle, and the ultimate success of that book was very very gratifying.

6 - During the worst moments what motivated you to continue?

I did often wonder if I would ever be published. John Kennedy Toole wrote A Confederacy of Dunces, and that wasn't published even though it's plainly a masterpiece. Something that kept me going was a line from an interview with Stephin Merritt from the Magnetic Fields (who at that time, the late nineties, was a big influence on my work). He said that he saw his songs as 'pretty objects to treasure forever'. That stopped me from throwing my manuscripts on the fire. Even if nobody else got me, I did.

7 - As clearly as you can remember, what was in the first successful book submission you wrote?

I don't write submissions per se. I write, and then show that writing to people and they either like it or they don't. The first piece of writing that I sold was to the anthology New Writing 8. That gave me a line on my CV that I was then able to use to leapfrog the slush pile.

8 - Your career shows a strong self-awareness and a sense of playing with expectations (especially when you appeared to retire as promised only to be replaced by Danuta), how much of this was pre-planned?

I saw stopping doing Dan Rhodes books as a way of breaking up a band. Retiring is standard showbiz practice (as is coming out of retirement). I did have a notion that I would publish all subsequent books under a series of pseudonyms, more for fun than anything else, but the reality was that when I wrote Gold I was able to get a workable amount of money publishing it under my own name, whereas if I'd published it under a cloak of secrecy I wouldn't have. Also, I felt I'd done that with Danuta already, so it might have been a bit old. I like to think Danuta will be back, but I'll probably leave it there when it comes to disguises. Who knows?

9 - You continue to thrive as a very individual author recognised for your talent and inventiveness that must be exciting but also hard to maintain. What do you do to remain motivated and confident in your work?
They call me The Lone Wolf... I think the trouble with ploughing my own furrow is that it makes my writing a bit of a nightmare to place in the market. We always have difficulty coming up with jackets that are both representative of the book and commercial enough to sell from the tables in Waterstone's - where, incidentally, I worked for some years after I was published. Ignore all stories you hear about authors achieving instant wealth because it almost never happens. I've worked in various jobs since, usually in warehouses, to pay the bills. What I've been doing is slogging on and hoping for a big commercial breakthrough on my own terms, i.e. being entirely happy with the words in the book. The look of the book, the way it's sold, etc, is something entirely separate, and what I care about most is that they still have a chance of reaching readers. As for motivation, bursts of good news keep me going - appearing in Heat magazine's Top 10, winning awards, having books translated, etc.. Without them I'm not sure I'd have made it this far.

10 - Your words will be read in a book about 'How to Get A Break as a Writer.' If your 21 year old self were reading that book what would you want him to know?
You'll get the girl but you won't get the money.

Interview: Sylvia Smith

1 - What first motivated you to take writing seriously?

I lived in Appleby House when I was 38 yrs old, the comings and goings there were really interesting and I thought it such a good story I decided to sit down and write it. I bashed out a book which I named Appleby House and sent it off to an agent.

2 - In three or four sentences; what experiences were central to honing your talent?

My manuscript was returned with the comment: 'It is clear you are not a professional writer.' I re-read my work realized precisely what the agent meant - books have to be written carefully. I wrote a second book entitled Misadventures, but this time I carefully chose every word I wrote. When the book was completed I sent thirty assorted pages to various agents. My tenth submission was successful. Jeremy Lewis 'the slush reader' in Caroline Dawney's office read through it. He was so pleased with my work he took the pages to Caroline saying: 'I must be crazy but I like this!' Caroline read through it and eventually phoned me. She told me later on that one of the reasons she took me on was because Misadventures didn't have a single spelling mistake in it.

3 - How important was recognition from others and what pieces of feedback most mattered when you were writing your first book?

I didn't get much recognition from others. I sent my work off to ten agents before I was taken on by Caroline Dawnay. I just kept going because I wanted to be a successful writer. The only feedback I'd had before being accepted was from the agent who pointed out the mistakes in Appleby House.

4 - How hard was it to put together the submission for your first published work?

It was quite simple, the hard work was just the writing. Sitting down and getting the words out. I didn't have to invent the story, because Misadventures is made up of events in my life up to that point.

5 - How many knock-backs did you receive on the way to that first deal and how badly did these knock you back?
Well, ten agents turned me down, and it took me about eight months to get the right agent. I just kept going because I wanted to get published. In the end it was the 'slush reader' at the agency - Jeremy Lewis - who read 30 pages of Misadventures, loved it and took it to Caroline Dawnay who decided to take me on. She got the book to Canongate, who published it.

6 - During the worst moments what motivated you to continue?
I didn't have any worst moments, I just continued. I was lucky to get the right agent and get a book placed with the right publisher.

7 - As clearly as you can remember, what was in the first successful book submission you wrote?
30 pages of the book Misadventures, a synopsis, and a covering letter.

8 - Your published writing revolves around a strong sense of finding yourself funny, and finding the funny side of things that happen around you. How much of this do you have to work on?
It just comes out naturally. I deliberately write with humour, all the way through I intend it to be funny. I am recapturing things I found funny when they happened. I keep the humour in mind all the time when I am writing.

9 - You have kept on writing and attempting different things. What do you do to remain motivated and confident in your work?
I've actually stopped writing at the moment, Caroline Dawnay

has got Longfield House which she thinks is my best work to date. So I don't just write all day. When I do write, I try other things and I have attempted books for children and a television sit-com which I loved and my neighbours thought was hilarious, but it didn't get a deal. I don't just keep going when I get knocked back, but I do keep going back to the things I do well, like the writing with humour.

10 - Your words will be read in a book about 'How to Get A Break as a Writer.' If your 21 year old self were reading that book what would you want her to know?

Just that I hit the jackpot and I had a wonderful time for three years. I used to love taxis turning up outside and taking me to lunch, and everyone around where I live wondering where I was going. There were great moments, like taxi drivers wondering why they were taking me to the BBC. I enjoyed giving copies of my books to taxi drivers, and I went to New York to promote Misadventures. I didn't expect to do things like that when I was 21, and I'm really glad I have done them.

6 Agents of Change

This is a chapter about: *getting and finding agents, also looking at other areas of help and mentorship available including websites, courses, professional mentors etc. Comments from agents and others involved in finding and managing talent.*

So it might make sense to start by defining what agents do. Your agent, in the simplest terminology is someone who has the right to represent you. In terms of your creative work this representation mainly revolves around helping you to secure the best deals for your original work and anything else you might be able to offer by way of creative work. The best deals will typically be those offering the highest prices, although in some cases a good price and very favourable terms with regard to controlling your work might represent a better deal than simply selling to highest cash bidder.

At the top end of the creative industries such trade-offs occur all the time, sometimes with stunning returns. A celebrated example occurred in 1987 when the band U2, who owed their signing and success to Island Records, were faced with a problem. Their record company had spent and lost so much money they were unable to pay the band $5million owed in royalties for the massive selling *Joshua Tree* album. The band agreed to waive the income but take a stake in the company.

The specifics of this agreement are not in the public domain but it is generally reported that the band settled for a 10% stake in the company. It is also generally accepted in the telling of this story that the 'band' in this case comprises five members; the four U2s who have been playing and recording together since the late seventies and their manager Paul McGuinness who is – apparently – a member of the band for the purposes of much of their business.

When the Island label was sold to Polygram in 1992 for £272million that suggests that at the moment the money in the deal transferred the 'band' was £27.2million richer; quite a good return on forgoing $5 million five years earlier. Bear in mind they gave up a figure in US dollars and earned one in pounds sterling, so the gain was more substantial than a casual glance at the numbers might suggest.

Agents and managers operate at all levels between the situation of an aspiring writer looking to get an agent interested in his or her work to the situation of the worlds leading rock bands, managed by a highly talented and far-sighted individual, striking an inspired and ambitious deal. If you consider your own situation, and try and think yourself into the situation faced by U2 when they decided to right off their money and acquire a stake in a company too poor to pay them, you understand something vitally important to all deals involving agents and managers. When you put your creative work into the commercial arena you are in business, and – whatever your ambitions – you should never lose sight of that fact.

This is a point made clearly in a book I would highly

recommend; *From Pitch to Publication* by Carole Blake. Blake is an experienced literary agent and her 1999 book is an attempt to teach hopeful writers everything she had learned up to that point. It is dated now, because the book doesn't take on board some aspects of the internet, but – other than that – it is full of sound advice and before she really gets stuck into discussing how a submission to an agent should look, she states: **'Learn the tools of your trade properly; it is a trade that requires a serious apprenticeship.'**

So, let's talk business for a short time, share an anecdote, and then think methodically about agents and where they fit into your ambitions. We can start by looking at the point made by Carole Blake in bold type above. Think about it for a second and it seems an odd phrase that you should learn *the tools of your trade*. Why not, the 'skills' or 'the reality.' In fact, it is the perfect phrase for this point. Perfect because it mimics the way other skilled tradespeople talk and makes it clear that writing for a living isn't that different from other areas of skilled employment. Builders, carpenters and others in the construction business who progress to managing their own companies talk about going back 'on the tools' on the occasions when they get involved again in the sharp end of the business. Being 'on the tools' describes a situation, the situation in which you are making things happen and producing work. When a carpenter or kitchen fitter moves back from managing a business he or she might be moving from one small job to another, using different skills and different tools to contribute to a complicated job. The 'tools' for a writer are different. But Carole Blake's advice to learn them means – in effect – know everything from how to research a market and put a submission together to how to put one brilliant sentence at the head of a letter of approach. Your tools, literally, might be a computer, paper and the rest. But your state of being 'on the tools' is one of knowing how every little part of your effort contributes to making a finished piece of work that does justice to your ideas and your ambition.

This matters because – of course – it is the whole job that is taken into consideration. For years I have been telling my students the story of the signing of author Jake Arnott and showing them a clip from a BBC documentary on first-time writers filmed at the end of the 20th century. Three writers are followed in the documentary but one is already successful. Jake Arnott's first novel *The Long Firm* earned him a two book deal worth £100,000 with Sceptre. The clip wasn't on YouTube as I wrote this chapter, though I have seen it there before. The documentary allows key people involved in the deal to talk and what they say is very illuminating in giving an insight into the whole process of getting an agent and getting a deal. To put this in context, in the late nineties when Jake Arnott signed to Sceptre the standard first deal for a writer of literary novels would be around £3000-£8000, the figure isn't much changed these days, having fallen significantly against inflation. So as Jonny Geller – the agent involved in signing Jake Arnott to the Curtis Brown Agency – succinctly puts it, the £100,000 deal is 'showing commitment.' Three people were involved in the deal. Arnott, the writer, had mapped out a very chequered and sporadic career, at the time of writing his first novel he had been working as a part-time props assistant in a theatre in Leeds and had found occasional acting work, notably by being wrapped in bandages and appearing in the title role in the movie *The Mummy*. By his own admission he was earning something in the region of £6000 per annum from his main job, but he did take the trouble of visiting the affluent Headingly district of Leeds and buying a Christian Dior suit in a charity shop. He was wearing the suit on the day he attended the London offices of Curtis Brown. Literary agent Jonny Geller had received Arnott's manuscript, read it, been hugely impressed and had sent it out to some publishers with the track record and financial power to turn the work into a best-seller. When filmed Geller made a telling comment about the manuscript, stating, 'I kept waiting for it to fall down…' He signed Arnott because the manuscript didn't 'fall down.'

In other words, Geller explains in his comments that literary agents read manuscripts and make signings the way you or I might buy a car. They start with a fairly clear idea of what they want, they know there may be flashy options, sensible options, cheap options and expensive options but in the end they balance these and only make a commitment when all the factors balance. Geller's phrase about waiting for *The Long Firm* to 'fall down' speaks volumes. By implication it says; 'I read lots of work that has potential.' Every working day agents across the UK reject work that has strong ideas, passages of exceptional prose and blatant ambition. They do this because the manuscripts in question 'fall down.' For example, a superbly crafted idea under-pinning a war novel is undermined because the military expert who wrote the book allows his characters to speak in huge chunks of exposition. A passage like; 'The Germans have 4000 men dug in around the ridge, adopting a standard defensive formation and supported by heavy artillery,' could be the point at which at agent feels the work falling down, and scribbles a note to his or her PA about a standard rejection letter. This letter may well be the standard 'thanks, no thanks, good luck somewhere else,' note that tells the writer nothing about why the manuscript failed. So Geller's point here is important for you. It matters that you pay attention to areas in which you work might fall down because it will have to be very close to saleable before a reputable agent will do you the courtesy of a constructive rejection. As a rule, a constructive rejection is a *very* good sign because it often indicates you have the potential for a deal with that agent if you take on board the advice.

The third person in the room when Jake Arnott got his deal was Editor Neil Taylor from Sceptre, a literary imprint of Hodder and Stoughton. Taylor was the first of a number of interested editors to meet Arnott and he did something that rarely happens. He walked out of the office with Geller and immediately turned to him and stated he wanted to make an offer Geller couldn't refuse. In other words, he asked Geller to stop anyone else meeting Arnott and backed this up with the promise he could deliver a large enough deal to make such a request acceptable to author and agent. Taylor would have had to discuss this deal with the top people in his company to get the authorization to make that statement at the offices of Curtis Brown. Offering £100,000 for Arnott's first two books was certainly a good enough deal to justify Taylor's request. Interviewed about this Taylor wouldn't be specific about the conversations at Sceptre that preceded his meeting with Geller and Arnott but he did say; 'We paid what we thought we might have to pay, which is more than we could have paid but not as much as we might have paid.' Should the clip ever reappear on YouTube you will be able to see the smiles that go along with the words, Taylor is communicating more than the words on paper suggest. Obviously the exact limit of his purchasing power that day was known only to a few people at Sceptre. But the point is clear. Taylor had set off for his meeting with the authority to offer a big deal. This could only have happened if the manuscript had impressed editors and managers at Sceptre. The other factor influencing Sceptre's interest was the reputation of Curtis Brown and Jonny Geller. We can't know the limits of the figures in Neil Taylor's head as he negotiated but we can make some educated guesses.

The book in question *The Long Firm* is an in-your-face crime thriller with several riveting elements. A narrative cleverly told from five perspectives, an obvious nod to the real life antics of the Kray Twins and a running theme around gay characters. The clever plotting puts it well into impressive literary novel territory. The resonance of real-life events adds another potential readership and the gay theme takes the book into another market. As a rule none of these potential markets get in each other's way, so the literary fiction readers don't find the gay theme off-putting etc. Neil Taylor knew he had a property on offer that could be sold in different ways to different readers, and it also had the potential – eventually realized – for television adaptation. The book was with Curtis Brown, a major agency representing writers, but also representing television and acting talent. The agency was the perfect home for a work that might be put on television. What Neil Taylor didn't know until he met the presentable author in the Dior suit was how easily he could work with Jake Arnott.

Consider the situation and you begin to grasp what we have to achieve in this chapter. Everyone in that room did their jobs well. Geller had generated interest in his client, enough interest to put Neil Taylor in a pressured situation. Taylor wanted that book for his company, and he knew that was going to cost major money. He didn't know Arnott had paid around £6 for the Dior suit, he simply saw the kind of author who looked like he was serious about making an impression and could be relied on to get out there and front the book if the deal went through. Taylor put up the money and secured the property for his company, cutting out other publishers. Jake Arnott also did his job to perfection. He was a poorly paid props assistant in a theatre with a CV unlikely to land him high paid professional work. Non of that mattered when he wrote a distinctive and highly innovative book, delivering a plot that looked fresh and dialogue that read so well an editor could already sense the potential for television. Above all, Jake Arnott carried off his part of the meeting well. It is a crass way of looking at it but you could say those few minutes of being the hopeful and highly talented author amount to the best paid performance of Arnott's acting career. Neil Taylor's comments; 'We paid what we thought we might have to pay…' suggest Arnott's part in convincing Neil Taylor may have been worth a few tens of thousands of pounds, and the meeting didn't last that long. That money truly matters here, not just because it changed Arnott's financial circumstances beyond all recognition. Once Sceptre were committed to £100,000 they had no option but to take the job seriously and work as hard as possible to recoup their outlay. Industry parlance for paying out advances like this is to be 'in the hole' for £100,000 which tells you all you need to know about how such sums are viewed. A company advancing money sees itself as having to haul itself back out of the hole made by the debt. Since profits are the point of a private publishing company there is no option but to put in the effort to turn the deficit around.

In a chapter about getting and finding agents we have to be considering how you might get into the same situation. The BBC focused on Jake Arnott in their documentary about first-time authors because he was a conspicuous and notable success. His would be an exceptional deal today, and it was signed in the final months of the last century. Most authors will never be able to sign the kind of deal that becomes hot gossip in the industry, but it still makes sense to aim that high. And it still makes sense to go about searching for an agent by getting *everything* right. So, if we look at the examples and quotes above, we can see that it pays to think about being 'on the tools,' in other words being in a state of working hard on the job and knowing you are capable of everything you might be expected to do. It pays to see your work as producing a package that includes a good submission, a good writer and some sense of focus and ambition driving both work and writer. Having achieved this, it pays to have everything checked in detail to ensure your submission doesn't fall down. Above all, it matters that you don't fall so far in love with your own ideas that you lose objectivity about what you are offering and to whom you are making the offer.

Jonny Geller's remarks about Jake Arnott's work make it clear that Geller sees a lot of work with potential, but rejects the material that falls down. As someone who has spent years working with hopeful writers and requiring them to produce submissions fit to be seen by authors as part of their course, I can confirm that there are loads of good ideas out there. Many of them with obvious potential, and a lot of them produced by people with clear talent. These ideas often crash and burn because some element of the package is lacking when it is finally submitted. If you stop and think about it for a few moments this is a depressing thought indeed. Why would someone spend well over a hundred hours working hard on a submission only to throw all that effort away because some part of the final package leaves an agent with a serious doubt about the potential of the whole idea? Believe me, people make mistakes on this scale every day of the year, and the tens of thousands of ideas are wasted every year in this country as a result of this behaviour. It is needless, and this chapter is an attempt to do something about that problem.

There is lots of advice out there, but it is amazing how much of it gets ignored.

For starters all of the major information sources for writers list most of the UK's agents, and all of the major agencies get a mention in each of the guides. *The Writers' & Artists' Yearbook*, *Writer's Market* and *The Writer's Handbook* all have a comprehensive section listing all of the UK's agents. All of these reference sources include in the listings a brief overview of the agencies, contact details and – frequently – some details of clients. They also provide information on US agencies and Irish agencies. These writing guides and other reference sources include simple and effective advice on dealing with agents. *The Writer's Handbook*'s page on making an approach to a literary agent includes the following words: '...before approaching an agent you must have *completed* the work in a draft you are happy with. No agent wants to see a draft you plan to rewrite; and no publisher will commission an unknown author to finish a book.'

All good advice, all of it frequently ignored by writers desperate to get a break. I once devoted hours of hard work to helping someone prepare a submission for an agent only for the author in question to throw in some random chapters he particularly liked just before the work went off. The confusion caused by the chapters and the indication it gave that the work and writer were disorganized effectively killed off the advantage this individual had gained by getting a personal contact with a very influential person in the book business.

As a rule, a fictional work – like a novel or full-length movie script – should be complete before submission to an agent. Even an agent wanting less than the full work in the first instance is likely to want to see the finished article before finally agreeing to front it. In the case of a non-fiction work, like a factual book, it *is* possible to submit less than the complete work, but it should be planned in detail and the sample material should be as good as you can possibly make it. You should also include a lot of material demonstrating that you have a sound grasp of the market into which your work will be launched.

If we assume you have something approaching a complete work and you want the best chance to move it forward we should look in detail at how you will get an agent and what will happen. It would be wonderful if at this point I could write a simple paragraph guaranteeing what response you will get and how the process will go on from the first reply. It isn't that simple, and the best thing to do is to line up the different views of agents and let you appreciate how dealing with an agent varies, depending on your point of view.

Definitions and Random Diversions About Agents

Most standard reference sources for writers and some general sources attempt to explain how agents work. In the simplest arguments found on sites like the Wikipedia you will discover that **literary agents typically act as a channel through which talent meets money and deals are made. Typically an agent's role in such deals combines two areas of specialist skill. The agent should know about his or her specialist market area to be able to make the right approaches on behalf of the writer.** So, the agent specializing in placing books for children should personally know all the major children's editors in the multinational publishers and should also have a clear idea of what those people are looking for. This market knowledge is generally a strength of the best agencies. It makes sense that an agent, dealing every working day with these publishers and producers is in the best place to know what is going on. The major publishers are unlikely to share sensitive market and editorial information with each other, and a hopeful author is unlikely to be able to access that information directly. **Along**

with the market knowledge it is generally the role of an agent to know enough about contracts to ensure his or her client gets the right deal. Not necessarily a huge deal, but certainly a fair one.

Christopher Little, who agreed to represent J K Rowling, secured her a four figure deal and both knew he had done his job well. He placed *Harry Potter and the Philosopher's Stone* with a company renowned for their high-quality, niche market books for children. Little's long history of work in this area and his personal contacts helped to secure the deal. It was a good deal, even if it is now discussed mainly for the purposes of indicating how far J K Rowling travelled after that first agreement. J K Rowling was pleased with the deal and pleased with Little's work on her behalf.

Beyond establishing the facts above about the role of agents almost every other area in which they operate varies. There are sole traders, individuals with contacts who typically specialize in one area of operation and handle a few clients. At the other end there are major agencies handling a range of talent. These major agencies can become involved in everything from selling a movie script from a first-time writer to freeing up time in the schedule of a busy celebrity so he or she can attend the opening of a supermarket. Curtis Brown and PFD are amongst the UK's biggest hitters in this area. We have already discussed Curtis Brown. PFD (Peters Fraser and Dunlop) were beyond dispute as the UK's biggest agency until a major falling out in 2007 led to some of its agents leaving to form United Agents, taking several household name authors with them. The story earned a great deal of national press attention. Some of the more detailed coverage went as far as to discuss the likely financial hit – in millions of pounds – faced by the depleted remains of PFD. One of the few times that the turnover of a major agency has been so openly discussed in a public arena.

Smaller agents typically restrict their work to placing the creations of their clients in the best hands and helping with the negotiations on contracts. Some agencies specialize in an area of work, like radio scripts, so despite their diminutive size it is wrong to regard such agencies as limited because in their own specific fields they have a reputation and ability to place work that compares well with much larger agencies. The smallest literary agents may have as few as a dozen active clients. The bigger the agency, the wider the range of work it can accommodate. **The very biggest employ staff who specialize in legal issues, licensing of the rights to work and other copyright issues.** Many of the bigger agencies represent dead clients and you will find these listed on their sites. PFD's client list includes Edmund Blunden (Estate). Blunden was a poet, academic and editor of others' work who died in 1974. His poetry still sells and his work is included in new anthologies, used for broadcast and otherwise kept alive to this day. Bigger agencies like PFD are better placed to negotiate on behalf of a client like the estate of Edmund Blunden because – typically – a range of quite random requests for his work will arrive and once the author is dead the work of an agency gradually comes to focus more and more on securing the best deals from these approaches. A bigger agency with access to legal expertise in areas like media rights and copyright law is the perfect place for a large literary estate.

Newly published writers who wish to grow their careers and discuss future directions may well find themselves happier in the first instance at a smaller agency where the personal attention they get in these negotiations is important in building their confidence.

The services offered by big and small agencies also vary depending on the skills of the individual agents and the range of expertise on offer in each agency. Becoming a literary agent is an ambition of many people working in editorial departments of publishing houses. These people often feel they have the expertise to do the job of an agent and they are also attracted by the chance to earn a percentage of the income of their clients. In other words, they are attracted by the opportunity of having no maximum cap on their salary.

It is generally agreed that the best agencies can be found amongst the membership of the Association of Authors' Agents. This is a voluntary body offering a forum for agents to discuss important industry matters and maintain a code of good practice. A 'survival of the fittest' law applies here in a small way, since three years experience is a pre-requisite of membership. All members must also be working in the UK at the time of membership and have a current client list. In this regard at least they differ from the Society of Authors, who do allow membership for those unpublished for many years and those without ongoing work or contracts. Agents are listed in the standard reference works for writers; *The Writers' & Artists' Yearbook*, *The Writer's Handbook* and *Writer's Market*. In these listings there is always a mark to denote the agencies affiliated to the Association of Authors' Agents.

For all the talk about what agents do and don't do there is one wholly practical reason for seeking out their services. **Many publishers, significant producers in areas like film and other big hitters simply refuse to consider work that isn't agented.** Whatever the rights and wrongs of this situation it is an unavoidable truth that over the last few decades the endorsement of an agent has become a quality mark for the unsigned and hopeful writers seeking a break in areas like book publishing and screen-writing. The cynical have often claimed this is simply down to laziness on the part of publishers and producers. Publishers and producers tend to hit back with the argument that so much unsolicited material directed to them is flawed rubbish with no chance of success in the form in which it is presented. Therefore; some form of quality control is essential if they are to sort out the potential winners.

You will find a few highly regarded publishers who don't work in this way. For example; Tindal Street Press, the following words come from the 'About' page of their website:

Tindal Street Press is an independent publisher of regional literary fiction with a national reputation for excellence and a prize-listing record that is the envy of many established imprints. (Three Booker nominations since 2003 and many other prizes and listings.)

Based in Birmingham, Tindal Street Press aims to find writers of national and international significance from places other than London and the South East – where nearly all of the English publishing industry is based.

Amongst the successes of this upwardly mobile and innovative company are works like Catherine O'Flynn's *What Was Lost* an ambitious and touching story set in two different time periods and revolving around a major shopping complex. Tindal Street also published *Never, Never* the first full-length novel by David Gaffney, set in Cleator Moor. Since Gaffney had already written his two books of flash fiction he became a three-times published fiction author without resorting to the services of an agent.

Tindal Street are very much an exception but the approach without agent option is generally the norm with companies with a very clear idea of what they do and little inclination to move beyond their areas of greatest success. One obvious example of this is Harlequin Mills and Boon, romance specialists. Though much derided by critics and sections of the reading public Mills and Boon (as they are generally referred to in the UK) have been pretty much a solid success story since their inception in 1908. In fact it was their decision to go directly into cheap romance books that set them on their way to an enviable turnover and prime position in a niche market they did a lot to create. Mills and Boon's website – *www.millsandboon.co.uk* – will show you two user friendly traits of the company; firstly they spell out the limits of each brand of book they produce, giving you word limits, ideas about how explicit to make the love scenes etc. Secondly, they explain exactly how to submit a manuscript specifying not only the number of chapters but also how to print and secure the paper.

If you shop around you will find other determined independents spread throughout every area of the media employing writers with an impressive track record and a sureness of touch in their selection of unsolicited work.

However, these operations are the exception in a world in which the services of an agent are increasingly essential. So it makes sense to take some time to look in detail at agents' websites, read down the small print in terms of how to submit to them and what they might be looking for and also to Google widely enough to establish in your own mind how useful an agent might be to your ambitions and who exactly might be the right agent for you.

For all the detail and precision in their web pages acquiring an agent can sometimes be a strange process and the eventual success of your joint venture can be down to unexpected factors. That much was true in my case. I had produced enough books and scripts without an agent to learn a lot of lessons the hard way before I found myself sitting around the office one afternoon and going into my fairly frequent; 'I'm bored, let's make something happen,' routine. What happened next was the thought entering my head that a particular celebrity lived locally and I couldn't recall reading a biography. I looked on Amazon and found nothing so I decided to cold call the individual and offer myself as a biographer. I'd love to say the next stage needed stealth and cunning but in fact it simply needed me to dial 118 118. Having secured the home phone number and made the call I ended up having a one to one meeting, agreeing the project on a handshake and starting work a week later. Once we had a couple of chapters and an introduction I offered it up to an agent and finally got representation with Guy Rose of Futerman Rose. This was the start of some frustrating adventures, the celebrity biography ran terminally off the rails when our subject moved management, took on a new team and made a determined effort at rebranding. Essential since this was a career in decline but one of the casualties was our biography agreement which went to a new writer, approved by the new management.

Having got a good agent and some notion of how this went a mutual contract put me in touch with someone involved closely at the top end of a major sport for years. A backroom person for sure, but one capable of dropping names and presenting the inside track on some well-worn stories. This project stalled because the offers of money didn't match the subject's own idea of what we should be receiving. As this book nosedived I was cold-called myself by a film director keen to turn one of my radio plays into a British film. I'd had several approaches about this idea in the past but almost all of them along the lines of; 'you write the script and we'll go looking for the money together.' This approach – at least – involved cash up front and an option purchase agreement[8]. So I agreed, wrote the script and signed the contract. There are three signatures on the contract, mine, the film director and my agent. You might ask at this point why did I bother including my agent when I had been approached personally and he didn't do anything to bring about the interest of the film director? My answer would be that Guy read the contract for me and pointed out areas of concern. Having avoided writing

8. Option Purchase Agreement: Standard deal for a movie script in which the purchaser (usually a production company or individual involved in production) secures an option on a script for an agreed period of time. The writer is tied into the contract for this period although such agreements tend to include regular payments, and an agreed percentage of the film budget. Typically this percentage is payable at the moment principal photography starts. In other words, once the money has moved, everyone is on set and the production is unstoppably on its way.

a screenplay before, mainly because the chances of success aren't that great, I had no experience of such contracts. Certainly they resemble book contracts and other script contracts I had signed but the crucial areas about net and gross income, percentages attached etc do vary in the film business and when Guy talked, I listened. I signed the contract when he thought I should. The other reason I was glad to have him involved, regardless of the 20% off the top fee, is that **a good agent represents a very useful friend when things finally get hugely successful**. Statistically speaking; the chances of my movie script coming back to me at the end of the agreement because the film hasn't started shooting are fairly strong. If the film does start shooting the chances of me making enough money to buy my next house for cash are fairly remote, but it pays to aim high, and that usually means it pays to have someone on your side who can help you focus on the important issues when things do go the right way. Bear in mind, my agent only gets paid when I get paid, so I don't have to pay out my own cash up front on the film deal.

My experience is typical of many others I have met over the years who find an agent, and then discover that things don't go simply. Agents get knocked back too, deals go astray and events intrude repeatedly. The relationship between an agent and writer can easily get strained. Cruel as it sounds a good analogy might be to picture the agent and writer as an animal trainer and his star performer, with the twist that each imagines the other one to be the animal. This isn't so far from an observation that Carole Blake makes in her book; '..agents must both protect and exploit their clients; protect their rights, exploit their work.'

I would add that the statement makes logical sense but the reality is that emotions can run high on both sides when things don't go well. A typical example of this might be a frustrated writer ringing up and arguing with an agent who doesn't appear to be moving a deal forward. The agent might counter with the view that 'leaving them to think it over' is the best course of action. The 'them' in this scenario might be a television company, film company or publisher. Each side in the argument between writer and agent might feel themselves to be 100% in the right when in reality both are relying totally on things they have learned the hard way in their working lives.

Beyond this as Carole Blake (again) notes; 'Agents vary a lot in the amount of editorial work they are prepared to do. We get paid for our sales, not our opinions.' In fact agents vary in many areas, percentages charged, telephone manner, even their genuine interest in writing. The best thing to do is shop around, the best place to start shopping is in one of the annual reference works written for writers and the best thing to do after finding a list of the likeliest contacts for yourself is to check them out online.

In terms of definitions I would make one final point before you do this work; **any agent asking for fees up front or looking to charge for basic services like photocopying is probably doing so because he or she isn't likely to make money any other way (i.e. by selling your idea to a publisher). If anyone asks for your money in these circumstances you could do better, so avoid working with them.**

Agents as seen by others

I once had a conversation with a person highly placed in a national organization involved with writers. 'What you've got to remember about agents,' he told me, 'is that they're all just grubby little fifteen percenters.' Predictably, he didn't want those words attributed to him when I told him I was writing this book. But, he was accurate about the standard 15% take on most domestic book deals[9]. That conversation does highlight one issue about agents. Many in the writing world view agents the way football fans view managers, often wondering exactly what they bring to the business and highlighting individual elements of their work that could be done differently and, arguably, improved as a result. From my point of view I think the comparison between agents and football managers fairly apt since those looking on and criticizing would often be crushed by the job were they faced with it for real, and also since a lot of what agents do involves grasping the complexity of a situation and working skillfully to achieve a result in difficult circumstances. However, if we move away from generalizing about agents and start to highlight individual examples it is possible to identify many things that *could* be improved.

9 – Whilst agent's fees vary the standard taken by most is 15% off the top of publishing deals and 20% of film deals. Translation deals also accrue higher percentages. Whilst this mystifies some the standard reasons offered to explain this revolve around the money lost as royalties move from one country to another and banks skim off fees to change it from one currency to another. This does have odd effects, especially in lengthy deals. When currencies fluctuate against each other, it is likely that payments due to a British writer will fall or rise, although the contract stipulates a number of equal payments. The higher agents' fees taken for works translated protect agents in such situations and also take account of the more complex legal arrangements that tend to apply when works are translated.

So, it is – at least – worth getting different opinions on the whole business of agents. One person paid to keep on top of developments in literary agencies and also at an objective distance from the business is Matt Shoard who writes the *Agent Secrets* column for *Writers' Forum* magazine.

1 - In your regular contact with UK literary agents are there any standard complaints/observations from agents on regular mistakes made by writers who approach them?

Most agents seem to treat their relationship with prospective authors as a kind of literary speed dating. So any submission that feels needy, pretentious, arrogant, boring, untidy, volatile, impersonal or patronising is an instant turnoff. A lack of self-awareness or understanding of how things work, or trying too hard to sound 'in' or savvy, will also get the delete button. To prolong the analogy to the second date - the more you chase, the more likely you are to be rejected. A well-known agent will receive hundreds of queries a month, so when they do find time to read through them, it helps to be concise, intriguing and attached to some brilliant prose. They also take a dislike to mocked-up artwork, endorsements from anyone who isn't famous, ideas without significant content, and under-research submissions – a thriller to a crime agency, for example, or a memoir to a literary fiction agent. They love to see that you've placed your work carefully in the context of their list. Agents often tell me that quiet confidence and profound humility, knowing that you're one of many, many hopefuls, is important. Once writers see that, they can begin sticking out for the right reasons.

2 - How many agents in your experience still insist on 'hard copy' approaches and how many are happy with emails?

It's about 90% email now. As a general rule, always check the website for guidelines. If there are none, then a two-line hello, a quarter-page biography that's fun and relevant, a half-page synopsis on the book, and two or three consecutive chapters should do the trick. No fancy fonts, no binding, nothing that detracts from your writing.

3 - Can you share any stories of submissions that were so interesting/unusual/blindingly brilliant that the agents concerned talk about them long after the event?
Agents talk about novels that worked from the first page. They want to be hooked, just as a reader does. I've heard stories of manuscripts arriving attached to a crate of champagne - even to a juggler, at one agency. It probably raises a smile, but it won't go down half as well as brilliant writing.

4 - If you were advising aspiring fiction authors and poets, are there any types of submission you would suggest they send directly to a publisher?
Poetry can go straight to the press. It's not a big earner and its publishers tend to be small and esoteric enough to care about the thousands of poems they receive. Anything very niche, controversial or experimental, like plot-free literary fiction, say, or a photographic history of salmon fishing that might retail for £50 a pressing, then you're better off seeking out the independents and the one-man bands. Someone like Constable & Robinson for the fishing, and Martin Rynja - an idiosyncratic and sometimes controversial publisher of whatever interests him - is worth a punt on an unusual memoir. Most publishers, however, need an agent to do the narrowing down for them.

5 - When you are dealing directly with agents for your column, do you find a great range of character and motivation amongst them?
They're an odd mix of thoughtful, ruthless and flirtatious. They

can also be very funny. If you find a good agent, you have a friend for life. A certain warmth and amiability is part of the job description. They believe in human beings, even if they say personality doesn't affect the deal. They're all bookish, unsurprisingly, but they do like to talk, especially if they're interested in your material. Then they're your champion, your confidant, and, as David Miller puts it, your Jiminy Cricket. Conversely, if you don't interest them, they can be almost silent. You might get a line or two but no more than that. They're always busy and it never seems to be with prospective material, always with something else. If you do get a longer email, or suggestions for changes to your pitch, then you can take it as a big compliment, and you should get editing and re-submitting straight away.

6 - Your editorship of Fleeting Magazine and involvement with writers through your teaching must make you party to a lot of stories about good and bad experiences with agents, care to share any of these?

Most horror stories come from the literary agents. There are some hilarious feeds at places like Slush Pile Hell, Secret Agent Man and the #queryfail tag on Twitter. Many agents' websites list their pet hates, too, which can be handy reminders about what not to do. One agent I've always wanted to track down is Andrew Wylie, aka the Jackal, well known for poaching authors and squeezing publishers and being a scary, old-money "card-carrying shit" — in some ways, exactly what you want from an agent, someone who never lets go, who isn't talking to you for fun. David Miller is my favourite agent. He tells of how he snagged a £1m advance for Magnus Mills' *The Restraint of Beasts*, an amount which turned out to be exaggerated but which drew in enough publicity to make the actual figure irrelevant.

And before we completely finish with agents we should also let one of them speak. Since I've liberally quoted Carole Blake's opinions, as culled from her book *From Pitch to Publication*, in this chapter the least I can do is let her speak for herself.

1 - There is lots of information available in the standard reference sources stating what agents do. How accurate is this in your opinion?
It is mostly accurate but most of the information out there is fairly general. Whilst many general rules are followed, every agency is different and anyone searching for an agent can appreciate these differences if he or she moves on from reading the reference books and follows up by looking at our individual websites.

2 - Which elements of an agents' work are least understood and least appreciated by writers?
This can vary too because of the differences between agencies but there are several areas of work I don't think many people truly understand or appreciate. The editing process on a client's manuscript can be long and detailed and you wouldn't necessarily want a publisher to know about that. Many would-be authors still think the process of placing a book involves ringing us up, checking we might take the work and then mailing it. They don't appreciate how much work we might have to do to make the work presentable to the right publisher.

It also matters that an agent maintains the right balance on a list and has the right hit-rate when it comes to getting work accepted. Obvious as it sounds, there is a quality of finesse to our work that will always matter and the reputation of an agency is vitally important. Retaining that reputation involves hard work.

Finally I think many people fail to appreciate the hard work that can be involved in keeping a relationship between a client and a publisher on the rails. Even when this relationship might involve a long-term contract there will be things to do, potential misunderstandings and disagreements and work for an agent in ensuring the deal continues. In this area, as with the editing work, a lot of our best work can be completely invisible as far as the public, and sometimes those working with us, are concerned.

3 - *From Pitch to Publication* must be the most authoritative book written from an agent's perspective, have any agents fed back to you about whether they agree or disagree with key points you made?

Everyone will disagree with some points but there are two things worth keeping in mind. So far as this country is concerned there isn't another similar book with a high-profile publisher and if From Pitch to Publication was very wide of the mark there would have been a gap for such a book. The book is also used to train young agents and editors, so the practices it describes continue to be relevant to the industry.

4 - If the your agency were going to draw up a list of the most common mistakes made by hopeful writers, how would the top three read?

1. Expectations very wide of the mark on the speed of the agenting process. Many writers don't realize how long it can take for an agent to find the right publisher for a book. Once the manuscript is accepted, many writers fail to appreciate how long it takes to prepare the market and do all the other work before a book is published.
2. Submission letters claiming far too much. For example; a book that is certain to be translated into 20 languages or a book that is bound to make a great film.

3. People who obviously lie or make otherwise inappropriate submissions. In the case of lies, I mean people who claim to know what an agent does and then submit something like science fiction when the agent's site makes it clear that science fiction is a category the agent doesn't touch. That is an example of an inappropriate submission. So is sending in a manuscript with little or no commercial potential to an agent who typically handles best-selling work.

5 - The last few decades have seen major producers and publishers relying more and more on agents to sort out the potential winners before approaching them. In your opinion; will this pattern continue, decline or remain where it is?

I think it will continue to get worse. The main factor behind this is that conditions in the industry are likely to get more challenging and so publishers will continue to want to avoid paying for the process of sifting the slushpile. That means the work will be left to agents. At the same time the number of people with access to the technology to write and submit books will continue to grow and the quantity of submissions will also continue to grow, meaning more documents, containing more words, year on year. Agents see this immediately after the summer holidays and Christmas break when the volume of submissions to us increases.

Because some of the people submitting don't fully understand how book publishing works they will end up submitting to agents because many publishers make it clear they won't look at unsolicited submissions. To get through this process a writer will have to develop a useful knowledge of the industry. I feel very strongly that if you want to be a professional writer you should do the industry the honour of learning about it.

Agent doesn't always mean 'Agent'

This chapter is called 'Agents of Change' and the title puns on the two meanings of 'agent' within the chapter. Firstly an agent is the literary, script-pushing variety. Secondly an agent is – in the broadest sense – 'a person or thing producing an effect'[10]. If we assume the effect we are chasing here is some strong sense of progress and achievement in your writing career it is worth looking at the range of agents of change out there to help you. You could – of course – grab at one of the standard reference works for writers and work through section after section, opening the book on your desk and going to every website mentioned as you rifle through the pages. My book can't match the tonnage of contacts available in tomes like *The Writers' & Artists' Yearbook* but I can provide some insightful studies of the kind of help and support out there. In each case I am presenting one case study, but I strongly suggest you look out all the options. Because, as the BBC would say in the same circumstances: 'Other options *are* available.'

Of *Course* You Can Change

One standard route to change and development for aspiring writers is to take a course in writing. Such courses vary immensely. Matt Shoard, featured in the interview above, was the first person to study for a PhD in Creative Writing at the University of Kent, Canterbury. He is one of a select few in

10. From *The Oxford Popular English Dictionary*, other definitions of the broader meaning of 'agent' vary, but not much.

the UK aiming for this qualification, but the numbers continue to grow. Others – myself included – are doing PhD work, but our qualifications will be branded as 'English,' 'Media Studies' or some other related area. The simplest Creative Writing courses are those run over a period of a few weeks by organizations like Adult Education. These courses typically certificate achievement, although the recognition doesn't technically count as a listed qualification in the United Kingdom. Creative Writing is a significant part of one widely available English A' level syllabus in the UK and once you get to graduate and post-graduate level there is lots of choice in terms of BA degrees and MA courses. There have been cynical suggestions – notably from some right-wing sections of the press and a few noted professional writers – that such courses amount to little more than amusement for the milder end of Care in the Community cases. As the instigator and leader of one such course I recall reading those comments and feeling genuinely annoyed. However, as someone obliged to be objective in presenting this book, I would have to admit that some of the students signed up for and passing writing programmes in British universities have virtually no hope of making it as writers. Others – by contrast – are superbly talented, use the courses to build on their raw talent, and go on to success on the terms they want.

If you are considering a course, you'll certainly want to have the best chance of success so the most objective thing I can do to help is to round up the main points, explain my own involvement as clearly as possible and let a few others with a different take on the whole business of writing courses have their say.

Basically, the courses on offer for UK writers fall into four categories:

1. Short-run and specialist programmes (generally certificated but some not technically 'qualifications' as defined by the QCDA – Qualifications and Curriculum Development Agency).[11]
2. Qualifications including Creative Writing but not specific to writers or aspiring writers (like A' level English Language).
3. General programmes strong enough to provide a powerful qualification in employment terms and specific to some element of writing (like BA courses in Creative Writing).
4. Specialist courses focused very closely on some element of writing and powerful enough to offer significant career advancement to the student, (like BA courses in Sports Journalism).

As you might expect me to say from this point, things aren't quite as simple as they seem from the potted definitions above. But I'll attempt to explain without confusing you too much. I'll also attempt to be even-handed and succinct by way of defining what each area covers and describing a 'perfect' and 'nightmare' student.

1 – Short-run and specialist

The thing that marks out most of these qualifications is the

11. Obviously they *are* qualifications in the most general sense and those gaining them have worked for their certificates. The problem of how valid they are lies in the degree to which they are accepted as accreditation of prior learning for other programmes and for entry to jobs

limited study time and their focus on a narrow band of skills. In some cases there are short-run and very general courses. Creative Writing programmes from Adult Education count as such, many of them being more like a social group in which a tutor works with a small group of students, sets general exercises and uses the results to bring out the 'voice' of each writer. Some of these courses also combine the added attraction of locating themselves in scenic splendour. The better venues, with tutors who have a significant record of publishing success, come at a price but the combination of holiday and hobby is appealing to many and some of the advice on offer is the best quality. For example; I had to wait a few days for my answers from Carole Blake because she was doing a session at a residential course for writers of romantic fiction. Her paying students on that course – quite rightly – got priority. Venues like Dartington Hall in Devon, Higham Hall in Cumbria and the Castle Hotel, Killeny (near Dublin) are worth visiting simply for the location.

Also included in the specialist and short-run training are the myriad of online, postal and commercially run courses in areas like screenwriting, copywriting and writing fiction. If you bought a copy of *Writers' Monthly* or *Writers' Forum* and studied the adverts and news on residential courses in any given month you would find lots of options along these lines. At the most general end of the market, and most prominent end of the advertising are organizations like *The Writers Bureau*, providers of longer-term one-to-one tuition and courses for hopeful writers. Advertising for organizations like these centres on the likely money to be earned once you have completed a course with them. The Writers Bureau offer a 'full refund guarantee,' something not generally available elsewhere.

I had experience of a similar course, run by the – now defunct – Writers School. This also offered a complete refund and asked only that you informed them of any earnings. My time as a student with them was in the mid-eighties. As I recall the fee for the whole 20 assignment course was £115 and whilst I was honest about my earnings I wasn't totally honest with them about what I was doing on their roll. The course did certainly provide some insight into the workings of the more ambitious end of the commercial writing course market.
My motivation was partly to get their materials, 'adapt' (i.e. steal) some of the more workable ideas that hadn't occurred to me, and add them to the growing amount of Creative Writing materials I was building for a college course I ran. The course fee also wasn't quite the hit that £115 back then would normally have been. For starters I was lecturing in a college and managed to get my line manager to agree to pay half the fee. I had also started submitting regular accounts as a writer so I was able to claim some of the half fee I did pay against tax.

For my money I got the standard first assignments which involved market research and some materials that gave me basic writing instructions to start sniping away at a range of standard markets. Writers then were – amongst other targets – directed to a section of the *Reader's Digest* magazine called 'Life's Like That.' I was already a working writer so earning money to match the fees wasn't a desperate problem and I did report earnings when they came in. Somewhere around assignment 7, I had covered my fees. By this time my assignments had progressed to me making decisions about what to chase and conversing with my tutor by post (the internet existed, but only for a few hundred people at that time). Once the final batch of materials arrived, I gave up.

I learned a few things I hadn't expected to know, both about specifics of some areas of writing and courses offering a full refund. Since enrolling for the course I have come across many others who have done similar courses, especially with The Writers Bureau, and heard some positive and negative things about the programmes. On the positive side I was impressed with the way my tutor – Sydney J Bounds, a writer of pulp sci-fi and already in his sixties when he acquired me as a student – managed to adapt himself to my demanding moves. Once I was calling the shots on the assignments I moved the agenda everywhere from serious academic writing to the edgy humour I was then starting to churn out for the likes of *Viz* comic. Sydney managed to make insightful comments in all eventualities and even responded with good humour when I stuck a cheeky 'hello – I wonder if you *do* read every word.' – right in the middle of a lengthy assignment. So he *did* read the lot, and I can't imagine he was being paid a fortune to do so.

It wasn't long before sentences from a letter I sent in, credited to 'NN,' were appearing in the publicity for The Writing School reporting the fees I had earned. This letter turned up for a few years in their publicity, causing regular hilarity amongst my friends who spotted it everywhere from *The Guardian* to the specialist magazines for writers. The fact my words continued in the publicity for so long left me wondering how many other students were earning money, and reporting it.

The positives of these courses shouldn't be underestimated, even if you are cynical about the profit-led motives and the hard-sell guarantees. If nothing else they line up the most obvious targets and make a sterling effort to teach you how to hit them. They also provide you with one-to-one help and oblige you to get out there and try to sell your work. These might be simple points, but they are easily over-looked. It is easy to be cynical and question whether you are being taught to be a writer, or simply being programmed to write. But I will freely admit that some of the things you'll find on these courses like these also turn up in modified form when I teach undergraduates on our Professional Writing programme. Some good practice is basic, and you can learn it online, or in a classroom.

On the down side I trust the 'catch' in securing they deliver on the guarantee of a full refund is obvious. I don't know how much work is involved in every single variant of these courses but had I failed to sell any work and insisted on my money back I would have had to slog my way through sixty separate pieces of original work, along with analytical studies of markets and… you get the point. The man-hours involved would have reduced it to a miserable and spiteful exercise.

My guess is there are some sharks out there. I would base this on the fact that I contacted a number of those involved in providing one-to-one help as I attempted to secure a brief interview for this book. Many were suspicious as soon as I started to explain this book on the phone. More suspicious and less helpful by far than film directors, agents and others who were on the end of my calls. Even those willing to consider talking to me didn't want to discuss drop-out rates on their programmes or exactly what level of qualification and aptitude they demanded before signing students up.

If you want to read a searing attack on such courses I strongly suggest you hunt down a copy of *Snake Oil* by John Diamond, turn to page 103 and read a piece originally written for *The Spectator* called 'Anyone Can Be a Wordsmith.' It starts with him receiving a flyer for a course, continues through a few pages of side-splitting but vicious invective and – close to the end – points out; 'Editors feel the same way about part-time dilettantes as policemen feel about Neighbourhood Watch schemes.' It's a serious point. If you're not prepared to put in the work and treat writing *very* seriously then no correspondence or online course will help you. This leads us to the perfect, and the nightmare, student in this area.

The perfect student would be someone with a solid background in some commercial area involved with dealing with the public. Also somebody intelligent, focused and not full of pre-conceived notions about how their wonderful writing will be received. So a university student with a retail background, a parent who sacrificed a career to raise children and sees writing as flexible working option etc. You need motivation and aptitude. A nightmare student – I guess – would be someone intent on staying indoors, taking most of their reality checks from online messageboards and other self-selecting social groups and harbouring the notion that he or she was an under-appreciated genius. It's only my opinion, but... the personal baggage carried by that second person is likely to be an impossible barrier when he or she is directed to the obvious targets and criticized by their tutor for being verbose and/or lacking the focus to hit the obvious targets.

But the above are my opinions. I also took the trouble to contact the highest profile of the current crop of programmes on offer. Diana Nadin, Director of Studies for The Writers Bureau provided the answers below:

1 - How long has The Writers Bureau been established and - approximately - how many students have passed through its courses?
The Writers Bureau was established in 1989 – so it's our 21st birthday this year. I'm afraid I can't be very precise about how many students we've enrolled (sensitive information) but it's in the thousands rather than the hundreds!

2 - I'm sure there is no such thing as a typical student but are there specific types of student you see again and again?
You're right, there is no 'typical' student. But the ratio of men to women is roughly 36% to 64%. As you can imagine, students come from all walks of life and represent all age groups. Some students think that it's an easy way to make money – those are the ones that usually fail to sell their work, because it's not! Many have had a life-long ambition to write about their life, or the life of someone close to them. Then there are the ones that are really determined to make a living (or healthy part-time living) from it. They work hard, are willing to turn their hand to anything, aren't precious about editors who change their work, accept rejection with stoicism and then keep trying. They're a joy to work with and usually succeed.

3 - You feature success stories in your adverts, if you had to identify the greatest successes ever achieved by The Writers Bureau, who would you pick?
I'm afraid I couldn't. We get as much pleasure out of a student in India who starts selling work regularly for a few rupees as we do from students like Christina Jones who has published many novels, has appeared on best-seller lists and been nominated for awards. In between are lots of people achieving their lifetime ambitions and earning a very welcome income from their work.

4 - Roughly speaking, what would a student be expected to do on their first assignment?
The first assignment on our comprehensive course only asks for two things: 1. Why the student wants to write and 2. a descriptive piece of approximately 300 words. We ask the first question because (together with the personal profile questionnaire that we ask students to complete) it helps the tutor to get to know their student. The descriptive piece allows the tutor to assess the current level of the student's writing. It also gives us the opportunity to pick up on any students that we think might struggle with the course because of poor grammar, punctuation or language problems (if they are overseas students). Although such cases are rare it means we can suggest that the student cancels the course and we refund the fees in full.

5 - In which areas of writing are you best able to help students to succeed and where would you find it hardest to do this?
I think that students have the best chance of success with articles. Probably memoirs/autobiographies are the most difficult to sell for anyone who isn't famous or notorious.

6 - Other than the obvious information covered by the questions above, what else would you want aspiring writers to know about The Writers Bureau?
We feel that all our courses are thorough and are updated

regularly. All our tutors are 'proper' writers – that is they write as a career and mark assignments as a secondary source of income. So, they are familiar with the writing world as it is now, and can offer constructive marketing advice. There's a great Student Services team to offer help and advice, where necessary. The student community on our website is vibrant and students there help each other. Finally, the fees we charge are excellent value for money. If you think about it, paying less than £300 to find out whether you've really got the makings of a writer in you is difficult to beat.

2 – Qualifications including Creative Writing

Bearing in mind this is a book about getting a break as a writer and I have pointed out a lot of the vagaries of trying to hold down employment in this area it is important to remind ourselves that the vast majority of professional writers – i.e. writers who earn some money for writing – earn small amounts of money. So it pays to be part-time and involved in other things.

It is not surprising – therefore – with so many part-time writers around that many of those studying something related to writing take a pragmatic attitude to their education and combine studies of writing with other subjects. This often precedes a career in which they *hope* to be able to write for a living but cover themselves in terms of financial security by taking work in another area. It was never the intention when we founded our own Professional Writing course to produce people with a wish to go into alternative employment but – to date – we have trained eight people who have gone into teaching of one sort or another from university lecturers to classroom assistants. In almost all of those cases the decision to teach was linked to childcare commitments and the holidays offered in education. Amongst our trained teachers are two people who have written radio plays (one of the plays produced going on to help a the digital station OneWord to win a Sony Award as Digital Station of the year), so – in one sense – they took the advice from their Professional Writing lecturers quite literally. If we'd told them to avoid combining writing and teaching for a living we would have been hypocrites.

A lot of qualifications combine creative writing with academic study in another area. Some of these use minimal creative writing so – for example – we don't really need to concern ourselves here with activities on History GCSE that ask you to write a letter from the perspective of a soldier in the trenches in 1916. It is certainly imaginative and useful to do this but in terms of a qualification that might equip you for some form of professional writing I suggest we start beyond GCSE.

If you are young enough to be looking at post-GCSE options there are two things worth a quick mention. If you are old enough for this not to apply to you the next three paragraphs are worth skipping. Some English A' level syllabuses offer a combined qualification, studying literature alongside a substantial part of creative writing and letting the creative writing contribute to the final A' level grade. If – as I did – you find yourself growing up in one of the most rural parts of the country then you may have little real choice about where to do your A' levels. On the other hand, most major towns and all major cities do offer choice and increasingly use different versions of A' levels to attract particular students. My youngest son moved from one grammar school to another after his GCSEs, moving from a specialist modern languages school to one offering more arts and creative subjects. His new school offers the version of English with creative writing. His old school doesn't.

Another option at post-GCSE is to take a more vocational course, usually in an FE (Further Education) college. Colleges vary in terms of the qualifications they offer but an obvious thing to look for is some variation of a BTEC National Extended Diploma offering work in Print or Radio. These courses usually demand a minimum 4 C grade at GCSE entry but the best ones provide a much better opportunity at post-GCSE level to develop skills and do genuine work likely to help with moving your career forward. BTEC National qualifications are designed to offer two options to post-GCSE students. Firstly, university entrance but secondly direct entry into the industry. It pays to imagine them as the opposite side of a coin to A' levels since each tends to have strengths and weaknesses that cancel out the other. The strength of A' levels is their wide acceptance, their long-track record and the fact they reward intelligence. The main weakness of A' levels is that they don't provide a substantial skills training, so it is very hard to go directly to work with A' levels as your main qualification unless you are taking advantage of a scheme offered by a large employer like the armed services. By contrast BTEC National qualifications *do* provide a substantial skills training. They also tend to be user-friendly by offering only continual assessment, with no formal exams. Their biggest weakness is their specialism. I have seen BTEC National Media students complete two years before opting to go into estate agency and – in two celebrated cases – work with animals. The 'animal' students had to go back two years in educational terms and start at post-GCSE level again when they started at agricultural college. Their skills in – for example – video editing, were not transferrable.

BTEC National qualifications do often provide substantial work in subjects related to writing. For example; I worked with some students at this level to write a book for a charity. This was a pilot project that tested out more complicated work I later brought into teaching my Professional Writing undergraduates. I got 19 students to write short items for the book and all of the students used the work to pass one unit on their 18 unit course. The whole notion of getting involved, making things happen, developing a portfolio and learning about your own professional capabilities is central to further education courses like BTEC Nationals. In the area of professional writing these courses typically feed people into 'entry level' (i.e. poorly paid and very short-term contract) work in the media or to university courses offering specialist training related to developing ideas and making things happen. Of the students who worked on the charity book project with me in their first year most went on to put in UCAS applications and most of the UCAS applications were in specialist areas of the media involving writing. So these students will eventually start their careers armed with BA (Hons) qualifications in Fashion Promotion, Event Management and the like.

Despite some university level courses being under-threat in the current financial climate, the area of the creative and media industries continues to be very strong in British higher education. The threat of cuts to budgets is likely to impact less on writing related areas than other courses because some of these courses can run themselves cheaply. Course tutors would sooner avoid the tough decisions of which production areas to cut, but it is possible to run a lot of writing activities on a very limited budget. Areas like Engineering and Physics, by contrast, demand expensive kit, labs and money for experimental work. If they can't attract large numbers of students, they can find themselves very vulnerable indeed because it is impossible to cut the budget and keep the course viable.

I could devote several thousand words to the possibilities spinning off the courses identified in this section but if I did I would be leading us in several directions, each of which only mattered to one or two people reading the section. So it is – I think – best to sum up this section with some general advice and move on. If you are finishing GCSEs anytime soon then the best thing to do is shop around, taking in as many VIth forms and local colleges as you can usefully reach. Check out what they offer in terms of writing work within A' level programmes and BTEC Nationals and remember that they have to keep and make available data on their inspection reports and the 'progression' (i.e. the universities and work places) to which their students have gone. If you are looking at courses including (but not limited to) Creative Writing at university, the best place to start is the UCAS (Universities Central Admissions Service) site; *www.ucas.ac.uk*. There is an entry on UCAS in chapter ten of this book, giving more details and also suggesting that if you do go there in search of more information, it pays to put time and effort into the search.

There are two points we need to make concluding this section:

1. There are options in education involving studying some elements of writing whilst gaining a wider qualification. All the places offering these options will be legally obliged to make available data on their performance.

2. Many of those taking these options are thinking pragmatically, they opt with their heart to do some writing and with their heads to place this in the context of a qualification likely to make them employable.

3 – General programmes strong enough to provide a powerful qualification in employment terms...

Such qualifications have been a major growth area in the UK's higher education market in the last couple of decades. There was a time when Creative Writing was the only game in town and this subject mainly came as an add-on to English. The United States remains the world's leader in writing related courses but the UK has adopted some of their models and theory and adapted other ideas for its own use. Virtually all the programmes that fall into this category are available in HE (i.e. above A' level). Increasingly they also include programmes offered at post-graduate level.

BA courses in Creative Writing are so plentiful that we don't need to concern ourselves here with wherever you might find them. Search the subject on UCAS and they will come tumbling out, along with joint-honours options of Creative Writing and..., or other minor/major combinations of Creative Writing with... Or subjects 'with' Creative Writing.

Creative Writing is so varied that I can only recommend you look specifically at any course you find interesting. The core of Creative Writing programmes is the base of artistic expression and the way writers – including yourself – can use the basic tools. When it is combined with literature Creative Writing typically looks at ground-breaking and highly regarded work. Writers like Angela Carter, who push boundaries on the use of tense, point-of-view and locating their text in a specific genre are a mainstay of the taught parts of such courses. Books like David Lodge's *The Art of Fiction* – a primer exploring different elements of the fiction writer's tool-kit – are standard general texts. Beyond this Creative Writing can be specific and pragmatic although most of it still tends to stay close to its roots in English departments. Creative Writing graduates have gained employment in teaching and other areas – like working with the Arts Council – where they can continue to work with writing. They also do well in areas like advertising and marketing. Creative Writing is an expanding and lucrative area of post-graduate work, especially in the form Master's Degrees, many of which run on a part-time basis and attract mature and very able students. Such courses are popular with lecturers because of the ability and self-discipline many students bring to their studies. At the very top end – i.e. the University of East Anglia – the courses have produced some of the best writers of recent years. The East Anglia (UEA) course has an alumni page to shame pretty much everyone else in the business. Ian McEwan was their first ever student and along with Kazuo Ishiguro went on from UEA to win the Booker Prize. The tonnage of published, performed and award-nominated writers linked to the UEA course continues to grow.

Less illustrious courses still produce published writers and – perhaps more importantly for the purposes of this book – a lot of people graduating from MA courses in Creative Writing feel significantly improved as writers. Even the less celebrated courses will immerse you in exercises to test your creative limits and study to widen your knowledge, though at undergraduate and post-graduate level this will almost certainly involve significant expense.

Alongside Creative Writing a number of other undergraduate and post-graduate courses have grown up related to writing. Some – like Journalism – have a long history and a fairly obvious application to the industry. In recent years changes to the industry have brought about new courses, many of them combining some element of writing with training in work for the creative industries. I started one such course in 1999. It was then an HND in Professional Writing, it was rebranded as a Foundation Degree in 2005 and it is typical of how the newer breed of courses work. We work directly with students who want to become paid writers, they have work experience, research their careers, work as a large group with a client to produce a published book and under-pin all of this with units on English Literature and media theory.

Roughly the same structure applies to other courses trading under names like Media Writing and Creative Industries. There are also specialist writing courses in areas like Screenwriting. In other areas – like Fashion Promotion – some standard journalistic practice and writing skills (such as the concoction of effective press releases) are on the curriculum. Navigating the complexities of this area is baffling to some and the problem isn't helped by the fact that courses tend to come and go very quickly. For example; our Professional Writing students became part of a Creative Industries package in 2005, meaning they could progress automatically to complete a third year in Creative Industries after two years with us. Four years later the degree in Creative Industries was scrapped, although much of the good practice developed on that course became part of another programme in Media Writing.

So, it *is* confusing. But there are positives. The newer courses tend to be practical and very pragmatic in their nature. Those of us running such courses make it our business to get the students doing real work. So far as my students are concerned; their books appear on Amazon whilst they still study with us and their other work is done for real clients. Other such courses manage events for clients, work directly with local authorities etc. The aim of many of the practically based courses is to get students equipped with a portfolio and a record of work experience so they can compete for jobs as soon as they leave. Once again, if you are interested there is no substitute for contacting courses directly after trawling through the UCAS site and checking out any public information available online, like inspection reports, contents of units and reading lists.

4 – Specialist courses focused very closely on some element of writing and powerful enough to offer significant career advancement...

The overlap between the 'specialist' and the general courses mentioned above is another area of confusion. I don't want to waste too much time on this, though it is worth pointing out where the confusion might arise. I run a general course, in that I make few pre-judgements about the particular work my students choose to do. Having said this, I am faced with students who have a special interest, follow this through all the practical assessments on the course and then use their portfolio to make them employable. This can be *very* specific. For example, a few students have made writing for a religious market a central element of their practical work looking into everything from how and where to submit work to the complicated distribution network that gets written material to British churches and into specialist Christian bookshops. They might have been on a general course, but some of these people didn't divert from their stated ambition and made the course very specialist as a result of their choices. But it suited them to do so.

The obvious specialist courses in terms of their branding and content are those preparing people for a job, clearly identified at the start of the course. There are a handful of specialized journalism courses in the UK covering areas like Fashion Journalism and Sports Journalism. If you graduate from one of these courses it would be hard to argue your way into a career too far removed from the content of the course. A BA graduate in Sports Journalism would – probably – be taken seriously by sports PR firms, the press office of a county cricket club etc. He or she might also find it relatively easy to secure interviews with people looking to develop sports in the community. But beyond the world of sports these interviews might quickly dry up. Having said this, the same graduate might well have such a strong portfolio of sports writing that he or she would be easily a better candidate than an English graduate if competing for a job on a major national football magazine. The specialist course would have looked into the workings of the sports publishing sector, considered issues like advertising revenue, changes to the sports industry etc. The Sports Journalism graduate could field those questions confidently at an interview, support their answers with a well presented portfolio and leave the English graduate trailing.

None of the above is an absolute truth. In the end we come back to the basic truths that it matters how much you want something and how hard you are prepared to work for it. But in terms of 'agents of change' we have identified some of the main points about courses available in the UK. These courses are certainly key to changing the lives of many, the commitment they put in, the skills they develop and the knowledge they gain all contributing to making them more employable as writers.

Other Agencies of Change

Beyond courses the other areas of help and support leading to change are harder to define with confidence. A simple point to keep in mind is that **a means of help and support to one writer might easily turn out to be a waste of time to many others.** This is certainly true of many websites, professional agencies and others who regularly advertise their skills in helping those intent on making a living with their words.

This is not meant as a put-down on anyone, merely

recognition of an age-old problem: when it comes to making progress as a writer. Commitment, focus and hard-work are all required to move you forward. Progress tends to come when everyone working on a project is heading in the same direction and fully understanding of their role. In this context agents trying to sell your work and courses offering a qualification have it easy. Once you are signed up with either there is an implicit recognition between yourself and the others involved regarding where they are taking you. The agent is taking you to deals and money, the course to a qualification and improved professional prospects. You might argue the ins and outs of this as you go, but – ultimately – the purpose of agents and courses is as I have just described it. They are agents of change for you, because of the targets they should bring within your range.

Outside of these options there are two other major areas I want to discuss briefly; websites offering a community to writers and professional helpers offering to improve your work. There are numerous examples of both. If you buy a copy of *Writers' Monthly* or *Writers' Forum* you will find numerous adverts for proofing, typing and editing services. All editions of the standard writers' reference books contain a section on websites for writers.

The best I can do here is to summarise what is on offer in both areas, consider the pros and cons, and let someone involved in each area speak for themselves. Writers' websites exist in a rapidly expanding array throughout the internet. At best they provide focused communities, informed debate, up to date news, job adverts and other vital information to keep you professionally updated. At worst they provide a self-indulgent, unproductive alternative to getting the job done. It is – of course – possible for one website to be both things because the degree to which such a site can help you depends mainly on how you use it. Simply joining a site won't make you a writer anymore than buying a racing car will make you a racing driver. Some online communities exist to do nothing more than post and swap work. Great if you want to make online friends, almost useless if you want to hone the skills that will bring money in for your writing. One obvious danger of such sites is that they represent the alternative to publishing. Their readership wouldn't have the inclination or the money to buy the work posted on the sites if it were commercially available. Whilst I don't want to insult everyone involved in such work I think it worth pointing out that some sites do exist mainly as a branch of social networking. It would be irresponsible to put names here but areas like fan-fiction (in which writers develop complicated narratives around characters already appearing in work produced by others), provide an obvious example. Some fan-fiction is inventive, clever, complex and entertaining. A lot of it isn't. And most of it isn't publishable because it centres around fictional characters and real life celebrities for whom image rights have already been claimed. For example, there was a spate in early fan-fiction for gay love stories involving characters from the first television series of *Star Trek*. Highly entertaining, but never likely to be sanctioned as official merchandise by the copyright holders to the lucrative *Star Trek* name.

Joining such sites and engaging with the membership might get you writing but I think any prospective professional writer should also consider how useful this is. If the primary motivation for members of a writers' site is to find people with the same obsessions and interests then it is possible that site will lead you *away* from being publishable. All the positive comments on your work may impress the people prepared to log on and read your comments for free but your appeal may be limited to these people, and you could spend years as a member and hundreds of hours writing for this audience, before you really consider how much better paid you could have been had you put the same effort into some other writing activities. So I strongly suggest to my *Professional* writing students that they limit their involvement to the kind of sites that present you with regular reality checks. A number of these sites are listed in publications like *The Writers' and Artists' Yearbook*.

The same publications also list a lot of agencies designed to help writers by offering professional services. Proofreading, editing, preparation of manuscripts for publication and reading manuscripts before advising on changes are all services offered widely. Some individuals and some companies provide such services. Others combine these services with publishing books, often at the expense of the author. We will consider self-funded 'vanity' publishing later in this book. But at this point it is worth looking at the professional help available at a price. I contacted a lot of people in compiling this book and didn't find many prepared to say kind things about the professional agencies out there offering help to aspiring writers. At the same time I didn't find anyone willing to put their name in print underneath some of the scurrilous comments I heard on the phone. It would be fair to say there is some cynicism about the kind of services offered. It would also be fair to say that most of the comments I heard were very general and often targeted *all* helping agencies without specifically naming any. You can probably imagine the kind of problems I unearthed.

There are agents and publishers who open submissions with covering letters suggesting the writer has paid for a professional edit of the manuscript and naming the 'professional' involved. A few sentences into the manuscript the agent or publisher targeted feels the whole thing is unpublishable because of some basic mistake, typically a flawed plot or turgid dialogue, and gives up. Put yourself in the position of the agent or publisher and you would probably accuse the 'professional' involved in editing the manuscript of being a rip-off merchant. Put yourself in the position of the author desperate for a break and you would probably understand why he or she would consider using such a service.

It is true there are some chancers out there. I once kept a letter from a 'freelance proofreader' and showed it to a few people because it was riddled with basic grammatical errors and a few spelling mistakes. I didn't contact the person responsible but it was obvious he hadn't intended this to be ironic.

On the other hand there are people in need of help, and some good help available. Freelance editors, proofreaders and the like do not tend to belong to any professional associations and they vary from sole traders who work by word-of-mouth to companies placing adverts in the newsstand writers' magazines. I heard lots of gripes about such people but at the same time there are lots of writers out there in clear need of help. At worst, it must be true, that there are desperate people going to other desperate people for help, paying for this help and still emerging well short of any standard acceptable to a publisher, media producer or agent. When this happens it is debateable who – if anyone – is at fault and doubtless everyone involved in the chain from idea to rejected submission could produce a well-argued paragraph explaining why everyone but themselves was at fault.

So, you have been warned, but the warnings do not mean everyone in the business is a crook. In fact, I would be a hypocrite to say that since I have done a couple of freelance jobs helping people prepare manuscripts for publication and also read manuscripts for publishers and done some editing work on other books and scripts. In almost all of these cases the people involved found me and asked for help. I have also turned down a number of others who have done the same. There is a clear need for the kind of services advertised in the writing magazines. If you want to avail yourself of such help it makes sense to treat the search in the same way you would treat running up any other substantial bill from a skilled tradesperson and stick to a few basic rules:

1. Enquire with more than one provider.
2. Get references or other evidence of these people having provided useful help.
3. Be really clear about what is 'in' and what is 'out' of any charge they make.
4. Make sure you get a few comparative prices from the people you approach to ensure you are not over-charged.

5. Discuss the job(s) thoroughly with them via phone or email before agreeing any payment.

A reputable operation will allow you to do all of the above. If people get difficult with you before you even start, that is probably a bad sign.

One provider who didn't get difficult and did provide answers about professional services when I asked them if they would help with this book project is Chapter One Promotions. Their website makes it clear they offer: 'Opportunities for aspiring and established writers.' In addition to providing critiques of manuscripts Chapter One are also involved in areas as diverse as literary agency and writing in prisons. Johanna Bernie at Chapter One answered the following questions.

1 - In four or five sentences can you give us an overview of the services provided by Chapter One?
At Chapter One Promotions we provide writing opportunities to develop both new and established writers and to support new writing talent.

We run highly structured workshops and a critiquing service for poetry, short stories and novels. Our International Short Story Competition and Novel Competition attract entries from around the world plus we host the Children's Story Competition and the Young Illustrator's Competition for upcoming writers and artists.

2 - I'm assuming there is no such thing as a typical customer, so could you outline the range of people accessing your services in a typical week?
Our clients are anything but typical but do hold similar traits

and that is to create strong pieces of writing, to learn how to write creatively and dramatically and to move closer to their goal of being a published author.

3 - Could you share one or two notable success stories from Chapter One and make clear what it was about these particular writers that helped them to achieve success?

Successes for those who have come through Chapter One Promotions have been in various guises. Some have managed to achieve their goal to be published, others have found a literary agent, and others have improved on their writing style and character development skills and feel that is where they need to be right now. We feel we are instrumental in helping writers to keep on writing, whether they chose to use our services or go to other providers to help them hone their skills. We've always strived to answer each submission to our literary agency, which not only highlights that we've read their manuscript but we also explain why the story works or doesn't quite work in a way that is not only constructive but positive and encouraging. No one likes a rejection letter so we try to offer a more personal response.

A relative newcomer to the field of writing, Jacqueline Walker attended our Pitch Your Novel Event a few years back and on the strength of the encouragement received sent her unfinished manuscript 'Pilgrim's State' out which was subsequently sold at auction to Hodder. Jacqueline is now in talks with production companies in regards to her book being made into a film.

Sally Siner came along to our Write Children's Fiction & Get Published workshop and on the strength of the work carried out at the workshop and previously written was taken on by the literary agent Pollinger Ltd.

These are just a few incidents that we know about that have filtered back to us. Some of our successes are seen as merely the stepping stone to bigger and greater achievements and in that process we are often overlooked, and sometimes even forgotten. But the key thing that we always remember are those that we help in small but meaningful ways. We have been a part of helping hundreds of writers in various guises, some to find their writing voice, to develop their skills, some we nurture and support and to guide and assist and that in itself is our greatest achievement.

4 - Without infringing privacy, what are the biggest problems you face with writers and what habits do your 'problem' cases present that put them beyond your help?

Writers are individuals who sometimes forget that others have been there before them and have survived the regiment of rejection letters, disappointments, frustrations and tensions of writing. Although their experiences aren't new, or unique, they are relevant and valid and sometimes writers need to be reassured, encouraged and listened to, as sometimes life gets in the way of that dream.

5 - What else would you want to explain about the services you offer that I haven't given you the opportunity to explain in the other questions?

Think like a writer, act like a writer. Write and rewrite. Place your work in a cupboard and forget about it. Come back to it with fresh eyes and read aloud. Listen to the nuances, the dialogue, and the tone. Is your mind drifting as you read, are you eager to turn the page? When your characters speak to you in your dreams or when you know what your protagonist would do in a real life situation then you are getting to grips with the essence of creative story telling. Learn the art of making a good story great and with those skills continue with your passion as it is this that makes you alive. Rejection is just a stepping stone that teaches you that you are not quite there yet. Believe in yourself, believe in your vision.

I have made several references to writewords.org.uk throughout the book. I should point out they are by no means the only online writers site offering membership of a community, access to contacts, mentorship and the like. In fact Anna Reynolds, editor of WriteWords points this out herself, namechecks a couple of competing sites and explains the differences between her operation and theirs in the interview that follows. There are a number of such sites listed in the sources section at the back of the book. But as a final example in this chapter on agents of change it is important that we look at the availability of writing communities online and let one explain how they help, and change, their members. Anna Reynolds of writewords.org.uk provided these answers:

1 - In four or five sentences can you give us an overview of the material offered at Writewords?

WriteWords has always aimed primarily to be a community for writers. So we offer a range of resources that we think writers at all stages might want, including; jobs, commissions, competitions, residencies and anything paid and unpaid. We have a comprehensive directory that lists publishers, editors, agents, literary consultancies, magazines, theatre and screen companies, poetry magazines and everything else writers need to help get their work out there, constantly updated through contacts with companies and individuals, and commented upon by members who've had a range of responses from sending their work out. We offer a huge range of online writing groups, where members can post their work- from a 4 line poem to chapters of a novel and everything in-between- all commented upon by other writers and by our Site Experts. There's a lively and active forum, where members post their writing concerns, queries, successes and worries. You can sell your work through us, do a course run by experts in their specific writing field, and showcase yourself to people who might be scouting for writers. We also run interviews with leading writers, agents, publishers and editors, and often have masterclasses with, for example, literary agencies, agents and publishers - recently Egmont and Cornerstones.

2 - It's obvious from the showcase pages there is no such thing as a typical member, so could you outline the range of people accessing your services?
Everyone from complete beginners, who post a forum thread saying they've just started their first ever piece of creative writing, through seasoned writers who are several drafts into a novel that they are workshopping on the site, through writers who are in the middle of the process of sending their work out for submission to publishers, agents, magazines, theatre/film companies, all the way to writers who are published/produced/often bestselling and still very much wanting to keep in touch with other writers and be part of our online community. It's a great benefit that people who've 'made it' stay with the site and give their advice, thoughts and experience to people who are very much at the beginning of that journey. And it works the other way too- it's easy to become jaundiced and fixated on whether the next book deal will come off or not, so to have that continuing dialogue with newer writers is refreshing and reminds us all why we're doing what we're doing.

3 - The site offers a lot of opportunities to update on news, chase up information on publishers etc. Do writers who use your site to achieve success ever feed back to you on how Writewords has contributed to this?
Yes, quite often- we've always encouraged members to feedback on their writing lives outside the site, and writers let us know, continually, when they have achieved success through the resources and workshopping features of the site. We've been credited in several books and short story collections. It's rare that people just disappear, in fact. If you have a look at the Successes

area, you'll see how often we've been involved in and thanked for providing the arena for writers, new and experienced, to try out their work before going public.

4 - Without infringing privacy, what are the biggest problems you face with writers and what habits do your 'problem' cases present?

We're an online community, so of course there have been people, throughout the years, who have been... challenging. Our challenges usually fit a pattern; people who are joining the site to express their discontent with not getting anywhere with their writing, and want to have a fight- they're not that bothered who it's with. Sometimes, this results in them being offensive to other members, and we politely warn them away from incendiary language, personal insults etc. If they don't heed this, we ask them to leave; our concern is for the majority, and to keep the site a safe place for writers to post their material and their thoughts and experiences. Often, people don't realise how their behaviour has been received, and they tone down their language and become part of the community. Writers putting their work online feel exposed if someone attacks their writing. We've adapted to this in various ways, for example, introducing a three tier system to feedback, so that if you ask for comments, you can choose from 'Be gentle with me', to 'Be tough- I can take it'. And we've got clear guidelines on what's acceptable and what's not.

5 - There are a lot of other writers' sites out there. Do you have any opinions on the kind of sites that are most useful to people looking to gain a break as a writer, and which might be the least useful?

I know from our members that some find YouWriteOn useful, others admire Authonomy- they do different things to us, which is great. We're less about trying to push people forward towards a book deal or some kind of agent/publisher attention, and more about working hard to foster a supportive, creative and mutually useful community. When we've considered changing things, it makes the site feel somehow divisive between the published and the not published- and in any case, lots of our members aren't actively seeking the approbation of the publisher/agent community, but simply wanting to be part of what often feels like a big, friendly, very mixed writing group. That's how we've always seen it anyway- as if it were real and not just virtual, a big commune with many differently themed rooms.

6 - What else would you want to explain about the services you offer that I haven't given you the opportunity to explain in the other questions?

I guess what we're most interested in developing is choice. We run a lot of online writers' groups, but if there isn't the exact one you want- Canadian Lesbian Vampire Fiction, say- then suggest it to us, and we'll set it up. We ask members to tell us what they want, and when we make changes to the site, whether creative or practical, we ask for feedback. We openly solicit people's experiences when they contact a publisher or agent- let us know if they treat you badly, or are delightful. We ask members to suggest themselves, or others they know, for interview- as long as they're interesting and their experience may be useful to others, we'll go for it. I think that's one of the most powerful aspects of the site. Creativity, choice, empowerment and support....just like your ideal, real-world writing group.

So, at the start of the chapter I said we would be looking at: *getting and finding agents, also looking at other areas of help and mentorship available including websites, courses, professional mentors etc. Comments from agents and others involved in finding and managing talent.* As with the other very long chapters in this book we could have done more. But, to my mind at least, we have done enough to cover the ground in this chapter. We have defined all the areas, considered pros and cons and allowed those involved to speak for themselves. As with the other chapters, this is just a start. If you need to follow up any of the routes outlined here I strongly advise you spend time on research, contacting the right people, comparing their responses and preparing your own work in a manner that best suits the people you choose to target.

7 Out of the Box

This chapter deals with: *Alternative strategies for making things happen. Case studies of writing success through unorthodox routes.*

The phrase 'thinking outside of the box' AKA 'thinking out of the box' has become something of a cliché in management speak for the art of generating ideas and solutions to problems which qualify as unconventional or different. Its main use here is to focus this short chapter and some of the ideas within the chapter. Like many writers I have had a love/hate relationship with the notion of thinking outside of the box. On the one hand, I have been fairly good at the unusual and unconventional work, even when some of my employment was highly conventional. On the other hand I have – like many others – become tired at the way 'thinking outside the box' has become an obligatory part of some planning meetings. One particularly annoying feature of the whole thing in some areas is the way *any* new idea with even the remotest sniff of novelty about it can be claimed as an example of thinking outside the box. The phrase is in danger of becoming so over-used as to be meaningless. But that shouldn't concern us here.

This chapter follows the work on how to get a break, how to sustain that break and how to get help from others – like agents – in helping you to achieve your most ambitious targets.

The main point of this chapter is to consider alternative, outrageous and unlikely options with the potential to take you closer to achieving your dreams. The terminology is less important than considering the options.

By its very nature thinking outside the box can often have a random, one-off, high-novelty and unique quality to it. So attempting to capture the essence of the spontaneity is a paradoxical act. The best I think we can achieve in this chapter is to look at some general approaches, with examples, and consider what these might mean for you.

In fact, we have already touched on some such examples in the chapters preceding this. Accidental as it was, the application letter I sent, signed as Idi Amin, to a training firm shows the most eye-catching and off the wall approaches might work in some circumstances. I also explained how I have twice approached high-street retail chains with suggestions about producing written material to sell in their shops and promote specific brands on sale there. Since there are confidentially agreements in place on both approaches I can't discuss this in more detail. But there is a general principle here. One type of thinking outside the box simply involves approaching someone who could benefit from your talents and having the front to point out why you, and they, are the perfect combination. One superb example of this in practice is provided by Davey Spens, the author of a book you may well have seen called *Frothy Tales*. The book sold for £1 in Costa Coffee shops in 2009 and marked the final phase of Davey's stint as the first ever Writer in Residence for Costa Coffee. Most writers in residence have to compete for their residencies and the perks involved. When I booked Davey to speak to a group of under-graduates he told a slightly different story.

Davey Spens was appointed the first ever Costa Coffee Writer in Residence because he approached them and suggested such a post might be a good idea. Davey also provided one of the best received and most entertaining short talks I have seen delivered to our students. The point he made repeatedly, and made well, was that it can pay to be innovative and follow your instincts. So, his Costa Coffee approach worked well, his attempt to gather a few like-minded individuals and plant a forest in Cornwall was less successful, but it was typical of his creativity which appears to recognize less boundaries on what should and shouldn't happen than many others recognize. Not surprisingly, Davey has worked successfully in writing and generating ideas across a range of projects, and it is highly likely his best and most eye-catching work is still ahead of him. A solid belief in future success often marks out those who think outside the box.

This book has centred on writing and being a writer but it is worth noting that publishing and producing work also lends itself to thinking creatively. One taboo area in publishing for years has involved older authors. Despite the odd breakthrough book, Sylvia Smith was 55 when *Misadventures* was finally published. Sid Smith had worked in manual labour, traveled widely and eventually become a journalist. He was sub-editing on *The Times* when – aged 50 – his first novel, *Something Like A House* became a critical success and won the Whitbread First Novel Award. These success stories were unusual but in recent years publishers have been more willing to take a risk on promoting much older authors. Diana Athill had spent a career in publishing and written her own books but it was the success of *Somewhere Towards the End* with its pragmatic and accepting considerations of old age that finally brought her a national profile, a few months short of her 90th birthday. Myrrah Stanford Smith had no track record as a published author. A retired teacher, her work in local drama and some vivid writing about an old fashioned swashbuckling hero – Nick Talbot – living in Elizabethan times secured her a three book deal, at the age of 82.

Publishers are in the business of long-term investment so the age of a writer is often taken into consideration when deals are being considered. But the age of an audience matters too and Diana Athill's work represented the elderly in a way largely ignored by British publishing beforehand. In the case of Myrrah Stanford Smith her age on signing the deal led to profile raising publicity.

One problem I have with the notion of thinking outside the box is that – on occasion – I am confronted with people, usually students, who appear incapable of doing anything else. They can endlessly generate clever, unusual and novel (as in original) ideas. For them 'thinking outside the box' might mean doing what everyone else does. Sometimes the simplest ideas can be examples of original thinking. Rosalinda Hutton wasn't one of the students I am talking about but she was one of the first to enrol when we started our course in 1999. She was also a notable success, by the end of her studies she had written a column for a local paper and had also begun the radio play *Constance* that would eventually help OneWord Radio to win the Sony Award for Digital Station of the Year. It took Rosalinda a few more years to make her major publishing breakthrough, landing a contract with an imprint of Random House for a 'misery memoir' *Cry and you Cry Alone*. When she emailed me to tell me the news I was stunned, not by the fact that Linda's talents had finally been recognized by one of the majors but by the story she told me about her upbringing. In two years of working with her on a range of assignments I had never heard her outline some of the strange events of her extremely varied childhood. I hadn't required students to share their life stories and Rosalinda had decided to focus on more elaborate projects than simply editing and presenting her past.

We will look at print-on-demand books in the next chapter but it is worth thinking about the possibilities they offer. We have already discussed charity projects, like the book I worked on for a hospice a few years ago. Print-on-demand books offer writers the chance to get work out for little or no money, the catch is that the books are only printed and sold when someone puts in a definite order. On the other hand, the outlay, even for a book generating an ISBN and – therefore – being orderable in bookshops and appearing on the main online sites like Amazon, can be negligible. The exact costs are discussed in the next chapter but the point when it comes to thinking outside the box is that writing and publishing books is now at a cost level allowing anyone with time, ambition and some money on hand, to take advantage. In the next chapter I'll explain some projects I was involved in, but at this stage it is worth pointing out that – even if you have no cash on hand – becoming a published author is now at the cost level of a fairly expensive birthday present. So if you want to think outside the box just ask yourself what you could write a book about, and how this book might enhance your CV, help you make contacts etc.

Cheap information technology drives print-on-demand publishing and it also drives most of the online opportunities for writers. In terms of thinking outside the box, one obvious strategy is simply to take your writing talents into areas you know nothing about and find sites, and online opportunities to write on subjects you have to research and check out. This isn't as stupid as it sounds, in fact: if you visited the offices of some publishers who specialize in trade journals aimed at very specialist areas of the working world, you would find a great many of their 'journalists' are far from expert on the subjects of the journals. For years I taught students near to such a publisher and there were teenagers being taken into the publishing house who would find themselves writing specialist trade journals in a matter of weeks. This made sense for several reasons, firstly the students had the skills to write and research, secondly they were cheap to employ, thirdly they worked to editors with some subject knowledge and finally a lot of the material in the journals was provided by experts from outside the publishing company. When this information arrived in the form of press releases or lengthy accounts of break-throughs in areas like the development of marine glue the students simply had to edit the words to fit the house style of the trade magazine(s) employing them.

So, if your thinking about your writing future hits barriers when you consider subjects, consider the approach above. Better still, visit a website like lifehack (*www.lifehack.org*), which works to find writers and get them covering the widest possible range of subjects. It would be fair to say that writing teachers have mixed feelings about such sites, but if you just want to tackle a short piece of writing and push yourself out of your comfort zone such sites are worth a look.

Sites like lifehack also give you basic tips on thinking outside the box. In their case they list strategies like taking a shower, studying a religion you know little about, taking a class on an unfamiliar subject and working backwards from a goal. My own favourite of their strategies, and one that has worked for me, involves asking a child about a subject.

One advantage of simply trying a target practice approach of lining up possible opportunities and sniping away is that it can produce opportunities you don't expect. Unfortunately the best personal story I can tell you here concerns what is – without any doubt – the stupidest decision I ever made as a writer. But please bear with me through this story because it will lead us to one wonderful fact about professional writing that hasn't been addressed in this book so far, and tends to be absent in most other books on writing for a living.

When I was just starting out as a writer I did adopt the literary target practice approach. Quite literally buying different magazines and papers, scouring them to figure out where the opportunities might be and then working up ideas I thought might be of interest and submitting them. It led to some interesting developments, for example: *Viz* comic took some of my work in the same week I sold my first piece to the *Times Educational Supplement*. *Viz* paid better and make less editorial changes and that led eventually to a period when I was working for a whole collection of comics, a stand up comedian and a range of other comedy markets. Some of my work involved parodying the styles of writers in a range of genres and this eventually brought an unusual offer. We don't need to bore ourselves with exactly how this happened but within a couple of years of starting serious comedy writing I was sent a section of a script in the post and asked if I could tweak it to make it funnier and solve a fairly obvious problem with the plot. I did both and sent it back at which point I was asked to attend a meeting in London. This had all happened quickly and in such a covert way that I hadn't really had time to think about what was going on, but the fee for the editing of the script was generous. It would still be generous today, and all of this happened over 20 years ago.

The meeting took place in a very plush office and I was told to address the person across the table by surname. Despite the formality, the discussions were very positive. They liked my work and wanted me to do more. The 'job' involved doctoring the scripts of other writers, mainly by way of devising plot devices to speed up the action, adding occasional jokes, and working to contract at very short notice. I was also to maintain confidentiality over the all the work I saw, including the script I'd tweaked as part of my interview for the job. It all sounded like a great opportunity. In writing terms you might regard such work as the equivalent of welding, you put in solid joins on the main structure of work and make every effort to hide your contribution. I had responded to the challenge I had been set but this work had found me, and I wasn't that experienced at the time. Because of the things that subsequently went wrong I have never been able to discover exactly how I was located and auditioned for this area of employment. I can't even say for certain who – as in the company or organization – I would have been working for.

The opportunity unraveled when I got my contract in the post. Most of it was as I expected but there was a clause stating I would indemnify my new employers against any legal action resulting from my work. In other words, any actionable mistakes on my part would come out of my pocket. I had ignored this issue on the few other occasions I had been faced with similar clauses in the past because – frankly – I wasn't worth suing. But this contract came a few weeks after I first took out a mortgage and there were others, as in my wife and eldest child, who were now in a position to be punished for my mistakes. I took the contract to a local law firm for a fixed fee interview, was advised to ask for changes and duly returned it unsigned with my request. That – pretty much – ended my chances, though I was paid for the first script. Over the years I've discussed this with others in the game and on the odd occasion I've come across somebody with an inkling of this secret area of 'welding' they've tended to look away and be diplomatic but leave me in no doubt this was monumental mistake on my part. Probably not quite on a par with a former work colleague of mine who turned down the chance to be the bass player in the band Queen, but certainly a mistake that could be counted in tens of thousands of pounds.

I would never have been so stupid as to knowingly create legal trouble and over the years such clauses in contracts have become more commonplace and I have signed plenty of contracts with them in. You'll notice the odd pulled punch in this book and the odd occasion when I don't name a particular person or organization, 'nuff said. I couldn't tell you which script I worked on if I wanted to. I can recall clearly what was happening in the pages I tweaked, and what changes I inserted, but I have never seen it produced and there was no writer's name or title of the work supplied. Though it was fairly obvious where it was placed in terms of market.

There are a few things to learn from this story in terms of thinking outside of the box as a writer. Firstly, there are potentially high earnings out there for people prepared to apply their skills in a general way and not be too precious about developing their own individual ideas. So literary 'target practice' can pay off in ways you don't always appreciate ahead of time. Secondly, this example proves that putting it about can pay. I was employable because my 'grab at any opportunity' approach to comedy writing had seen me mimicking writing styles as diverse as Leonard Cohen's prose style and dispatches from the Crimean War; I know this much because that discussion was part of the interview. Thirdly this example leads us to one fact often over-looked by many hopeful writers; **it is possible to earn very good money producing work nobody ever sees.**

Given the uncertainties involved this isn't recommended as a career strategy, but it is worth considering. In addition to script doctoring there are also companies buying in works, like complete scripts, and some others simply needing people to work covertly on material. At the top end this work is lucrative, and it tends to find people who have proven they can turn their hand to a range of things. I have done some of this work over the years, though nothing in the financial league of the work I turned down after buying my first house.

It is also worth considering a close relative to the covert editing and doctoring work, the literary mash-up. 'Mashing' or colliding material from a number of sources has been a feature of the music industry for years. Some performers have built careers on their skills, notably The Artful Dodger, who based his stage name on his ability to sample work and hide the original sample so well in the finished product that the original creators and – crucially – their record company couldn't spot it. There have been literary equivalents of such work for years, the underground press of the late sixties followed by photocopying and fanzine culture brought about lots of busy looking pages and lively productions but until recently this approach has been largely confined to the less profitable areas of writing work. Perhaps because most of those copying and reinventing work haven't seen it as their main area of writing. In the music industry the rich rewards available for sampling, mashing and re-inventing over the last 25 years have led many of the strongest talents in the industry into that area and performers like Eminem and Jay Z have come to be seen as much more than musicians. One notable example, Danger Mouse, openly states in interviews he is an 'auteur' in other words, someone with an overall guiding vision for his work. In one interview he went as far as to say: 'Musically, there is no one who has the career I want. That's why I have to use film directors as a model.'

Danger Mouse's work is generally high profile, though his

most celebrated album has never been legally released. *The Grey Album* features vocal tracks from Jay Z's *Black Album* mashed with musical loops taken mainly from The Beatles album *The Beatles*, and better known as 'The White Album.' The sheer conceit of artists like Danger Mouse has brought them attention and notoriety and the better able talents amongst these acts have managed to turn that into opportunities and income.

For all the imaginative genius shown by the highest profile writers using words as their medium the same lateral thinking hasn't always been evident. There are a few glorious examples of mashing ideas to create new work that do show the potential value of thinking well outside the box. One obvious trend at the moment involves the same mashing approach used by musicians in which an original work is – quite literally – cut and pasted with new material. Perhaps the best example of the current crop is *Pride and Prejudice and Zombies,* credited to Jane Austen and Seth Grahame-Smith. Seth Grahame-Smith took the original text and rewrote it. So the original opens with the classic line:

IT is a truth universally acknowledged, that a single man in possession of a good fortune must be in want of a wife.

The *Zombies* book opens with:

IT is a truth universally acknowledged that a zombie in possession of brains must be in want of more brains.

The joke is obvious, but also impressive, especially given the multiple imitations spawned and the advancement of Grahame-Smith's career to include a sizeable movie deal for his mash-up novel. In fact, anyone with reasonable computer skills can attempt something similar because a number of online sites like Project Gutenberg include complete texts for many out of copyright works. How long this particular gimmick will last is anyone's guess, but the potential to deface history and generate new meanings is far from exhausted.

Mashing up of a different kind has always been central to some of the most original thinking amongst writers. Another best-selling book, continually in print since 1982, is *The Tao of Pooh.* A gently funny gem that attempts to explain the way of Taoism through the example of Winnie the Pooh. The running joke being that Pooh himself appears as a character, continually discusses the subject with the author and remains unconvinced he is the perfect means by which to explain the whole subject. The readers get to be amused because – in classic comedy fashion – they are smarter than the main character and can see all along that Pooh is indeed an embodiment of the whole idea. This unlikely combination became a cult best-seller, promoted mainly by word of mouth and given as gift.

The same 'gift book' market also saw a more recent unlikely best seller with Nicey and Wifey's *A Nice Sit Down and a Cup of Tea.* The book offers pretty much what it says on the cover. An entire chapter is devoted to little more than the various means of storing biscuits, loving descriptions of cake varieties abound and the joys of simply sitting down and enjoying a cuppa are never far away. Like Rosalinda Hutton's revelation that her best-seller lurked in a place so obvious she hadn't looked there before *A Nice Sit Down...* comes from a brand of thinking outside the box that celebrates the simple and obvious. There is a website covering the same ground at *www.nicecupofteaandasitdown.com*.

Seeing the obvious in a new way has been something of a trend in new writing in recent years. There have been detailed books devoted to subjects like a history of Cod, as in the fish, and salt. The *Cod* book in particular was a success because it brought up a fascinating history. Exploiting cod stocks, the dietary benefits of eating fish and the seas in which they flourish have all influenced the development of western civilization. Where other histories put this point in the margins, *Cod* pushed the history of societies like the Vikings to the margins and put the fish in the spotlight.

Areas like television develop, exploit and ditch ideas at such a fast rate that there is no real dividing line between thinking to develop new product and thinking outside of the box. Pretty much every conceivable type of work is being developed somewhere by somebody all the time. For all that there is scope for people capable of generating different and interesting ideas to get noticed. One idea of mine that got a 'bite' (i.e. some attention) but was ultimately rejected was little more than a novelty. Back in the days when the channel Live TV combined 24 hour broadcasting with all manner of budget novelty presentations I put an idea to them. Bear in mind this channel had a glove puppet bunny – called Newsy Rabbit – that 'reacted' to the news bulletins. The same channel also pioneered topless darts and showed live pictures of a fish tank in the early hours of the morning. I wrote to them suggesting they interrupt the fish tank with live pictures from a roving camera and the camera went out specifically to find security guards and others sleeping on the job in the middle of the night. The strength of the idea was its ability to find an audience for a channel that was apparently broadcasting to almost nobody at that time of day. The idea died because even the minimal budget required to make my idea work was too much for their graveyard shift. But the interest I had showed that on the fringes of the media there will always be someone willing to listen if you can find a way of increasing an audience.

These days the opportunity reach that audience is open to anyone capable of producing material and loading it onto youtube, myspace and their ilk. Given the range and diversity of material on these sites it is hard to say exactly where thinking outside of the box on these sites stops and starts. Basically, everything is available all the time and the problem isn't one of producing work so much as producing work that will find an audience, when there are millions of options available and attention spans are short. From a writing point of view the best option is probably to produce something that has strength as an idea and the ability to develop its own narrative. Certainly, the longer term successes in areas like youtube seem to combine both of these. For example; Where the Hell is Matt? A sequence of short dance videos in which a chunky young American travels the globe before facing the camera and performing the same bizarre dance routine. These videos have developed to the point that people around the world now recognize Matt and the video clips show them joining in. One clip filmed in central Barcelona shows Matt starting to dance before being rushed and engulfed by a mob who pour in from both sides of the screen. Matt's work appears as an unofficial and well-intentioned goodwill mission. The whole thing began as a joke but two world-wide trips have now been financed by Stride Gum and Matt's celebrity continues to grow. *www.wherethehellismatt.com*.

There is also the work of US singer/songwriter Bo Burnham. Burnham specializes in lyrically complex and clever comedy songs, often built around twisted views of romance and mature observations on life. It is cynical but also gloriously funny, the videos earned him a massive following partly because he was a teenager when he started to post them. He was still, just, in his teens when he signed to do his first, and triumphant, season at the Edinburgh Festival in 2010. By the end of that season he had been shortlised for their annual comedy award.

Matt and Bo Burnham offer the kind of skills that have been available in entertainment for years but at least the cleverness of their thinking made each a word of mouth success and allowed them to find a massive audience without having to pass all the usual obstacles of auditions, having their acts shaped by managers and the like.

One element of thinking outside the box that has worked for a few creative people over the years involves creating work covertly, or using an indirect or stealthy approach to getting contacts and getting a break. Anonymous work can serve a range of purposes and some high-profile people have used anonymity. Stephen King, consistently one of the best selling writers in the world, spent a few years producing additional novels as Richard Bachman. The move served one main purpose, to allow King to publish more than one book a year. It also allowed him and his publisher to examine how much of his success was down to branding and how much to talent. One Bachman novel – *Thinner* – sold 28,000 copies (impressive for an unknown author with little publicity support), the same book achieved ten times that sale when King's involvement became public knowledge.

By their very nature those thinking outside the box to do covert work or similar are hard to identify whilst they are working to achieve an aim. I did come across a few examples in compiling this book and on condition of maintaining the anonymity of the instigator of the following project I can share one such story. Unusually this project is a literary agency, but one that started in a slightly different way to others.

"I think I should lay my cards on the table straight away and fill you in about this agency. The agency was formed to help to promote the writing of two unpublished authors. One of them had just completed a novel, had canvassed all available UK publishers, and found that without exception they would only accept work via an agent; she then approached every single literary agent in the country and was turned down by them all. The only course of action open seemed to be to form a new literary agency! That's where I came in; I had been involved in a range of work in the literary sector, I knew a lot about tracking down rare books, niche markets and had a lot of other useful background knowledge. I was also aware of the way the internet was eating away at some of the work I did, so forming an agency seemed a positive move. To establish bona fides in the field, I put the business "out there", got an entry in *The Writer's Handbook*, established a web site, and started to consider other authors – in short we acted as professionally as possible. In some ways we are like any other agency, we have taken on clients, kept other details on file and responded politely to everyone who has approached us. However, the main point of starting and, to some extent the point of continuing, is to use the bona-fides now established to push the careers of the writers we initially identified, because we continue to believe in their work. In reality we really need a major success with one of the original clients for this to become viable and to be more than a hobby. However, for fairly obvious reasons, our presence online and in *The Writer's Handbook* doesn't make an issue of this fact."

So the agency in question has become a regular agency somewhat by default, having set-up, and attracted clients in the same way as the others. The thinking outside the box element – relating to the original clients – still continues. When I showed the copy above to a few people involved in the writing world their initial reaction was to grab a copy of one of the main writing reference books and try and spot the agency. To date I have heard nine guesses, all of them wrong. So the agency in question appear to have achieved their aim of looking like any other small operation when approached by the general public. Creating a front whilst pursuing a personal agenda, with a passion for what you are doing, ranks amongst the most dedicated approaches when it comes to thinking outside of the box. But, the previous chapters have made it obvious that dedication and attention to detail under-pin a lot of success stories. I wish them well and thank them for allowing me to share the story above. If they ever declare their real intentions and name the authors they formed the agency to help, remember where you read it first.

One final example I want to present makes a key point about thinking outside the box: sometimes this strategy is best used in a developing situation. Spontaneity and adaptability can be key components of the whole thing. There are lots of examples of this in writing history and doubtless you have experienced incidents in your own life when someone just reacted to a situation in a creative way and achieved something positive as a result. One developing story I have been aware of concerns a friend of mine and his daughter. Dick is a writer, his daughter Megan has been involved in a number of different areas of work, including working for a magazine linked to the film industry. The pair of them tried one of the most difficult jobs for any creative writers, getting money for a film. One element of their lives is that Dick retains his original US accent; Megan – brought up in the UK – passes easily for British. Megan is married so they have different surnames. Therefore, many of those dealing with them as they sought film funding didn't see a father and daughter. Dick explains two key moments in their work:

1 - Could you briefly explain the situation that led to you re-inventing yourself in terms of appearance as you sought funding?

We had a good story to turn in to a script; it took place in another country, which meant some travel in the beginning and it was historical, requiring research, to me always more pleasurable than the job of writing. Serious investors want to know where they go from the first pitch, meaning that we needed a slate of four films, so that along with the original script I got busy with at least the synopses and outlines of another three, hoping to look thoroughly professional. The other country was China and the stated 'we' was myself and my daughter, who by that time had lived in Shanghai a number of years. As producer, hers was the job of finding the money; I had no experience of asking for a gigantic sum for something I had written, but together we went around London banks, production companies, distribution companies, and almost anyone who looked like he might have paid off his mortgage. Over several years we even traveled to LA and San Francisco, coming away with some compliments about being able to work together harmoniously, otherwise it was the smell of one-star hotels in our luggage and no money.

A word about my daughter: she knows the language of movies, having worked on trade magazines for film; she is knowledgeable, determined and voluble with a definite British accent and knows theatrical windows, presales, and how to value territories. I am by her definition an old guy who speaks American and I tended to let her do the heavy lifting in our pitches. I rarely said I was the writer unless asked; if it happened I would admit it and there would often be a kind of curious respect for anyone wandering into money circles without a sidearm. Nobody really wants the writer around after he leaves his script and gets his money; the Hollywood definition of stupidity is the actress who sleeps with the scriptwriter.

2 - Could you give us a succinct version of the story about you trailing around LA and Dick doing the talking, whilst those talking to you failed to realise you were father and daughter?

Next came Cannes; my daughter had gone there for several years representing her magazine so it was a natural. She said when we pitch together I notice they turn to you. I said maybe they like me more – anyway you do most of the talking; maybe they just get tired. No, she said, you have a certain gravitas. I said only when I wear a tie, and I'm not doing that again. (Very early, when we had an appointment with the finance director at an upscale London bank filled with frock coats I wore a suit only to find that the technical expert we had with us came in a tie-dyed shirt and a vest embroidered with Looney Tunes figures – he was the one who was listened to intently.)

No, she said, it's the gravitas. We are not related and you are going to be the finance expert. I'll shut up except to fill in for you. You're the American, I'm English. And I'll defer. It was thus that we had many meetings, a few good times and we got a commitment for $250,000 from a co-producer that year at Cannes.

Thinking about that later I sometimes wonder whether we would have gone on without that kind of boost, so the fact that the producer's company went belly up nine months later is immaterial.

The point of this chapter is to explain: *Alternative strategies for making things happen. Case studies of writing success through unorthodox routes.* We have covered all of these areas. We could cover them for another 10,000 words without even scratching the surface of what it means to think outside the box. I hope something in the examples collected here has made you think, or inspired you to try something a little different in your writing.

8 In POD We Trust

This chapter covers: *Print-on-demand publishing, and other developing areas of low-cost independent publication for writers. Interviews and comments from authors using this method.*

It also rounds off the chapters covering how to get a break as a writer. All that remains after this are details of contacts and a glossary of useful terms. This chapter belongs at the end because the work discussed here is best employed by writers with some sense of their own skills, what they want and how they intend to achieve it. In terms of low-cost and developing areas of publishing we need to cover three different elements **vanity publishing, self-publishing** and **print-on-demand (POD) publishing.**

It should be obvious if you have read this book from the start that I worked hard to find interviewees involved in all the major subject areas covered. I did the same when it came to vanity publishing but finding anyone who would admit to being involved in vanity publishing proved impossible. I spoke to people I was convinced were involved in it, they disagreed, and I am not about to name them here. We should – however – consider why these three areas of publishing form the final chapter and what they might mean for you. We should start by defining what each term means.

Johnathon Clifford claims to have coined the term 'vanity publishing' in 1959, a claim supported by his own site and Wikipedia. The term had been around before then but the timing of Clifford's usage of the term to describe book publishers is significant. Book publishing has been getting steadily cheaper as the technology involved becomes easier to use and offers more copies for less money. By the early 1960s there were firms, especially in the USA and UK, capable of turning the words of aspiring writers into product, if the writers paid. Prior to this time the term had generally been used to refer to an individual and – usually – rich individual publishing a single work.

Such behaviour wasn't limited to book publishing. The same era saw the first significant developments of recording studios allowing anyone with the money and inclination to cut their own record. For all the low quality dross that resulted we shouldn't forget that Elvis Presley was discovered when he went to cut a record for his mother. So vanity projects have unearthed significant talents.

'Vanity' when applied to book publishing has become something of a pejorative term. Nobody I know uses it in a positive context. The reasons for this are fairly obvious. The Wikipedia – for example – stating: *Although vanity presses are a legitimate publishing option, the term "vanity press" has become derogatory, and is often used to imply that an author who self-publishes using such a service is only publishing out of vanity, and that his or her work could not be commercially successful, an assumption that is not true in all cases. In other words, a work published by a vanity press is typically assumed to be unpublishable elsewhere.*

I will second that observation, and point out that in researching this chapter I rang some operations I thought were obvious vanity presses. As with all the other cold-calling I did for this book I explained who I was and what I was doing. In general this part of the conversation went well, most of the companies were keen on free publicity and keen to tell someone who they were and what they did. The problems started when I explained I was looking for an example of the kind of operation regarded as a vanity publisher. At this point about half the operations I contacted denied they were vanity publishers and either sought to end the call or explained that I *had to* explain how their case was different. Many of these publishers had strong opinions on other companies who were vanity publishers. One irony being that – three or four phone calls into this research – I had already spoken to some of the companies outed by their competitors as vanity operations, and – of course – they had gone to great trouble to explain why they weren't.

I'm assuming you are still following this. But I understand that the arguments get circular and hard to follow very quickly.

My job throughout this book has been to explain things and try and let those involved have the chance to speak directly to you. For fairly obvious reasons, this fails when it comes to vanity publishing. The truth as I experienced it seems to be that everyone involved in operations that are regarded throughout publishing as vanity publishers has their own take on what they do, their own arguments about why they are *not* vanity publishers and why others *are* vanity publishers. From my experience calling and asking questions, these arguments often fail to address the main points that lead others to identify an operation as vanity publishing. The usual arguments about why a company is NOT involved in vanity publishing revolve around a few key points. Firstly, many companies define themselves as doing something else. I have heard partnership publishing (i.e. they are in 'partnership' with the author, the author gives money, they give time). 'Specialist' publishing (i.e. all their projects are specific and unique and would therefore be handled without sympathy at a major publisher) and many 'vanity' publishers say they are providing a 'self-publishing' service. The last one, I think, is a fair point and one we will investigate soon. Self-publishing and vanity publishing exist side by side, often in a very uneasy relationship.

The one thing you discover quickly in trying to research vanity publishing concerns the low standing it maintains in the publishing industry. Many of those involved in commercial publishing, book reviewing, self-publishing and related areas have a particular hatred of vanity publishing and are happy to express it in forthright terms, so long as they aren't quoted directly in books like this. 'Parasites,' 'crooks,' 'bastards' and 'scum' were amongst the words I heard, and these words came from all ends of the publishing industry, and sometimes from people not prone to swearing.

Interestingly, I once had a conversation with the editor of a magazine which – in my opinion at least – takes significant advertising from vanity publishers. The conversation resulted from me ringing them up a few years ago and trying to convince them to cover the story of the book I had written with hospice patients. The magazine lost interest very quickly when they realized the publishing had been paid for by a charity grant, informing me the book was a 'vanity project' and on principle they didn't do articles on vanity projects. I made the mistake of hitting back with a question about why they took so much advertising from vanity publishers if they had such an aversion to writing about their works. Let's just say the conversation went downhill very quickly after that. Thankfully we did get some national coverage for that hospice book but the fact that a magazine being supported by adverts from publishers who ask authors for cash upfront was still averse to writing about vanity publishing says a lot about the way nobody wants to be associated, or tainted, with any involvement in the whole thing.

In the absence of a vanity publisher standing up and defining the sector the best we can do is to use the definition developed by Johnathon Clifford. Since first coining the phrase Clifford has devoted much of his time to combating the worst practices of vanity publishing and his site *www.vanitypublishing.info* contains a user's guide to vanity publishing and offers free download documents containing advice for authors. This is more than work to Clifford, it is something of a crusade, and his efforts have changed the law, and protected writers from some rogue traders. Clifford's site notes:

Since 1994 I have organised a one-man campaign to insist on truth and honesty in the publishing world and – at last – in 2008 the law was changed to enable the authorities to deal with the rogues in the publishing world.

During the last 18 years I have been instrumental in closing down the 13 worst vanity publishers and – according to an independent report – have with my "voluntary help, guidance and advice, saved or retrieved in excess of £25 million for authors world wide."

The free download guides available from vanitypublishing.info include a definition of vanity publishing accepted by the Advertising Standards Authority: *Vanity publishing, also self-styled (often inaccurately) as "subsidy", "joint-venture", "shared-responsibility" or even "self" publishing is a service whereby authors are charged to have their work published. Vanity publishers generally offer to publish a book for a specific fee, or offer to include short stories, poems or other literary or artistic material in an anthology which the authors are then invited to buy.* Johnathon Clifford's document goes on to state:

Therefore any company that wants to charge to publish your book is – by definition – a vanity publisher, whatever they may try to tell you to the contrary.

We will examine the contrary arguments of publishers in areas like self-publishing and print-on-demand later in this chapter, and look at case studies from authors who have used these services.

At its worst vanity publishing exploits the ambitions we all have as writers. It preys on naïve people who want to get their work out to an audience. Interviewing potential undergraduates I have been presented with their 'published' works and seen material with spelling mistakes, crudely laid out and clearly unfit for commercial sale. Vanity publishing is at its worst when the unwary are led by the unscrupulous to fund deals that serve only to sustain the parasitic operations of a pariah sector of the publishing industry, hell-bent on little other than its own survival.

Johnathon Clifford's site, and – hopefully – the opportunities identified and explained in this book, should help you avoid this world. But before we move on to consider sectors who offer different services, I think it worth our while to stop and consider vanity.

Technically speaking vanity can mean 'conceit' or 'futility'. In terms of vanity publishing it is obvious that in the worst cases, the two are combined to tragic effect. The difference between conceit and futility isn't always easy to spot ahead of time. If a book submission praised by your friends and family gets knocked back 20 times, was it futile to write it? That isn't an easy question to answer, and some of the greatest literary works of all time have been rejected with cruel condemnations. If you get a copy of the book *Rotten Rejections* by Andre Bernard or go to the page on writersservices.com dealing with rejections you'll find quotes from one publisher's stating Anne Frank's Diary lacks any; 'special perception or feeling which would lift that book above the "curiosity" level.' Another publisher noting that Joseph Heller's *Catch 22*: '…is really not funny on any intellectual level.'

Writing for an audience has always had, and always will have, random elements in terms of who gets discovered and reaches an audience. Some innovative and passionate work will never achieve its potential, some cynical and unimaginative work will always achieve success, and writers will write for both the best and worst of reasons. Somewhere in the middle of this vanity will always play a part. And I'm not having a go; I would be a hypocrite to attack anyone else for vanity in their writing. By the time this paragraph was underway in this book I could hit the word count option to see I was almost 100,000 words into the project. Sure, I wanted the book deal for the right reasons, but I was also vain enough to think my experience and my words counted for something. There have been other times, notably in my commercial PR work when we've done something so well that a champagne cork has taken flight, or – as a television crew departed having filmed in our foyer – an office door was shut, high fives were exchanged and the odd shout of 'yes, get in!' was heard. As writers we might excuse such behaviour with logical arguments such as; we are celebrating a job well-done, we care about our work and/or we've worked hard enough to earn the rewards. But vanity, i.e. the self-belief that our work matters, and so do we, is there for most of us. And I think denying that is dishonest.

So vanity, as in the personal quality of being vain, must be everywhere in professional writing. This explains why vanity publishing continues to thrive and why people end up paying to be published. Remember: *...<u>any</u> company that wants to charge to publish your book is – by definition – a vanity publisher, whatever they may try to tell you to the contrary.*

The definition is logical but it comes from a site dedicated to warning you about the hazards of vanity publishing. I am writing a book on how to get a break as a writer and the agenda here is different. I strongly suggest you visit *www.vanitypublishing.info* and avail yourself of the free download documents. I also suggest you carefully study the examples that follow. If you want to get a break as a writer my succinct advice would be to treat paid-for publication as a dangerous sport. Should you feel the need to participate, make sure you do all the safety checks necessary for your own protection. By this, I mean only work with a company that allows you to check with their other customers, provides clear evidence of what you get for your money and – above all – takes on board what you want and responds appropriately. Anyone taking your money to publish a book and suggesting, for example, that the national press might review it, isn't to be trusted. But if we regard paying for your own publication like a dangerous sport, we can also see it provides some of the same rewards as such sports. Those taking risks but remaining mindful of the dangers can learn about themselves, and achieve things denied to those who stand back and glibly declare the whole thing too risky.

Johnathon Clifford looked over the words on vanity publishing above, helped with some points of factual accuracy, and added his own comments:

The phrase 'vanity publishing' has come to have very bad connotations because there are so many dishonest vanity publishers. When Minerva Press went into voluntary liquidation they left well over 9,000 victims world wide who had lost anything from £1,800 to (in one case of a lady living in Paris) £21,000 for one book. Their total indebtedness was reported as being £2.6 million.

Where the dishonesty comes in is where a publisher knowingly lies to the unsuspecting author simply to get money out of them. There is nothing wrong with charging someone to publish their book as long as what you as the publisher promise the author, is exactly what you provide, and there are those who do exactly that.

As you have found, no vanity publisher wants to be called that themselves, and have invented a number of alternative terms. This is not acceptable because (after the publication of my books Metric Feet & Other Gang Members *and* Vanity Press & The Proper Poetry Publishers*) in 1991 the Advertising Standards Authority sent a directive to all vanity publishers instructing them that they must desist from referring to themselves as "joint or partnership, or any other term that suggested that they made a financial input to a book they published." They don't! That directive is obviously still in force. Whatever 'reasoning' these companies use, they are still being dishonest with their possible clients, which they have been told to stop doing.*

Johnathon Clifford's work continues, because the dishonesty and deceit continue. Enough of the horror stories; let's look at some more positive outcomes.

I once dealt with a company who see themselves as a 'self-publishing' operation. I found Amherst Publishing via the local Yellow Pages when I was looking for someone to take on the publishing of the anthology of work written by hospice patients. I had a fairly clear idea of what I wanted. I would collect the work and edit the book, I already had clear ideas about the page count and contents. I also had a specific budget. In the end the choice to go with Amherst Publishing was made because I couldn't find a local printer capable of doing the job for the same price and also including the ISBN. The online options were cheaper but involved me doing a lot more of the work. Amherst was a local company, they listened, they showed me other work they had produced and I was aware of another author who had used their service and was happy with the results. In effect, Amherst Publishing delivered a service. In this case the job had very clear aims.

I was editing a book written by hospice patients, we wanted all of our copies available for a book launch, we had a deal with the local Waterstone's to take copies and the remaining copies would be sold via the hospice's own chain of shops, or online via outlets like Amazon. This wasn't about making money. It certainly fell into the 'paid-for' definition of vanity publishing outlined above, but most of the words in our book *Dreams Wander On* were written by terminally ill hospice patients. This book was the end of a project aiming to give focus and meaning to those experiencing limited options because their health was failing. To term this as 'vanity' is cruel. My own first-hand experience of liaising with Amherst is that I got what they claim to offer; a self-publishing *service*. This was never a commercial project, the whole thing had been underwritten by a charity grant and whilst Amherst, the hospice and Waterstone's went on to make money the sums involved were not massive. Amherst knew our budget from the start, and also knew we would shop around with local printers, consider buying our own ISBN etc. They had to compete for the job.

The outcome we wanted was the celebration of the achievement of our group, and the existence of a book that would help people understand something about terminal illness, and the work of the hospice.

We established a few chapters back that organizing a project and generally making something happen can be one means of getting a break as a writer. In those circumstances, self-publishing in the form delivered by companies like Amherst Publishing still has a role to play. You pay more than you would approaching a print-on-demand company, but you tend to deal directly with people who handle the areas you would find hardest to handle yourself. You will find 'self-publishing' operations with client lists that include local schools, churches and the like. Technically speaking they are well within the definition of vanity publishing accepted by the Advertising Standards Authority, but if you shop for their services with the same caution you would use shopping for a major purchase, like a house or a car, you can still find some reasonable and helpful operators out there. And you can create work that adds to your CV.

Roger Wickham, who continues to run Amherst Publishing agreed to be interviewed for this book:

1 - In a few sentences can you explain how you help authors to self-publish and the specific benefits of the service you offer?
We look after our authors by designing and producing their books for them, producing their publicity material, such as leaflets, posters, and other pos material, and advising them on the best sales channels to follow. We offer a first class production service and extensive experience in the publishing and marketing of books.

2 - How many books are you publishing each year, and how varied are the subjects of these books?
We don't publish books. We produce books for others to publish

– about 50 or 60 new titles per year plus reprints, plus a wide range of marketing material. The subjects range for children's to novels, from family history to poetry, from a history of the early fire brigades to a book of sermons, from a thesis on Cromwell to a book on the final capture of Napoleon. A fantastic array of subjects that often only see the light of day by being self-published.

3 - As print-on-demand advances and self-publishing gets cheaper how much of a threat do you think it might become to traditional publishing?
I don't know if self-publishing will ever threaten the traditional publishing market, but what it does do is allow writers to produce titles for a niche market. Not forgetting of course all those people who don't want to sell their book but just want to produce a book of family history or autobiography for distribution to family and friends. And as we can now offer hardback print runs of as few as one hundred, at a reasonable cost, this is becoming increasingly popular.

4 - Are there any specific types of author who could usefully spend their entire careers using a service like yours?
Yes, and they do. I have many authors who have come back four, five, six times with new titles. For one client who concentrates on books for the canal market, we have produced 11 tiles, with three more on the way. Authors can make more money this way than settling for a small royalty from traditional publishers.

5 – Self-publishing rubs shoulders with the world of vanity publishing, can you explain your take on the dividing line between the two?
The dividing line between vanity publishing and self-publishing is really quite simple. With vanity publishing you are paying for publication of your book. You may or may not receive royalties depending on whether any copies are sold. With self-publishing

you are buying a chosen quantity of books which you either give away or sell and take all the profit. There are no royalties because all the profit is yours. The Society of Authors suggests that you consider self-publishing before vanity/subsidy publishing, and that you are very clear what your money is buying before handing any of it over.

6 - Could you share at least one conspicuous success story from your own company, and explain how this came about?
We have another author who we helped to set up his own publishing imprint, and in the last six years have produced ten books for him. Six of them are a set of children's hardback titles which he takes around primary/middle schools where he gives presentations and sells his books. This has been very successful, and over the last five years, we have printed 70,000 copies. We also design and produce all his direct mail shots, leaflets, book marks, posters, and other pos material. This has developed into a good full time business, and there are now plans to introduce new titles for younger school readers. See the website on www.kernowland.com.

7 - If someone came to you and said they were desperate to get a break as a writer and wanted to know how you might help them, what would you say?
Too big a subject to cover in a few words. What sort of writer? What subject? Novels are very difficult, but we could certainly advise on the best routes into niche markets.

An alternative to self-publishing is growing in strength and becoming the first option of choice for a range of writers. Print-on-Demand (POD) is very much the new kid on the block, growing rapidly in the last ten years. POD took hold as the internet grew and software packages offered writers the option of moving entire manuscripts around by email. The gist of print-on-demand is simple to understand. Copies of works, like books, are only printed when someone demands them. So costs are kept to a minimum. Works like books are 'published' in the sense of being paginated, given an ISBN, printed off and posted to the British Library to meet the requirements of copyright law and made available for order to bookshops, and online via outlets like Amazon. At this point individual copies are printed to order. To an Amazon customer the whole process makes no difference at all, but POD does present some problems to bookshops. Most bookshops negotiate discounts with publishers, bigger publishers have the financial power to agree major discounts when supplying large numbers of individual titles to a chain. This is the basis of deals like the '3 for 2' promotion which has been a popular part of Waterstone's offer for years. Bookshops prefer stock on a 'sale or return' basis, allowing them to send back unsold items. Because POD producers only print to order it is hard to get bookshops to take POD stock, but it is possible.

The bookshop problem aside, POD has brought book publishing, as in becoming a published author, down to a level of affordability on a par with a generous birthday present. It has also made specific areas of publishing more vibrant and diverse than ever. For example, academic publishing, traditionally an area rife with niche market titles offering hugely detailed works on subjects of minority interest. These days PhD dissertations, the proceedings of academic conferences and other related works are easily loaded into files and made available via POD. The cheapest POD operations offer services that simply require you to load a file, offer you a choice of pre-programmed cover designs, and leave you to buy your own copies.

For the last few years I have done an exercise in class involving getting students to write a 500 word story, loading all the stories into one Word document, and 'publishing' the resulting book on the world's biggest POD site, Lulu.com, in a matter of minutes. Lulu is a recent and rapid success story, founded in 2002 in Raleigh, North Carolina, the company grew quickly on the back of POD book publishing but now refers to itself as a 'technology company' and offers diverse services including publishing CDs and producing calendars. As of this writing they have offices in 12 countries, it may well be more by the time this book is published.

POD publishers won't thank me for putting it so crudely, but the genius of their business is its accessibility. They may be online but their offer is something akin to the drop-in service available at high street chains like Kall Kwik. Most of the major POD operators display their price-lists and varied services prominently. Some – like Lulu – offer their services through pre-set interactive options on their sites, others – like Authors Online – are approachable by phone and email and deal directly with authors.

POD has brought book publishing, and associated benefits, to a range of people who couldn't afford it any other way. For starters, POD has revolutionized options for people like me who teach writing and one reason for the UK posting over 200,000 new ISBNs a year is the rapidly increasing use of

POD. In the last few years I have used POD services in two distinct ways, firstly getting students into small groups, getting my employer to under-write the production costs of POD books and then charging the small groups of students with writing and promoting their own books. However good or bad the results it is a useful way to teach subjects like copyright law and those students who generate sales via Amazon are invariably excited as copies start to move. The aim of this work is to generate portfolio material for the students, and let them learn about writing and promoting books by *doing* something, even if it is only to establish a Facebook group, link in their book's page on Amazon and then watch as a few of their friends buy copies.

I have also got larger groups of students involved in producing POD titles for clients. In these cases we work directly with an organization, like the local Mencap group, write a book to help them raise awareness of their work and then hand over the copyright so any profits go to the client. I work in a department including Art and Design and Video courses, our book publishing is cheaper than the other areas of work. The project for the local Mencap group, completed in June 2010, provides one useful case study. My second year undergraduates met individuals who have been helped by the charity, they interviewed these people who had a range of learning difficulties and each interview formed a chapter in the book *Choices*. We sourced photographs from the charity and were given the clearance to use three other professional pictures by photographer Richard Hamilton from his touring exhibition *Shifting Perspectives*. We only started incurring costs when it came to the POD publishing. I bought in a stock of

100 ISBNs, cutting out our need to buy these for individual books. Our 74 page book cost £249-00 to 'publish' via POD and the end result left us able to buy individual copies from Authors Online at £3-30 with black and white photos or £5-50 with colour pictures. Any order over £100 came post free. At this point we informed the publisher that the charity was now the 'author' and should have these author prices when ordering in their own stock for their own charity shops. In addition, any royalties from Amazon and other online sales were to go to the charity.

Book publishing on this local level, for reasons like this, has only become possible via POD. It will get cheaper against inflation, and it isn't exactly expensive now. If you want a break as a writer, it is now possible to organize a project like the one I have just outlined, and deliver it for very low costs. Consultants, subject experts and others who have audiences so small in number they make niche markets look vibrant now use POD as an extension of their work. POD offers options unavailable in traditional publishing, many POD operations – for example – allowing authors to change the master files of books repeatedly if information goes out of date, or mistakes are spotted.

Richard Fitt, who runs Authors Online, one of the UK's leading POD specialists, agreed to be interviewed for this book.

1 - In four or five sentences can you explain how print-on-demand works at your company.

First and foremost POD is perfect for authors wishing to self-publish, simply because there is no investment in stock required. Authors can order books from a single copy upwards. Secondly it perfectly suits internet selling through companies such as Amazon, who can list the titles without holding stock, knowing that the fulfillment time is only marginally longer. Thirdly it suits worldwide distribution as once the book is setup on a server it can be downloaded anywhere in the world and delivered at local prices. No more shipping books worldwide from centralised plants in only one country

2 - How many books are you publishing each year, and how varied are the subjects of these books?

We publish in excess of 200 titles a year and rising. With approaching 1000 titles I doubt if there is a subject we haven't now published something on. If it's legal we will publish it.

3 - As print-on-demand advances how much of a threat do you think it might become to traditional publishing?

It is huge threat to publishers. The average sale of a traditionally published book is around 2000, and we pulp over 60 million books a year in this country alone. So the amount of wasted resources and money is enormous. The problem is the book retail trade still has its sale-or-return agreement in place, the only industry in the country (other than newspapers) to do so. Sooner or later that will have to end and then traditional publishers will be able to supply bookshops on demand. Also I firmly believe that as POD is so inexpensive, sooner or later established authors are going to wake up to the fact that they could publish themselves, using companies such as ours to prepare the book for them, and then self-publish using POD and keep all the profits to themselves

4 - Are there any specific types of author who could usefully spend their entire careers using POD?
All of them as far as I can see, but for anybody writing for a niche market, uncommercial to the big boys, this is the perfect answer.

5 - Could you share at least one conspicuous success story from your own company, and explain how this came about?
We published a book on The Yoothspeek guide to Shakespeare in 2008, To Be Or Not To Be, Innit by Martin Baum, which was picked up by a Reuters journalist who lived in the same village as the author, he sold the story, which was picked up by every newspaper in the country and even many abroad, such as *The New York Times*. Two days later the author was on the BBC breakfast programme explaining what he had done to the language of the Bard! By lunchtime the books was Amazon ranked in the top 20. We went on to sell thousands.

In 2007 we published an excellent work on Michael Jackson, *Michael Jackson: for the Record* by Chris Cadman and Craig Halstead. It always sold well, but when the star died in 2009, the book went on to become the number one best selling book on Michael Jackson in the World, and it is a hardback! Not bad for two self-published books!

6 - If someone came to you and said they were desperate to get a break as a writer and wanted to know how you might help them, what would you say?
Writing a book is only half the story, you still have to go out and sell it. So many authors think they can publish a book and sit back and watch the royalties roll in. Sadly not true. Identify who you are writing for, aim your marketing at your target readership and then go out and sell it to them. But above all the book has to be of a high enough standard to want that market to buy it.

And then, like it or not, lady luck will come into play. Martin Baum would not have had his success if that journalist hadn't bought his local newspaper carrying Martin's story. Chris and Craig, of course, benefited from Michael Jackson's untimely death. But if you don't go out and create activity about the book it is unlikely to go anywhere.

This chapter set out to cover: *Print-on-demand publishing, and other developing areas of low-cost independent publication for writers. Interviews and comments from those closely involved in these areas of work.*

We have done that and in completing this round up we have almost finished discussing how to get a break as a writer. To some extent we have come full-circle. I started in the opening chapters by suggesting ways you could do something, anything, to get your work out there. With POD publishing you can do that. Don't let me stop you going directly to a site like Lulu, loading up some of your words and bagging yourself an online book for sale, complete with a cover design featuring your own photographs, inside the next hour. That – at least – should give you a buzz, which is a significant part of what drives most people seeking to be a professional writer.

However, we have also come a long way, discussed detailed examples, heard from many of those involved in professional writing and considered activities in a range of areas. If I re-wrote this book in ten years time I can guarantee you that the world of professional writing will have become more diverse, and developed new offshoots. My sincere hope is that somewhere in this complex and changing world there is work, and income, available for you. I have tried my best to explain how this might happen but the extent to which this makes a difference to you will depend entirely on your own efforts.

Good luck!

9 The Write Stuff – AKA 'Sources'

This chapter covers: *Round up of major contacts and sources with ideas of how to use these contacts. Discussion of how to build on work covered in book through use of reference works and web sites.*

I'm grateful to the many writers, administrators, and others involved in the creative industries who gave time and effort to answering questions, and helping to create this book. The least I can do is allow them a moment of their own at the end. If you've read this far and thought about what their example might mean for you, you could take some time to check out online what they are currently doing. The list below is by no means exhaustive, it is intended as a 'sources' section to end the book. In other words, I hope you follow up something or someone in the list below and find some help, inspiration or validation for your own work.

In addition, I have name checked a number of high-profile and public organizations likely to be of help to writers and added a few personal touches relating to examples – like the master haiku poet Basho – I hope you find inspiring.

All of these examples are collected here. The information was correct as this book went to press.

In numerical and then alphabetical order:

433 Magazine is an online home for drama based audio files. It provides a first opportunity and showcase for those prepared to write and record their own work. Other sites also offer this service but it remains rare. As of this writing the site was in preparation and did not have a clickable presence online.

Amherst Publishing: Kent-based specialists in self-publishing especially in *books for authors, businesses, schools, churches, and other organisations, both locally and throughout the UK, who want to self-publish their own books.* Established since 1995, their published works include *Dreams Wander On*, for the Heart of Kent Hospice. They produce a booklet, *The Amherst Guide to Self Publishing* explaining the stages of book publishing. Temporarily without a website as these words went to press. Tel: 01959 525600, books@amherstpublishing.co.uk

Jake Arnott remains one of the UK's most compelling and celebrated novelists. His first book deal, netting him £100,000 for two novels, with Sceptre was one of the last major deals signed in the twentieth century. Arnott remains on the books of the Curtis Brown Literary Agency, with whom he signed ahead of that deal.

Arts Council of England, Wales etc: *www.artscouncil.org.uk* Online home of the agency funding, administering and leading a range of the UK's creative arts. Useful as a source of policy information, funding advice and a reality check on what is being funded and developed. Wales *www.acw-ccc.org.uk* and Northern Ireland *www.artscouncil-ni.org* have their own versions of the same. The **Scottish Arts Council** has its own site at; *www.sac.org.uk*

Association of Authors' Agents: In their own words from the FAQ section of their site: *The Association is a voluntary body to provide a*

forum for member agencies to discuss industry matters, to uphold a code of good practice, and to provide a vehicle for representing the interests of agents and authors. Our members have each practiced as literary agents for a period of three years or more, are based in the UK, have a list of clients who are actively engaged in writing, and abide by a code of practice… http://www.agentsassoc.co.uk/

Authonomy: *www.authonomy.com* A hothouse for aspiring writing talent that earned news coverage when it was established. Set up by Harper Collins, i.e. a major publishing house, the following words come from their FAQ's page:

authonomy invites unpublished and self published authors to post their manuscripts for visitors to read online. Authors create their own personal page on the site to host their project – and must make at least 10,000 words available for the public to read.

Visitors to authonomy can comment on these submissions – and can personally recommend their favourites to the community. authonomy counts the number of recommendations each book receives, and uses it to rank the books on the site. It also spots which visitors consistently recommend the best books – and uses that info to rank the most influential trend spotters.

As with You Write On – listed later in this section – this isn't a home for the casual or faint hearted. But it has continually found new talent willing to submit work and people willing to get involved in commenting on work. Whatever the similarities to talent shows like *The X Factor* this initiative is – at least – innovative and it does offer a progression route all the way to full-blown commercial publication by a major publisher to anyone with work capable of surviving the whole process that far.

Authors' Licensing and Collecting Society: ALCS, *www.alcs.co.uk*. Established 1977, this organization collects and distributes copyright fees due to authors from the use of their work. Affiliated to the Society of Authors, the ALCS is dedicated to promoting the rights of authors, and – in particular – works to identify monies due, collect them and distribute them to their rightful owners. In the words of its own website the organization seeks to achieve its aims: '…by encouraging the establishment of collective licensing schemes, where appropriate, and ensuring that fees resulting from such schemes are efficiently collected and distributed.' And also; '...by building an understanding of the contribution writers make to the economy and society as a whole.'

Author-Network: *www.author-network.com* One of the better UK authors' sites, containing up to date news, lots of easily accessible information on topics like agents and Creative Writing courses and monthly opinion columns to give any writer a reality check. Highly recommended.

Authors Online: *www.authorsonline.co.uk* One of the UK's leading print-on-demand (POD) publishers and interviewed on this subject for chapter eight of this book.

BAFTA: The British Academy of Film and Television Arts. www.bafta.org. Technically speaking this is an independent charity with a brief to promote the arts with relation to moving images and time-based media, like television. As part of its remit BAFTA has spent over a decade running the Rocliffe Forums, a series of events and initiatives dedicated to bringing new talent – including writers – into the industry.

Basho: Matsuo Bash (1644 – 1694) master haiku poet and travel writer of the Edo period in Japan. Frankly, he is mentioned in this section because this is personal, one of the greatest writers in history, in my opinion at least. Anyone who sees their craft as an extension of themselves could usefull study Basho's example. A more balanced view is provided by Wikipedia: *During his lifetime, Basho was recognized for his works in the collaborative haikai no renga form; today, after centuries of commentary, he is recognized as a master of brief and clear haiku. His poetry is internationally renowned, and within Japan many of his poems are reproduced on monuments and traditional sites.*

Carole Blake: Continues as one of the UK's leading literary agents and is Joint Managing Director of the Blake Friedmann Literary Agency. Clients include Jane Asher and Barbara Erskine, along with a major stable of talent. *www.blakefriedmann.co.uk*

Sydney J Bounds: British writer of pulp sci-fi titles and sometime tutor to writing students including yours truly. He died in 2006 but his work is listed at: *www.fantasticfiction.co.uk/b/sydney-j-bounds*.

Bo Burnham: Young American comedy singer/songwriter. His fame and prestigious bookings for events like the Edinburgh Festival were achieved largely on the back of a series of highly popular videos posted on youtube. *www.boburnham.com*.

Angela Carter: 1940-1992, influential and highly regarded UK novelist, writer of short-fiction and journalism. Her ground-breaking and innovative published works continue to be a mainstay of 'literature' elements of taught courses in Creative Writing. A *Times* poll in 2008 ranked Carter as tenth in a list of the '50 Greatest British Writers since 1945.'

Chapter One Promotions: *www.chapteronepromotions.com* One of the better online homes of a popular service for writers. There are some sharks out there but Chapter One are not among them. They offer proofreading services and other paid-for elements of help likely to shape a manuscript and take it closer to publishable standard. As with others in the area, including some writers' magazines, Chapter One also run competitions for writing.

Jai Claire: Is British author noted for her intense, challenging and dark fictional style. Her first published book – *The Cusp of Something* – is a collection of short stories. One anonymous Amazon reviewer noting:

Prose that fizzes, sings, aches and exhilarates. Full of uncomfortable, challenging perspectives this collection is the opposite of relaxing but in story after story the succulent, voluptuous language keeps you hooked. I'll second that. *www.goodreads.com/author/show/502930.Jai_Clare*

Jenny Colgan: Prolific and highly successful purveyor of 'Chick-lit.' Jenny's romantic comedy writing earned her a contract with the big-hitting Simon and Schuster and impressive sales throughout the 21st century. Her pragmatic and insightful responses to interview questions about how she achieved the all-important first break appear at the end of chapter five of this book. *www.jennycolgan.com*

Cream Communications: Is a communications agency covering a range of media and communications work including PR, marketing, consultancy, crisis management and internal engagement (basically, getting your own staff on board as ambassadors for what you do and why you do it). Established in 2004, their clients include Galaxy Fireworks and one of their press releases for Galaxy Fireworks appears in chapter two. *www.creamcommunications.co.uk*

The Downs Mail: From the late nineties to the second decade of the 21st century local papers faced a series of threats to their existence. During the same period *The Downs Mail* went from one edition to four different editions aimed at different parts of the Maidstone area. The circulation rose from 13,000 to 88,000, so they must be doing something right. Billing itself as 'Maidstone's local paper' (in fact, depending on how you count them, Maidstone has two or three local papers, some with more than one regional edition), *The Downs Mail* continues to thrive. *www.downsmail.co.uk*

Fiction Factory: Independent production company based in London, one of leading independent production specialists dealing with radio drama. Sony Award winners, and notable for a series of innovative and high-quality productions in recent years. *www.fictionfactory.co.uk.*

Film Angels: Is one of the UK's premier meeting spaces for film producers with money (the 'angels' of the title) and hopeful writers with ideas to pitch. The site offers online meetings but requires a fee from the hopeful writer. Whilst some grumble about this, it does serve to keep the site free from most of those with half-baked ideas and restrict it to the point that some film producers do come and acquire work. *www.filmangel.co.uk*

David Gaffney is living proof that it is possible to sustain part of your working life in the most eclectic and creative areas of writing. From gathering stories via a mobile confessional booth to becoming published and acclaimed as one of the UK's leading exponents of the ultra-short form of flash fiction David continues to succeed in the most marginal and inventive corners of the writing world. His website *www.davidgaffney.weebly.com* has doubtless added some more incredible and surprising examples of his work since these words were written.

Jonny Geller: Is one of the UK's leading literary agents, having risen through the ranks at Curtis Brown to become managing director of their books division and developed a track record of deft signings and distinctive deals. Amongst Geller's discoveries is Jake

Arnott, his other clients include Sasha Baron-Cohen and John Le Carre. Geller has also posted video clips online discussing the basics of the relationship between writers and agents. Try *www.notesfromtheslushpile.co.uk*.

Harlequin Mills and Boon: *www.millsandboon.co.uk* The planet's leading publisher of romantic fiction and an operation so famous for their ongoing niche market success that their name has become a byword for an entire area of work, similar to the ubiquity of brand names like Hoover and Google. In production for over a century and still the brand leader by some considerable margin. Though much maligned by critics and sections of the reading public 'Mills and Boon' offer two user-friendly options to a hopeful writer that are hard to find elsewhere. Firstly, they positively encourage approaches without an agent. Secondly, their site includes very specific instructions on what to send, the length of their various categories of book and how to present the manuscript (no fixed bindings, printed on one side of the paper and secured with elastic bands).

Rosalinda Hutton: Is a British writer, journalist, radio playwright and – sometime – lecturer in English. Given her many talents it was always likely her work would find a high-profile home. As of this writing she is finishing a misery memoir (title still to be agreed) for Mainstream, an imprint of Random House. If you Google her after reading this it is likely the book will be making its presence known online.

Rae Louise Jones: Continues writing and performing poetry and working to form the band she needs to put the right sounds behind her unique words. She has a Facebook group:
http://www.facebook.com/group.php?v=wall&gid=73760287806

Jennifer Kingsley Publishers: World leaders in books on areas like autism and living with disability. A particularly user-friendly publisher to the authors interested in their specialist market since in the first instance the company want a clearly outlined idea, and a CV from the prospective author. They also provide a downloadable form for use when approaching them. *www.jkp.com*

London Creative: Remain amongst the biggest and best agencies specializing in communication solutions for business. Doubtless the clients featured on the front page of their site, and the testimonials from satisfied customers will have changed from those available when this book went to print. But that turnover of clients, and achievement of results is the point for London Creative and their competitors. *www.londoncreative.com*

Literataturetraining: *www.literaturetraining.com* Highly recommended site. One-stop shop for help with professional development. In the context of this book Literature Training is especially useful in two ways, firstly by providing up to date information on specific training you can apply for and access to help develop particular skills. Secondly, by providing a window into the rich and varied world covered by the catch-all term 'literature.' If you were to take on board the suggestion made repeatedly in this book that you simply 'get involved' then this site may well be a valuable source to help you decide when and where that involvement might take place.

Erica Longdon: Has probably carved out the most individual and eclectic career of any of those interviewed for this book. Voice over artist, prime-time radio host and – currently – holistic therapist. As her interview in the book makes clear, her writing skills and ability to communicate succinctly have been central to all aspects of her professional life, along with her own desire to do the work she wants to do. Her website can be found at: *www.Angelhandsheal.com*.

Lulu.com: The biggest provider of print-on-demand titles in the world. Lulu is US based but offers services internationally. Based in Raleigh, Carolina Lulu's operation has grown to have offices in a dozen countries. The company publishes books, CDs, calendars and a range of other POD materials.

Maidstone Borough Council: Continue to support the arts in their local area, an activity permanently fraught with difficulty when many other areas also compete for a finite amount of money. Their arts page can be found at: *www.maidstonearts.com/?65,Default*

Of course, you may want to Google your own local authority and find the right contacts to help you.

Marjacq: UK based literary agency founded in 1974 and – in 1984 – the first such agency to set up a specific division for game developers. *www.marjacq.com*

Tamsyn Murray: Is a British author who achieved a 'double whammy' breakthrough in 2010 landing major publisher contracts for her adult fiction and work for children. Her previous – and highly eclectic career – is detailed on her website which also notes: *After moving around a lot when she was growing up, she now lives in London with her husband and her daughter. At least her body does. Her mind tends to prefer imaginary places and wanders off whenever it can but that's not necessarily a bad thing in a writer. www.tamsynmurray.co.uk*

National Council for the Training of Journalists: NCTJ *www.nctj.com* is an educational charity offering a range of training programmes, both in class and online, for aspiring journalists. The organization boasts a strong and impressive past, stays on top of the many developments in a rapidly changing working world and provides specific training courses in areas like sub-editing and sports journalism that continue to change the lives of working journalists for the better. Short and long courses are available and 'journalism' within the remit of the NCTJ covers all the major media and takes into account the changes being brought about through the increasing use of the internet as the main source of news for many people.

National Union of Journalists: *http://www.nuj.org.uk/.* Is the main trade union for journalists in England and Wales. Scotland has its own affiliated branch, but both the NUJ and its Scots partner specialize in the same work. The union campaigns on behalf of all members, safeguarding rights and – increasingly – fighting to save existing jobs and pension entitlements. For a snapshot of current concerns over journalistic employment a quick visit to the NUJ site, or the Scots equivalent is probably the best option.

NERD – New Entertainment Research and Design. Recently formed and high-profile development production company serving British television. NERD's site makes clear the company: *specialises in developing and producing documentary and entertainment formats as well as scripted projects in comedy and factual drama.* John Farrar of NERD is interviewed in Chapter Five of this book. The company was founded by people with a lot of experience but is willing to represent a select few new clients, the site noting: *We occasionally represent the ideas of third parties and offer a transparent, simple deal at the point of engagement. We do this only where we believe we can add value and help harness the full commercial potential of an idea. www.nerdsite.co.uk*

The Never Ending Story: *www.TheNeverEndingStory.co.uk* A bold and complex site offering writers the chance to establish their own publications online, network with others and generally develop their ideas in an environment that encourages writers to produce and hone their talents. All of which sounds very general. I could bang on, but – in this case – clicking their site and navigating what is on offer would give you a clear idea of whether it might work for you.

New Novelist: *www.newnovelist.com* Basically an online shop but one potentially of great use to the kind of aspiring writer motivated to read this book down to the fine details of this listings section. New Novelist sells software packages designed to help writers with everything from professional looking page layouts to character development.

Jonathan Newman is one of Britain's most compelling and watchable film makers. Chapter two of this book spends time considering his first full-length feature *Being Considered*. His other works include *Teeth*, *Swinging with the Finkels* and *Foster*. He is writer/director of all of these full-length movies and also combines those roles on a series of short movies. Newman has worked in television and is one of the talents behind the 'boutique' production company Serendipity Films: *www.serendipity-films.com*.

The New Writer Magazine: *www.thenewwriter.com*. Is a magazine combining innovative and interesting new prose and poetry with articles on the 'nuts and bolts' of creative writing. For a recent FREE back issue which contains Guidelines send an A4 SAE stamped at 81p (Large Letter) or 5 IRCs if overseas to The New Writer, PO Box 60, Cranbrook, Kent TN17 2ZR UK

Poot! Comic: *www.pootcomic.com* continues to set about breaking taboos and reducing sensible people to convulsive laughter. Relaunched in 2009 after an 18 year break, circulation was steadily rising as of this writing.

Pressbox

An online meeting place for PR and press people. Intended mainly as a resource to disseminate good business to business stories

Pressbox is also home to a rapidly changing series of press releases, most of them well written and – therefore – a useful learning resource for anyone thinking of sharpening their writing skills in this area. *www.pressbox.co.uk*

Project Gutenberg: Massive site and one of the most celebrated projects involving digitizing books, and other documents. Project Gutenberg pre-dates most of its competitors, having been founded in 1971. Its online collection offers free downloads of a vast array of out of copyright material and also includes sound files. The downloads are available in a range of formats. www.gutenberg.org

Matt Shoard is a man of many literary parts. The first person signed up to study for a PhD in Creative Writing at The University of Kent, he continues his studies, teaches at the university, writes the regular *Agent Secrets* column for *Writers' Monthly* and also edits *Fleeting* magazine, an online repository of the best in short fiction and poetry. *www.fleetingmagazine.com* He blogs with *The Guardian*: *www.guardian.co.uk/profile/matt-shoard*

Shopper Anonymous: *www.shopperanonymous.co.uk* remains active in the area of mystery shopping and operates at a level likely to offer opportunities to aspiring writers. This is a professional job requiring professional skills but the rewards in terms of adding an unusual element to your CV and gaining an insight into areas of life you would otherwise miss, can be extremely useful in career terms.

Skillset: *www.skillset.org*, an excellent site from the Sector Skills Council for creative media. The site has a wealth of detail looking at the routes into different areas – like radio, advertising and computer games – the training available, the qualifications you will need and the career structures you are likely to face if you commit yourself to the futures explored by Skillset.

Sylvia Smith: Sylvia Smith is one of the most individual and unusual authors to emerge in the UK this century. Her first book *Misadventures* is an autobiography chronicling a series of funny, and sometimes worrying events in her life, focused on the small day to day details other authors often miss. Praise for her work has centred on the humour she creates and the way her writing concentrates on characters and events usually ignored by autobiographical writing. *Misadventures* caused something of a sensation when it was first published in 2001, becoming a cult best-seller and prompting press coverage. Whilst journalists refrained from openly stating it, many thought the book – combing terse and funny writing with tales of a life revolving around office jobs and the minutiae of relationships – an elaborate hoax, believing it to be the work of an anonymous 'name' author. It isn't, and Smith's subsequent books *Appleby House* and *My Holidays* have continued in the same style. She has completed two further works, *Longfield House* (considered by her agent to be her finest work to date) and *The Men in my Life* both of which are seeking publishers as this book goes to press. Smith avoids Facebook, MySpace and other online presence stating she is; 'Not on anything apart from the phone.'

Society of Authors: *www.societyofauthors.org*. Over a century old, a large and robust organization that has grown from a genteel and exclusive band to become an effective and muscular presence representing the interests of authors of all kinds. Whilst the high-profile novelists in the society tend to make more headlines the Society of Authors is also very active in areas like ensuring writers of textbooks get their due from photocopying. Technically speaking, the Society of Authors is not a trade union. However, their services to individual members duplicate the interest in pay, conditions and working arrangements of many unions. As their website states: 'The staff are ready to help members with any query, however trivial or obscure, relating to the business of writing. Our services include the confidential, individual vetting of contracts, and help with professional disputes.' A quarterly magazine, *The Author* provides a digest of news and feature articles concerned with current conditions in the working life of authors. Regular meetings take place at their London headquarters and regional groups also meet.

Kevin F Sutherland: Is one of the most innovative and inventive comic performers to have sustained a career in the UK in recent years. His drawing of famous comic characters like *The Bash Street Kids* and his stand up comedy work are the nearest things to a normal job in a CV that also boasts unique creations like the Scottish Falsetto Sock Puppet Theatre (sold out at the Edinburgh Festival from 2007 to 2009 and winner of Best Comedy Show in 2009) and his own Comic Art Masterclass (a live event showing how to write and draw comic characters). I could go on, but there will doubtless be something new and equally unique to find if you look at his site: *www.comicfestival.co.uk*

UCAS: Universities Central Admissions Service. Organisation handling applications to British universities and providing an online resource detailing all available courses and allowing candidates to apply directly online. From the point of view of those interested in studying writing there are lots of choices. It pays to look at BA courses (i.e. full-degrees) and also the HND/Foundation Degree options. The latter represent less powerful qualifications but often offer lower fees and suit those with substantial experience of the working world who are keen to get a higher education qualification with a practical base and move quickly back to work. Log on at *www.ucas.ac.uj* and you can search by subject, by level of qualification and by institution. A long time spent checking out options in Creative Writing and the related specialist areas – Event Management, Marketing, Journalism, and Professional Writing – and also looking at the possibilities of combining these subjects with others is strongly recommended to anyone intent on following up this book with study in a university.

Vanity Publishing Info: *www.vanitypublishing.info* Is the online home of the ongoing work of Johnathon Clifford. Clifford has been a steady and dedicated campaigner against dishonesty and deception in the murky 'vanity' end of the publishing sector. His work has resulted in the demise of some of the most infamous operations, but – as anyone visiting his site and availing themselves of his free to download documents will soon realize – the sector continues to ignore directives, and still provides a home for disreputable operators.

Where the Hell is Matt? Continues as an ongoing amusement/occupation for its founder. An FAQ's page on the official site gives some history on how the project came about and how it is financed. *www.wherethehellismatt.com.*

The Writers' Guild: *www.writersguild.org.uk* is the UK's leading organization helping salaried and part-time writers in areas like the broadcast industry. Technically speaking it is pretty much the only trade union for writers in such an area, although some writers belong to the non-union Society of Authors and get some of the same support from that organization as is offered by The Writers' Guild. In areas like television and film the Guild is the recognized body for negotiating minimum terms of pay and conditions and the regular upgrades in – for example – minimum fees for one-line comedy sold to BBC Radio are the result of the Guild's ongoing work. The Writers' Guild also offers general services, including reading and vetting contracts, legal help for members and an area of their site allowing people to find and contact members with offers of work.

The Writers in Prison Network: Continue to place writers in

residency, dealing directly with inmates – both male and female – serving time at all levels of security. Their site gives details of their work and also includes details of current vacancies.
www.writersinprisonnetwork.org

Writewords.org.uk: One of many writers' sites online. Writewords is amongst the better British sites and I will confess to being a long-term member and very happy with what's on offer. Like the best sites it combines regularly updated information, regular news, a jobs column, showcase pages for individual writers and forums on which writers of all abilities can meet and discuss aspects of their work, from mutual critical appraisals to the best contacts to further a career. The general rule online is that you get what you pay for and Writewords – as of this writing – offers up a full menu of its services for £35 annually. You can access the site for free, though interacting and accessing the jobs column is not available without payment.

You Write On: *www.youwriteon.com* Online writing community, highly popular with some and high-profile in the context of such communities. The profile has largely been achieved because You Write On has a fairly clear remit and has managed to deliver on its promises. As their site explains: *YouWriteOn's premise is simple: members upload opening chapters or short stories and the YouWriteOn system randomly assigns these to another member to review. You then review another member's story excerpt – assigned to you at random – each time you want to receive a new review back in return. After 5 reviews a story enters our chart system and the highest rated writers receive free feedback each month from editors for leading publishers Orion and Random House.* To a certain extent you might describe this as a 'put up or shut up' type operation and I have seen the prospect of submitting to this site terrify a few people who were happy to talk about their novels in progress. For those wishing to make a serious commitment, however, the site has often proven very useful.

Glossary

Account Handling: Usually associated with advertising and public relations, this is an area of work that asks a person to provide a channel of communication between a client and a company. The creative industries need account handlers because clients can fail to understand creative people and creative people can fail to understand clients. An account handler often acts to explain the misunderstandings and make sure a job goes as smoothly as possible. So, for example, if a breakfast cereal manufacturer asked an advertising agency for ideas to celebrate a century of making cereals the agency might respond with a campaign based around other things that have existed for 100 years and the caption 'Some things are as good as ever.' The cereal makers might not understand the genius of this idea, especially if they found themselves looking at mocked up adverts featuring the Manchester United team from before World War One. A good account handler would be able to explain the thinking behind the campaign, and would also have the tact and diplomacy to make sure the creative team didn't present ideas that were unsuitable. Account handlers usually start in the creative teams of advertising and PR agencies and work their way up to their jobs.

Aspirational Brand: A product or service to which customers aspire. For example; owning a high performance car. Working with aspirational brands often offers creatives involved in PR a greater range of opportunities in terms of things to be done in communicating ideas about the brand. This is because it's important for many aspirational brands to remain in the public eye and be discussed. Some brands – notably the likes of Rolls Royce cars – are above such marketing. Many aspirational brands achieve their sought after status largely because their marketing and regular high profile in the public mind works to keep them there. In some cases an aspirational brand can be a small business, for example; a hairdressers. See the discussion of Pennies Day Nurseries in chapter two.

Boutique: Dictionary definitions of the word still link it to a small shop, usually one selling fashionable clothing. In writing/media terms the word has come to take on a related meaning. Small production companies or events combine talents as a means of accessing some central facilities and reducing the costs to each individual. The link to the original meaning is the presence in the writing/event 'boutique' of a small but significant range of talent or live events. So a 'boutique festival' is a festival linking a series of themed concerts or live events, and tending to use one central office for publicity/ ticket sales etc. A boutique media production company does a similar job, but links the talents of a number of people usually working in similar areas. Chapter two includes an interview with film director Jonathan Newman who forms part of the boutique production company Serendipity Films.

Chick lit: AKA 'Chick-Lit/ Chick-lit. Generic term for fiction focused on lifestyle issues linked to modern women. Chick lit novels typically base themselves around a modern female main character, explore her dilemmas with a great deal of humour and some observations on the state of relationships. Chick lit novels bear some resemblance to romantic fiction but tend to be regarded as different in a few key areas. Firstly, they typically explore relationships in a family as well as romantic relationships, secondly they tend to be less focused on the style of a particular publisher and are typically valued for the skilful writing and personal style elements of their authors. Thirdly Chick lit novels tend to be longer than the romantic novels of a publisher like Mills and Boon. The best known Chick lit writers enjoy massive sales and regularly feature amongst the best-selling fiction writers in any genre. One notable Chick lit author – Jenny Colgan – is interviewed in this book.

Development Production: An area of creative work usually associated with television but also going on in other parts of the creative industries. Development production is a term used to describe the work of developing ideas to the point at which they can be seriously considered for production. Some large media organizations – like the BBC – have many people involved in development production. These people have often been employed for a particular job, and their contracts may not include the words development production. So, for example, the people working in the BBC Writersroom who are charged with finding new talent and bringing it on are all helping with typical development production tasks; like identifying ideas with commercial potential and trying to shape them to fit schedules and budgets. Smaller companies, like independent production companies, often describe themselves as working in development production. Their work often involves generating ideas, working up scripts and other support materials and then producing sample material, like 'pilot' shows to be seen by others who have the power to commission the work and offer serious money for its production. The down side of working in development production is the pressure to keep developing ideas and the danger of burning out. There can also be huge frustrations when a lot of work and effort appears to be wasted because it gets rejected by the people with the power and money to turn it into a production. Work in this area can also be short-term and poorly paid, especially for a new graduate. The good news is that your talent can be spotted at this level and you have the chance to network and build contacts.

This area is also a very good training ground, teaching you a lot very quickly about the workings of the creative industries.

Elevator Speech: Aka; elevator pitch. A short presentation about yourself and your ambitions, suitable for delivery to someone in a position to help you achieve your ambitions. Wikipedia's page includes the line: 'concise, and compelling description of a product, service, person, group or organization, or project.' In terms of writing work and aspiring writers it should be added that an elevator pitch should offer some clear insight into the likely benefit to the person on the end of the pitch. One common reason for ideas and work to be rejected in this context is that those pitching simply explain the work and their talent as they themselves see it, ignoring the views of the person(s) to whom they are talking.

Flash Fiction: Fiction of an exceptionally short length, aka; microfiction, short short story, sudden fiction. There is no accepted maximum or minimum length for such fiction. The form has increased greatly in popularity with the rise of the internet. Tweets on the Twitter site, posts on messageboards and status updates on social networking sites all merge with flash fiction's edges but – at heart – flash fiction retains an identity based on the clear attempt to tell a story and provide insight into character and situation. Noted practitioners in the UK include David Gaffney and noted works include Dan Rhodes' *Anthropology* a collection of 101 chapters each exactly 101 words long. Ostensibly a novel chronicling a series of largely disastrous relationships *Anthropology* can easily be read as a series of 101 darkly comic flash fictions. Another notable, though hard to find, title is *BRUTE*, a short fiction anthology based on a cult comic of the 1980s. Notable because one story – 'The Angler' – is one word long. Attempts to locate the authors of *BRUTE* ahead of publication proved unsuccessful so printing the one word might constitute an infringement of copyright since it is a complete copyrightable work in its own right. Perhaps it's best if you imagine what that word might be.

Free Sheet: Aka: free-sheet. A term applied to free publications. Usually associated with local newspapers. The history of free local papers is usually traced back to California in the 1940s and in particular to the work of enterprising publisher Dean Lesher. The basis of a free newspaper is usually a collection of advertisers paying all production and distribution costs in return for having their adverts placed in front of the readership. Occasional exceptions to this involve one advertiser paying all costs and using a one-off or semi-regular free paper as a part of an advertising strategy. Free newspapers have been a significant part of UK local news for over 30 years but their prominence has increased in recent years as the traditional model of paid for local papers has come under threat from the internet. The free-sheet business model has some advantages over the internet, particularly so for local services who advertise knowing the paper may lie around a home for a week, or a month, and be used instead of a phone book should the reader need to ring a local plumber, take-away restaurant etc. Some papers have experimented with occasional free editions, sometimes making one issue per month free in a local area. Whilst the future of the local press in the UK remains uncertain most commentators and experts on the subject assume free-sheet papers will be part of any future enjoyed by printed local newspapers in the UK.

High-Concept Pitch: AKA High-concept pitch/ High Concept Pitch etc. Distilling a complex idea into a very brief form of words containing the 'concept' behind the complete work. High-Concept pitches typically occur when both parties involved in agreeing the deal have a track record of success. Isolating verified examples of such deals is hard, probably because it doesn't do the sales chances of a film or novel much good if the public know the contract was agreed over a bottle of wine on the terrace of a fashionable eaterie. However, persistent rumours surround several notable media successes, particularly the story told to the day on sites like venturehacks.com suggesting the deal for the movie *Alien* was secured on the back of a High-concept pitch claiming it to be '*Jaws*, in space.'

ISBN: (International Standard Book Number), unique number allocated to most published books. Since 2007 these identifiers have been 13 digits long. Divided into different parts, the numbers represent an identifying code for each fully published work. Different number groups in the code identify publisher, language sharing country group (i.e. English speaking etc), specific item number of the book and a 'checksum character' or check digit. Books with an ISBN are automatically picked up in standard cataloguing systems, allowing them to be ordered by retail chains, collected for sale by online outlets by Amazon and easily accessed in library reference systems.

Mystery Shopping: Catch all term for an area of work involving posing as a customer or service user, investigating a product or service industry and reporting back on your findings. Companies exist to provide mystery shopping services, these companies are employed by a wide range of operations – from shops to airlines and theme parks – and the reports generated feed into areas like quality control and annual appraisals. A detailed example of one mystery shopping organization in chapter three explains why this area of work might be a useful part of the CV of an aspiring writer. Whilst the example and this paragraph look at mystery shopping largely in terms of its potential use for an aspiring writer it pays to remember that mystery shopping operations – like Shopper Anonymous – describe themselves in terms of providing: 'independent feedback to a business about their customer service'.

Open mic: Aka: open-mic. General term usually applied to live events involving the reciting or performance of creative written work. 'Open mic' distinguishes the fact that writers are free to apply for the right to perform at such events. On some occasions anyone is welcome to get up from the audience and perform, on other occasions it is advisable to pre-arrange a performance. Some venues – for example; Covent Garden's Poetry Café – include regular open mic events in their schedule.

Press Agency: Organisation – usually employing a number of staff – based around gathering and reporting stories. Press agencies vary from individuals to major organizations like Associated Press and Reuters. For aspiring writers the best chance of a break comes from working with local agencies, usually concentrating on finding and reporting stories from a small geographical area. Press agencies earn money from sourcing stories and taking payment when others – like newspapers and magazines – opt to use these stories.

Press Release: Short presentation of the main elements of a news or public relations story. Intended for reading by journalists and news teams. Press releases have been used for over a century and still form a major element in the trafficking of news from those hoping to feature in the news to those writing and reporting it.

Production Management: The meaning of this term varies from one creative industry to another but the basic idea remains the same. Production management is, literally, managing a production like a stage show, and making sure things are organized properly. People working successfully in this area typically combine some creative vision; like the ability to know when an idea will succeed, with a sound business sense, the ability not to get too overwhelmed by small details and excellent communication skills. The downside of this work is often that others become famous and get attention if a production succeeds; typically writers and performers take this attention. The upside of this work is that the skills can transfer from one area of the creative world to another, so someone working in the theatre could easily move to the music industry or even work for a county council arranging live events.

Reflective Practice: A process of continuing monitoring and review involving a person considering aspects of their life, usually their working life, and applying analytical thoughts. Reflective practice typically involves a mentor although some areas of the working world offer online options for help and some people prefer to work alone. Major users of reflective practice include healthcare professionals and educators. Education linked to subjects like Creative Writing often emphasizes reflective practice, both via tutorial and group sessions, encouraging writers to be critical and place their work and practice in the widest possible context.

Script Factory: Name for a team of people all working on the scripts for one production; like a comedy series. Script factories work in a number of different ways. The least stressful is often a well managed meeting at the start of a series where the storyline for the whole run is established before the writing of individual episodes is farmed out to particular writers or teams of writers. Script factories can also be pressured and extremely hard working, sometimes involving last minute rewrites involving a team of people working in one large room overnight. In the days of typewriters this last option was sometimes unavoidable. It can be done today via a live web conference, though some producers still prefer the old tactic of putting everyone together and watching them work hard. Good things about this work include the valuable training it gives, forcing writers to produce work on the spot and giving them constant feedback on their best and worst ideas. It is also the kind of training ground that allows real talent to emerge and writers to learn from each other. The down side of this work is the stress, the level of burn out and the constant feeling that you are only as good as your last idea.

Spin: Basically the art of bringing about a specific interpretation of facts or events. Usually achieved by selectively making available elements of a story, emphasizing specific facts over others, or using suggestion and insinuation to lead people into certain beliefs. Though often associated with national and international politics and major corporations, the production of spin on very low key and local news events offers a career opportunity to aspiring writers.

Word Slam: Aka: word-slam, WordSlam, Wordslam etc. Basically, a loose set of very similar terms used in promotion of live events themed around the performance of creative written work, like poetry. Word Slam events often overlap with 'open mic' poetry nights. Such events are a vital opportunity for those intent on producing work towards the more 'arty' end of writing and poetry and flash fiction are typically well represented at Word Slam events. Such events often attract public funding or take place because an organization – like a local borough council – has diverted public funds into making them happen.

Writer's Voice: AKA 'Writers' Voice' a general term usually used to denote individual writing style. The term is widely used on writing courses and also by critics, especially those dealing with literary fiction. The source of an individual 'voice' for any writer can be identified via their use of grammar, syntax, imagery, dialogue, character development etc. So – in reality – the term is an attempt to identify specifics of a writer's style and link them to that writer's personal intent to convey ideas. The term can cause confusion for students, not least because it is often used in classes to describe both the voice of an individual writer and to describe the phenomena of the writers' voice (i.e. the notion that such a thing exists at all). In class, you need to pay attention closely to know which is being discussed. On paper this separation is made easier because a reader can check the placing of the possessive apostrophe: writer's (so we're talking about an individual), writers' (*all* writers).

About the Author

Neil Nixon has been writing professionally since he was a student. His published works include non-fiction books on the media, the paranormal, and football. He has written fiction including published novels, a series of radio plays and one complete movie script (currently optioned). His other writing activities have included more comedy scripts and published jokes than he can usefully count, work writing for a greeting card company, work as an obituaries correspondent, salaried work in corporate PR and work as an advertising creative.

In 1999 he started the UK's first full-time university programme in Professional Writing, a course he continues to lead. Neil has a website at *www.neilnixon.com*.